SECULARISM, ISLAM AND EDUCATION
IN INDIA, 1830–1910

Empires in Perspective

Series Editor: *Jayeeta Sharma*
Advisory Editor: *Masaie Matsumura*

Titles in this Series

SECULARISM, ISLAM AND EDUCATION IN INDIA, 1830–1910

BY

Robert Ivermee

Routledge
Taylor & Francis Group
LONDON AND NEW YORK

First published 2015 by Pickering & Chatto (Publishers) Limited

Published 2016 by Routledge
2 Park Square, Milton Park, Abingdon, Oxon OX14 4RN
711 Third Avenue, New York, NY 10017, USA

First issued in paperback 2017

Routledge is an imprint of the Taylor & Francis Group, an informa business

BRITISH LIBRARY CATALOGUING IN PUBLICATION DATA

Ivermee, Robert, author.
Secularism, Islam and education in India, 1830–1910. – (Empires in perspective)
1. Education – Religious aspects – History – 19th century. 2. Education – India
– History – 19th century. 3. Islam and secularism – India – History – 19th
century.
I. Title II. Series
379.2'8'0954'09034-dc23

ISBN 13: 978-1-138-09949-4 (pbk)
ISBN 13: 978-1-8489-3547-1 (hbk)

Typeset by Pickering & Chatto (Publishers) Limited

CONTENTS

ACKNOWLEDGEMENTS

This book was made possible by a grant from the UK Arts and Humanities Research Council to support my doctorate at the University of Kent. Research was carried out in libraries and archives in Britain, Ireland and India. The staff of the following institutions are thanked for their kind advice and patience. In Britain, the library of SOAS, University of London; the Bodleian Library, University of Oxford; the Borthwick Institute, University of York; the Robinson Library, Newcastle University; the Department of Manuscripts and Special Collections, University of Nottingham; the Cambridge University Library; the Templeman Library, University of Kent; and particularly the British Library, London. In Ireland, the National Library of Ireland, Dublin. In India, the Bihar State Archives, Patna; the Andhra Pradesh State Archives, Hyderabad; the State Archives of West Bengal, Kolkata; the National Library of India, Kolkata; the National Archives of India, New Delhi; the Nehru Memorial Library, New Delhi; and the Maulana Azad Library and Sir Syed Academy, Aligarh Muslim University. The papers of Charles Edward Trevelyan have been used by permission of the librarian at Robinson Library, Newcastle University; the India Office Records, the Ripon Papers and the George Nathaniel Curzon Papers by permission of the British Library, London; the two collections of Lord Mayo's papers by permission of the National Library of Ireland, Dublin, and the Manuscripts Department, Cambridge University Library; the Portland (Welbeck) Collection by permission of the Department of Manuscripts and Special Collections, University of Nottingham; and Charles Wood's Papers by permission of the Borthwick Institute, University of York. Parts of the research have been presented at conferences at the University of Leeds, the University of Kent, the University of Hyderabad, SOAS, the University of Copenhagen, Heythrop College, University of London and the Institute for Historical Research. The organizers of these conferences are thanked, as are participants kind enough to have offered responses. An earlier draft of part of chapter five was published as 'Islamic Education and Colonial Secularism: The Amroha Experiment of 1895–6', *South Asian History and Culture*, 5:1 (2014), pp. 21–36.

A large number of debts have been incurred during research and writing. For their continued support, I would like to thank David Ivermee and Emma Mojarab, Christine Reedijk, Clare Ivermee and James Bedford, William Parrott – and above all my parents, Sue and Fred Ivermee. Kieran Porter was the first to read a number of the drafts. Jeanne Constans has been an unfailing source of conversation, encouragement and welcome distraction. At SOAS, Avril Powell first suggested that I undertake doctoral research and has since offered invaluable advice. Abdulrazak Gurnah helped to elucidate major ideas and must be thanked along with other members of the School of English at Kent. Pratik Chakrabarti and Javed Majeed asked important questions and provoked me to clarify parts of the study, as did the anonymous reviewers at Pickering & Chatto, whose editorial team, in particular Janka Romero and Alex Douglas, have been a pleasure to work with. Conversations with colleagues at Heythrop College helped enormously as the process of turning a doctoral thesis into a book progressed. My biggest intellectual debt is to Alex Padamsee. Without his insight, suggestions and queries, consistently challenging my approach to voluminous archive material, the book could not have been written.

INTRODUCTION: SECULARISM CONSIDERED

I look upon our Indian educational system as one of the most appalling experiments on the largest scale that the world has ever seen ... [We] are dealing annually with over two and a half millions of children. We catch them young; we keep them during the school-going age; the longer we keep them the more we destroy their religion; and then we turn them out loose upon society without any religion at all.[1]

'[A] godless system of bringing up the youths of the country was sure one day to land us in disaster'.[2]

In the early nineteenth century, British administrators in India determined that education in schools and colleges supported by the colonial state would be exclusively secular: no religious instruction would be imparted in educational institutions under government patronage. The repercussions of this decision are felt today. Though the Government of India's commitment to sponsor only secular education has been partly compromised since, the educational provisions of the postcolonial Indian state remain organized around a distinction between religious and secular instruction, and the prohibition of the teaching of religion in government schools and colleges. Article 28 (1) of the Indian constitution dictates that 'No religious instruction shall be provided in any educational institution wholly maintained out of State funds'.[3]

In spite of its continued impact on Indian education and society, little research has yet been undertaken into the origins and development of the Indian government's secular education commitment.[4] Fewer studies still have sought to document and interpret reactions to the exclusion of religion from state education in India. This book is conceived as a corrective to the absence of cogent critical enquiry into the impact of the religious-secular distinction entering Indian education during the colonial period. Its focus is the engagement of Indian Muslims with British authorities on the subject of colonial pedagogy and the responses of British and Muslim parties to the restrictions placed on religious instruction in the colonial educational system. It reveals the extent to which Muslim elites challenging the exclusion of religious teaching from government institutions secured revisions of state educational provisions, and exposes the contribution of Muslim-British negotiations of colonial education to the historical development of Indian secularism.

Secularism has been the subject of intensive academic scrutiny in recent years, as scholars have come to realize the shortcomings of the thesis of secularization, once widely accepted in the western academy. According to that thesis, conceived with the history and progress of Europe in mind, the advance of rationality from the Enlightenment onwards would render religion subordinate to the claims of reason. Faith would be confined to the private domain of individual belief and no longer contribute to the political, economic and social activities of actors in public.[5] The concept of secularism was imagined to denote the institutional arrangements reflecting this new mode of human consciousness, including the separation of state and religion and the divorce of government and politics from religious belief, while also indicating the individual's relegation of faith to the private sphere.[6] In the present day, however, religion remains important to the activities of individuals and organizations across the globe, informing political and social activity to an unexpected degree.[7] The anticipated restriction of religion to individual belief has not materialized and, amid what is widely described as the public resurgence of religion, the concept of secularism is now examined anew. In the humanities and social sciences, scholars reconsider the origins, meaning and impact of secularism,[8] while philosophers and sociologists work towards the theoretical accommodation of religious actors and ideas in the public sphere.[9]

In contemporary India, religion remains a public affair. During the past three decades a proliferation of local and national political movements have asserted the importance both of religious identity and faith in the public domain, culminating in the re-election of the Bharatiya Janata Party to government in May 2014. This was not how the country's post-independence political elite imagined it would be. When the Indian constitution was framed, the rights to freedom of conscience and religious worship were guaranteed, but it was expected that religion would be practised privately – at a distance from politics and other public activities.[10] While in some quarters the endurance of religion in the public sphere has been viewed as a sign of India's failed or incomplete transition to modernity, a growing number of academics and intellectuals have embarked upon the critique of secularism itself. Scholars have suggested that the narratives and practices of India as a secular state, imposing uniformity over its subjects, have compromised the position of minority religious groups;[11] the emergence of aggressive religious politics has been explained as a consequence of the failure of entrenched political elites to grant religion a legitimate role in the public arena and as a reaction to the homogenizing practices of the secular state.[12] Profound scepticism has been expressed over the suitability of secularism as a precept of Indian government, as the attempt is made to devise other principles for ensuring the protection and peaceful coexistence of multiple religions in Indian politics and society.[13]

To consider the historical development of secularism in India is a particularly important endeavour in light of the 'dissolution' of the Indian national consensus on the concept.[14] This study takes as its starting point the insight that secularism is not a concept possessing a fixed and universal meaning, but one rooted in the specificities of time and place.[15] It assumes that meanings of secularism have been produced and modified in different locations and time periods as the result of particular historical circumstances. I take up the challenge outlined recently by several scholars of re-examining the production and development of secularism in colonial India, not so that a 'correct' meaning of Indian secularism might be unearthed, but to shed further light on the concept's contested complexity and contingency on historical events.[16] Rather than measuring the Indian experience of secularism against a supposedly universal norm emerging from western narratives of secularization and modernity's advance, I focus on specific events and people, discerning their contribution to the construction of secularism on the subcontinent.

Throughout the nineteenth century, the term most commonly used by British administrators to describe the relationship of the colonial state to the religions of India was 'neutrality'. Existing research suggests that as liberal explanations of the British imperial role on the subcontinent – centred on notions of reform and improvement – gave way to more conservative or paternalist justifications for empire after the Indian Rebellion of 1857–8, a new justification for colonial rule emerged: the preservation of a government external to India that would maintain neutrality between subsets of the indigenous population in perpetual competition and conflict with each other.[17] An important element of the British claim to impartiality was the idea of arbitrating from a position of neutrality between India's heterogeneous religious groups. Deriving in part from developments in nineteenth-century Britain, where the gradual removal of civil disabilities on non-Anglican parties forced national governments to respond to the demands of multiple religious constituencies, the pretence of religious neutrality has been identified in recent scholarship as a significant way in which the British Indian polity resembled a modern secular state.[18]

What, however, about the specific relationship or set of relationships between the colonial state and religious faith? The designation of a state as 'secular' is broadly conceived as meaning one of two things: either the complete, formal separation of state from religion – reflected most often by the absence of public funding for religious institutions – or the impartial and equal state support of a plurality of religions.[19] In Victorian Britain the enfranchisement of religious minorities was accompanied by a movement towards the state support of multiple denominations – a development which ought to put to bed the simplistic notion, common to contemporary Indian debate, that secularism in Europe has uniformly meant the removal of religion from the public domain. Scholarship on British India usually posits the withdrawal of the colonial state from the support of Indian religions during the first half of the nineteenth century. Prior to 1830, it is observed, colonial governments endowed religious institutions belonging to Hindu and Muslim groups, sponsored religious education and administered Hindu and Muslim law in colonial courts – all aspects of an 'orientalist' administrative approach. Under pressure from evangelical and utilitarian influences in Britain, this support was gradually withdrawn and the colonial state manoeuvred towards a model of religious neutrality involving the separation of governmental practice from Indian religion.[20]

Though the fact of a partial withdrawal of the colonial state from the support of Indian religions is often recognized, its extent and nature remain unclear. The process of separating state from religion was slow, continuing beyond the 1858 transfer of authority from the East India Company to the British crown, fragmented and incomplete. Take for example the government management of Hindu and Muslim religious endowments or the administration of religious law in colonial courts, both of which continued through the nineteenth century in spite of the burgeoning British rhetoric of 'non-interference' in Indian religious customs and beliefs.[21] To attain a fuller understanding of secularism in nineteenth-century India it is necessary to focus critical attention on the specific practices of the colonial state as it encountered Indian religions. The decisions of British administrators seeking to distance governments from religion must be historicized alongside the debates and counter-movements that they provoked. Studies of the colonial state and religion have often concentrated on Christianity, with the support of British officials for Christian missionaries and the public endowment of Indian churches as particular objects of attention.[22] If the development of Indian secularism is to be understood, however, the connection of the colonial state to Christianity must be studied as just one part of its complex and often contradictory wider relationship with religion in India.

The term 'secularism' was first coined in England in 1846 to denote the organization of society through principles independent of religious belief. As it was adopted and utilized in the metropolis thereafter its principal focus became the impartiality of the state in matters of religion – particularly after the foundation of the National Secular Society in 1866.[23] Only in the twentieth century did the term enter into political discourse and commonplace use in India. Nevertheless, as scholars have recently noted, it is quite possible, indeed imperative, to study the evolution of Indian secularism through enquiry into discourses where the word is not itself used, in a period preceding its popularization.[24] Contesting the exclusion of religious instruction from the colonial educational system, British and Muslim parties encouraged colonial authorities to offer the support of the Indian state for all of the religions of India, rather than none. Some argued explicitly for a redefinition of the relationship between religion and state towards that end. The British-Muslim exchanges considered in this study interrogated and moulded conceptions of the relationship of state to religion in India, contributing to the development of understandings of Indian secularism, even when the term 'secularism' was not directly employed.

An enquiry into the relationship between colonial education and Indian secularism is long overdue. As chapter one explores, the non-patronage of religious instruction was announced as a government principle in 1835 and confirmed when the term 'secular' was first inscribed into state policy in 1854. For the remainder of the nineteenth century and beyond, European and Indian parties were forced to contend with a colonial state refusing to endow religious teaching – whether Christian, Hindu, Muslim or of any other religious group – making education the policy area in which British professions of 'non-interference' in religious matters were most closely matched by administrative practice. The resolution of the British government of India to avoid the patronage of religious education is referred to in what follows as the 'colonial secular education commitment'. Responses to that commitment included attempts to organize religious instruction privately and the wholesale denunciation of the government's approach, provoking the critique and rethinking of prevailing understandings of the relationship between religion and state.

Secular Education and Colonial Governmentality

The earliest educational institutions supported by British authorities in India were colleges founded in the late eighteenth century for the instruction of Muslim and Hindu elites in Arabic, Persian and Sanscrit subjects. From the early nineteenth century, however, a growing body of colonial officials, sustained by evangelical and utilitarian ideas of the transformation and improvement of Indian peoples, sought the introduction of western education to the subcontinent, culminating in the March 1835 announcement that instruction in European subjects would be the 'great object' of state pedagogical efforts.[25] For reasons that chapter one makes clear, British administrators determined that western scientific and literary subjects would be the vehicle of Indian progress; no religious instruction would be imparted in colonial educational institutions. Commitments to the intellectual and moral improvement of the Indian population and the exclusive provision of secular education thereafter developed conjointly as the colonial system of public instruction expanded. Charles Wood's dispatch of 1854 established an extensive state educational system from school to university level and affirmed that the British government would concern itself with the provision of secular education alone.

If the development of a colonial educational system in the decades after 1830 is to be fully understood, it should be located within the context of wider changes to the British governance of India during the period. In the work of

Michel Foucault the advance of governmental rationality, denoted by the neologism 'governmentality', was a transition taking place in seventeenth- and eighteenth-century Europe by which a rational art of government was first devised and effected.[26] Foucault traced the governmentalization of European states from a starting point with the French theorists of raison d'état, through the German eighteenth-century state of 'police', to the establishment of more liberal forms of government – particularly in Britain– after 1800.[27] With each of these developments, he proposed, European states moved away from an older form of sovereignty according to which the highest power of the state lay in its capacity to take and grant life and raised a new object – population – as the ultimate end of government. The governmentalized state acted from an awareness that its strength derived from that of its subjects and undertook to encourage the wealth, well-being and longevity of the population under its rule. Through a multiplicity of institutions, new techniques and rationalities of government were introduced for the disciplining of individuals and regulation of populations.[28] The governmentalization of European states, Foucault posited, was accompanied by the proliferation of new measures for the collection of information on subject populations. New governmental practices, in turn, were productive of knowledge employed in the acts of governing.[29]

That major parallels exist between the governmentalization of European states described by Foucault and the advent of a modern regime of power in colonial India has been readily noted in research.[30] During the course of the nineteenth century the colonial state became increasingly interventionist, extending the scope of its activities and impacting more profoundly on Indian society. An East India Company government committed in the first instance to the administration of law, and extraction of revenue from land gave way to a bureaucratic Raj visible to and encountered by a growing number of Indian subjects. The governor generalship of Lord Dalhousie (1848–56) should be considered a watershed, during which modern state practices including the building of roads, canals and railways, the creation of postal and telegraph systems and the undertaking of large-scale public works were begun, and after the events of the Indian Rebellion colonial government was augmented by military reinforcement, administrative rationalization and the codification of law.[31] Accompanying the extension of governmental technologies was a proliferation of efforts to study, measure and classify India's natural environment and people, involving the harnessing of the sciences of geography, geology, botany, archaeology, anthropology, ethnography, demography and epidemiology to colonial rule.[32] The production of knowledge about India went hand-in-hand with the expansion and reinforcement of British government.

Over the past two decades, scholars inspired by Foucault's contribution have paid significant attention to the multifarious practices of the colonial state, tending towards the disciplining of individual conduct and the regulation of the Indian population. In his groundbreaking study, David Arnold has shown how the introduction to India of a state-centred system of western medicine positioned the body as a site for the construction of colonial authority, legitimacy and control. The coercive practices of the British state, he argues, extended to include the regulation of the colonised as physical beings.[33] Gyan Prakash has built upon the foundation laid by Arnold to consider colonial attempts to improve sanitation, counter epidemic disease and instruct Indian subjects in the principles of health and hygiene.[34] Centred on the macro-level study and management of an Indian population, these endeavours resonate greatly with the Foucauldian concept of governmentality. Other colonial practices studied for their contribution to subject formation include the planning and construction of cities,[35] policing and penology,[36] the management of labour[37] and the organisation of the economy.[38] In his final writings, Foucault extended his work on governmentality to consider the government of the self.[39] His insight has provoked attempts to explain the ways in which British norms of dress, manners, speech and behaviour underpinned colonial rule.[40]

To consider the extension of colonial education a part of the governmentalization of British rule is instructive.[41] In nineteenth-century India, public instruction possessed considerable potential for the exercise of colonial governmentality, a form of rule which, in short, regulated conduct and fashioned subjectivities at both micro (individual) and macro (population) level, through multiple practices. By the middle part of the century, as one scholar has recently noted, the British government of India had come to be viewed as an essentially 'pedagogic enterprise' – pedagogic effects and benefits were ascribed to most colonial practices, such as the administration of law in government courts.[42] Accompanying this ascription was a dramatic extension of the formal spaces of colonial education, state-supported schools and colleges, in which the regulation of conduct and fashioning of subjectivities could take place. The development of a state educational system proceeded alongside, and encouraged, the conceptualization of wider colonial government as possessing fundamentally pedagogic ends.

The writings of Charles Trevelyan constitute a compelling example of early nineteenth-century colonial government conceived as a pedagogic undertaking. Arriving in India in 1826, Trevelyan represented a new class of British administrator convinced that the aim of colonial government should be the moral and intellectual improvement of Indian peoples in preparation for eventual self-rule. Trevelyan conceived that wider colonial reforms, including the introduction to India of a codified body of law, would engender the transformation of Indian subjects, but in his view it was chiefly via the introduction of a colonial system of public instruction that the improvement of India would be attained.[43] That the educational plans advanced by Trevelyan should be considered part of the governmentalization of the colonial state is clear. Alongside a growing number of his contemporaries, Trevelyan conceived of colonial education as vital to the fashioning of a modern Indian subjectivity. Detailing the foundation of an extensive network of schools and colleges extending to every division and district, he viewed the people of India as a population to be acted upon by government. For Trevelyan, that population would be enlightened and ultimately rendered a nation by colonial public instruction; Hindu and Muslim identities would be superseded by the production of an anglicized Indian subject.[44] In parallel with his conviction that educating Indians was a duty of government, Trevelyan held that colonial public instruction would strengthen the British position in India, creating loyal subjects.[45] As in the governmentalized states studied by Foucault, the security of the British administration in India would be ensured by the regulation of the population under its rule.

After 1835 the zealous liberal vision articulated by Charles Trevelyan and other reformers arguing for the dramatic extension of colonial public instruction was less often heard. However, the conviction continued to prevail that the colonial state should extend its pedagogical efforts; the expectation remained that western education would reshape and improve its Indian recipients. After Wood's dispatch of 1854, government educational departments established in each of the British Indian provinces took responsibility for the widespread establishment and management of schools delivering European scientific and literary instruction, while also awarding funding to private institutions in which prescribed curricula were taught. Withstanding a brief hiatus during the Indian Rebellion, the colonial system of public instruction expanded rapidly and by 1871 in excess of 400,000 pupils received instruction in government-managed schools alongside approximately 250,000 studying in private institutions that submitted to regular inspection in return for state funds.[46]

Within fifty years the plan for an extensive colonial educational system advanced by British figures from the second quarter of the nineteenth century had been realized. That system targeted an Indian population increasingly identified and measured by other governmental technologies – including provincial and imperial censuses – that employed an emergent science of statistics.[47] Government-funded institutions taught secular scientific and literary curricula with the aim of producing modern Indian subjects. Both the content and form of colonial public instruction were held conducive to Indian progress: not only would acquaintance with European knowledge and ideas expose the errors of indigenous learning, but 'modern' pedagogical techniques such as translation and essay-writing would embed rationality in the Indian mind.[48] Colonial education promised to regulate behaviour while refashioning subjects – a development captured by Foucault's notion of government as the 'conduct of conduct'.[49] The progress of individuals through the colonial system was measured by regular examinations. Data on scholars and institutions was passed from local, to provincial, to all-India level, allowing colonial administrators to chart, with a claim to scientific accuracy, the impact of education on the populations under their rule.

The history of colonial education is not, however, one of the straightforward, uncontested advance of western learning.[50] This study explores the concerted negotiations in which British and Muslim parties engaged on the subject of colonial public instruction. Focused on the colonial secular education commitment, it reveals the complexity and contestation surrounding the formation and development of state educational provisions. To understand Muslim-British negotiations of colonial pedagogy we must first consider in more detail the operation of colonial governmentality, and the relationship between state and civil society in British India.

Pedagogy and Civil Society

Though broadly sharing in the belief that colonial public instruction would effect improvement among Indian subjects, British individuals disagreed profoundly over aspects of state educational provisions. Independently and in cooperation with Muslim parties, they campaigned for the revision of colonial educational policies including the exclusive government patronage of secular instruction. Muslim parties confronted with state pedagogical provisions entered in dialogue with British figures, negotiated with government and secured revisions of colonial education, among them the introduction of means for the reconciliation of religious and secular instruction, to an extent previously unnoticed in research. The formulation of Muslim and British opinion, exchanges between Muslim and British parties and the representation of views to government took place in emerging public spheres populated by civil institutions in each of the Indian provinces.

Recent critical enquiry into the concept of the public sphere has been profoundly influenced by the contribution of the German philosopher and sociologist Jurgen Habermas, who identifies the public sphere as a site for the discussion of affairs of popular interest located between society and the structures of the state.[51] For Habermas, the emergence of the public sphere in Europe created a new conception of government as a communal affair, whereby citizens participating in civic deliberations were no longer the inert recipients of state decrees but active participants in their formulation. Habermas traces the development of the public sphere in eighteenth century Europe through the construction and articulation of 'public opinion' in an array of emergent institutions, including the salon, the coffee house, the literary society, the journal and the newspaper.[52] After 1700, he argues, the power of European states was checked by the exercise of reason in the institutions of a new public space. C. A. Bayly, among others, has shown how many of the features identified by Habermas as characteristic of a European public sphere, including political theory, individuality, rationality and social communication, were present in Indian society before the advent

of colonial rule. The introduction of lithography in the 1820s built upon existing indigenous structures to produce the circulation of knowledge and views in
printed form and the exercise of public opinion as a curb on government in a way
that Habermas would recognise.[53] What the Habermasian concept of the public
sphere lacks, however, is an appreciation that civil institutions not only constrain
the exercise of government but also participate in the act of governing, shaping
individuals and aggregations through measures often reflecting the imperatives
of modern states. Foucault's representation of civil society as a domain in which
the regulation of conduct and fashioning of subjects is carried out, but also
opposed and negotiated, offers a more convincing explanation of the relationship between state and society, particularly apposite to an understanding of the
development and impact of colonial education in India.

Elevated by Habermas and other theorists as a site separate from the state, civil
society was for Foucault simultaneously a domain for analysis and intervention on
the part of governmentalized polities. With the emergence of new governmental
technologies, he contended, civil society developed as the 'necessary correlate' of
the state, the target of its interventions in the art of governing.[54] Driven by the
imperative of political economy, European states came increasingly to exercise
governmentality, regulating and normalizing populations, through the institutions of civil society. Civil society was put to work in the service of the modern
state as a domain on which governmentality was exercised in a manner consistent
with economic requirements and the juridical concept of rights.[55] Significantly,
however, the exercise of governmentality was for Foucault rarely straightforward
or uncontested. Preceding his interest in the normalising actions of modern
states was a distinct turn in his thought towards a relational understanding of
power, revealed first in *The Will to Knowledge* (1975).[56] In Foucault's work from
this point onwards, power is presented as something not hegemonic but fundamentally unstable and dependent on the interplay of multiple relationships in
perpetual flux. Wherever governmentality is exercised, the possibility exists of
resistance or negotiation on the part of actors in civil society, best understood as
a transactional domain for the interplay of relations of power between governors
and the governed. The institutions of civil society are locations for the contestation of governmentality, between forces of conduct and counter-conduct.[57]

Developed with the genealogy of eighteenth century European states in
mind, Foucault's conception of civil society enhances our understanding of the
practice and negotiation of colonial government in India. Under British rule,
the development of modern civil institutions including membership clubs, public associations, newspapers and journals took place from the early nineteenth
century alongside the creation of a modern state apparatus. In parallel to new
governmental technologies, these institutions participated in the regulation of
conduct and fashioning of subjectivities, shaping how Indian (and European)

parties thought and behaved. Concurrently, however, they provided the location for individuals and aggregations to negotiate governmental practices and initiate movements of counter-conduct. Public education provides one of the standout examples of colonial governmentality exercised by both the state and civil institutions. While a large number of schools, printing presses, newspapers and journals contributing to the dissemination of western learning were controlled by government authorities, multiple equivalents of each were maintained by parties acting in civil society. European-style literary and cultural associations participated in the task of educating India through, for example, the maintenance of libraries and staging of debates, and as the century progressed a growing number of civil institutions contributing to the advance of western education, including schools, newspapers and associations, were established and managed by Indian elites. However, British and Indian actors also found in civil society a site for negotiating and responding to state educational provisions. Specific government practices, such as the exclusion of religious teaching from state institutions, were contested and alternative educational initiatives were launched.

This study follows the path of other recent scholarship on colonial governmentality provoked by the later Foucault's understanding of the instability of power relations to consider the ways in which British government in South Asia was opposed and negotiated by indigenous parties. While many earlier contributions to the field, including David Scott's influential essay on the colonial government of Sri Lanka, explored the role of technologies of rule in the regulation of population and fashioning of modern subjects without regard for manifestations of opposition, scholars of colonial governmentality have lately begun to address questions of resistance and negotiation.[58] One avenue explored has been the ways in which Indian parties co-opted and mutated the practices of the colonial state for their own ends: Gyan Prakash has argued that Indian nationalists confronted with British medicine subverted governmentality by pursuing their own programme directed towards the population's 'welfare',[59] while C. A. Bayly suggests that Indian liberals challenged the legitimacy of the colonial science of statistics by accumulating empirical facts and producing alternative statistical series.[60] A growing number of studies focus on the failure of colonial governmentality to regulate subjectivities effectively, suggesting the weakness of colonial agencies in relationships of power. Diana Heath, for example, cogently traces the limitations of governmental power in regulating obscenity in nineteenth century India and other British imperial sites.[61] James S. Duncan reveals the continuous opposition thwarting colonial efforts to exercise power on coffee plantations in Sri Lanka.[62] David Arnold suggests that the state-centred system of western medicine in colonial India failed to impact upon all but a tiny proportion of subjects;[63] and Uday Kalpagam contends that colonial authorities failed to control opinion and regulate conduct in indigenous public spheres.[64]

To varying degrees, each of these studies acknowledges not only the presence or possibility of opposition to government technologies; by integrating acts of negotiation into understandings of the operation of colonial governmentality they suggest that the development of governmental practices was itself informed by negotiations between multiple agencies, indigenous and European.[65]

Colonial public instruction possessed major potential as a field for regulating the conduct of individuals and fashioning subjectivities; it promised to constitute a particularly significant set of practices for the exercise of colonial governmentality. With each successful negotiation of government education, however, that set of practices was modified; through concerted negotiation, new governmental practices were devised. This study examines the history of a set of government technologies, colonial public instruction, taking as its object the formation of subjects. Consistent with the scholarship noted above, however, it considers processes of debate and negotiation a crucial part of that history, through which new governmental practices were developed and the nature of colonial governmentality revised. At the heart of the colonial project to produce a new kind of Indian subject through government education was instruction in secular western scientific and literary disciplines. Most officials considered the colonial secular education commitment vital to the success of government pedagogical efforts and the security of British rule. Negotiating with colonial authorities, however, dissenting Muslim and British figures concerned for the provision of religious education secured substantial revisions of government educational policies. In emergent civil institutions, technologies contributing to the exercise of colonial governmentality were modified and the nature of Indian secularism was brought under scrutiny.

Scope and Limits

The second half of the nineteenth century was a period of great vitality for Muslim education in South Asia, as parties responded to the changing circumstances of colonial rule. Across the Indian subcontinent, institutions were founded outside of the state educational system – inspired to varying degrees by British, Indo-Muslim and Islamic forms. In her seminal study, Barbara Metcalf has shown how a small madrasa established at Deoband in 1867 grew into the centre of an extensive network of seminaries disseminating Islamic instruction in places as distant as Peshawar, Chittagong and Madras.[66] Other groups of ulama concerned for the provision of religious education included the Ahl-i-hadith, the Barelwis and the Nadwat-ul-ulama, all of which founded educational institutions set apart from the state.[67] For a majority of Muslims in the nineteenth century, religious education meant instruction in madrasas outside of government structures, or in the home. The related but distinct focus of this study is

Muslim parties engaging with British authorities to ensure the provision of religious instruction within the colonial system.

For most of the period studied, those Muslims were predominantly members of an elite Persian- and Urdu-speaking sharif class employed in government service or landowning occupations. Many identified themselves as *ashraf*, claiming descent from outside of India and a family history of service to Mughal and other Indian governments. After 1875 they were joined by a small but growing professional class of Muslims employed as teachers, lawyers, doctors and public officials, who also entered into exchanges with government. The study is for the most part confined to the northern Indian territories of Bengal, the North-Western Provinces (NWP) and the Punjab. I concentrate on emerging civil society in each of these locations, exploring the participation of Muslim elites in associations and societies that negotiated state educational provisions and contested the colonial secular education commitment. By analyzing not one province, but the breadth of northern India, the study reveals how Muslim parties across geographically dispersed areas – in both Muslim majority and minority regions – shared similar concerns for the provision of religious instruction and, later in the period, acted together to contest the separation of religion from government instruction. At the turn of the twentieth century, some of the individuals I consider turned their attention to the education of Muslim girls. Scholarship has shown that as they did so, they emphasized the necessity of religious instruction being provided to female children alongside the teaching of other subjects.[68] In an earlier period, however, the education of boys was Muslim leaders' major or exclusive concern, and is accordingly the focus here.

On account of their acceptance of western education and willingness to enter into dialogue with representatives of the colonial state, some of the Muslim individuals featured in this study have been regularly labelled 'reformers' or 'modernists' in scholarship on South Asian Islam and contrasted with those 'traditionalists' or 'revivalists' concerned for the protection and propagation of religion.[69] The examination of Muslim demands for the provision of religious instruction within the colonial system problematizes such simple binaries, showing how Muslim parties encouraged their co-religionists to study western subjects, while simultaneously acting on account and furthering the cause of their faith. Each of the Muslim organizations I consider represented a broad coalition of interests. Within them, individuals could be found with quite divergent religious ideas and beliefs. Take for example the Muslim Educational Conference (MEC), an institution that, as we shall see, brought together Muslim parties from across northern India after 1886. The MEC was founded at Aligarh by Sayyid Ahmad Khan, whose religious thought, based on independent reasoning and the rational interpretation of the Qur'an, set him theologically apart from many contemporaries.[70] The term 'Muslim' does not denote something uniform.

In what follows, a degree of insight is gained into changing Muslim religious practices and ideas, including a growing acceptance that religious instruction might be imparted in vernacular media and a new emphasis among several Muslim scholars on the ethical dimensions of Islam. First and foremost, however, the study is an intellectual history of the role played by Muslim and British parties, who were responding to the colonial secular education commitment, in changing the course of government educational policy and the history of Indian secularism. To trace extensively the changing nature of Islamic customs and beliefs in colonial South Asia, in the manner of several excellent recent studies, is beyond its scope.[71] Muslim social and political organizations are introduced and their role negotiating colonial educational provisions is explored. However, no detailed analysis of the social history of the networks identified in the research is attempted; the experiences of Muslim students and teachers in schools and colleges within the colonial system are not elaborated on. With the exception of the Calcutta Madrasa, a state-managed college for Bengali Muslim elites (considered at length in chapter three), and the Muhammadan Anglo-Oriental (MAO) College at Aligarh (a focus of chapter five), the history of particular educational institutions is detailed only briefly.

The study is based on English-language sources, including substantial volumes of Persian and Urdu material translated during the colonial period or more recently. In addition to a wealth of official records from archives in India and Britain, published and unpublished non-official sources are relied upon heavily, enabling British and Muslim perspectives to be represented in a far more nuanced way than is found in the colonial archive. They include newspapers and periodicals; books and pamphlets; the proceedings and reports of civil institutions; and the private papers of influential Muslim and British figures, some of which have been utilized rarely – if at all – in existing scholarship. As Muslim parties responded to the colonial secular education commitment, concerns for the provision of religious education in the state educational system were undoubtedly an influence on their resolution to act publicly on behalf of a distinct religious group. Alongside competition for public employment, the explosion of the vernacular press, Christian missionary activity and the practices of a colonial state conceiving of Indian society as composed of multiple religious groups – to mention just several key factors – it appears that restrictions on the teaching of religion in colonial education contributed inadvertently, but substantially, to developing Muslim understandings of religious community.[72] The task for scholars working with vernacular sources is to substantiate or refute this claim. It is hoped that this study will be the starting point for more detailed regional enquiries into the networks established by Muslim leaders responding to the colonial secular commitment, and the impact of concerns for the provision of religious instruction in state education on Muslim community formation. The reception of secular colonial pedagogy by other Indian constituencies, intermittently considered in what follows, also demands further attention.

The start and end points of the study are a little more fluid than its title suggests. The year 1830 marks the start of the decade in which the systematic introduction of western learning to India began and the colonial secular education commitment was announced. 1910 was the end of the decade witnessing the foundation of the first all-India Muslim political association, and the advent of popular politics to compete for government attention with the model of negotiation between British officials and Muslim elites characteristic of earlier years. Chapters one and three retreat further in time to fill in important background, beginning with the foundation of the Calcutta Madrasa, the first school or college patronized by the East India Company for the instruction of Indian subjects, in 1780. The conclusion considers the 1920 chartering of a Muslim university at Aligarh: the culmination of Muslim opposition to the exclusion of religion from colonial educational institutions.

Methodology and Structure

Enquiring into the historical development of Indian secularism, this study explores what Edward Said termed the 'intertwined histories' of Europe and its colonies.[73] It takes as a foundation and confirms that the histories of Britain and sites within its empire are more intimately related to each other than is recognized in most studies of metropolitan or colonial locations. The chapters that follow consider the importing of metropolitan ideas and concepts to India, chart their adoption and mutation, and highlight the multiple points of departure for actors on the colonial stage. Said's insight has been developed by scholars concerned to map not only the transfer of ideas between colonial centre and metropolitan periphery, but also between different colonial sites in Britain's empire. In this study, new insight is obtained into what has been termed the 'mobile' and 'intertextual' nature of knowledge in the British imperial world;[74] European and Indian Muslim parties engaging in debates over secular education and the relationship between religion and state derived ideas and information from England and, additionally, locations as far-flung as Ireland, continental Europe and the Ottoman Empire.

The use of several terms in the study should be clarified. The word 'liberal' is employed, following multiple precedents, to denote justifications for the British imperial role centred on the transformation and improvement of India.[75] Evangelical and utilitarian parties arguing that the duty of the British in India was to inculcate progress are included within this descriptive category. The term 'denominational' is used, in the absence of a better alternative, to denote institutions including schools, colleges and membership organizations, intended for the exclusive or near exclusive participation of members of one religious group. Chapter five considers the popularization in Indian debate of the terms 'denominational' and 'denominationalism', used pejoratively by European parties to describe the demand for a Muslim university, before being appropriated and imbued with new meanings by Muslim elites. The term 'denominationalism' is utilized outside of this discussion to denote the phenomenon of denominational institutions; like 'denominational', it is employed in a positive rather than a normative sense.

It is not the intention of this study to perpetuate the binaries found in many colonial sources on the education of India between 'modern', 'western' or 'useful' knowledge or learning on the one hand, and 'traditional', 'Indian' or 'indigenous' knowledge or learning on the other. As scholarship has shown, the production of knowledge – particularly scientific knowledge – in post-Enlightenment Europe relied heavily on developments in the non-European world; the attempt to disseminate 'western' learning in colonial India involved multiple exchanges through which new knowledge was created.[76] In short, the intertextuality of knowledge is such that it cannot be unproblematically confined to a particular spatial domain. The terms 'western', 'European' and 'English' are used in this study in conjunction with 'knowledge', 'learning', 'education' or 'science' in order to represent the views of those who, to varying degrees, considered colonial public instruction to involve the introduction to India of something new and different to learning in which colonial agencies played no part. Wherever possible, exactly what individuals understood by, for example, 'western education' or 'European science' is dissected and explained. Of course, some colonial figures were aware that 'western' learning could not be claimed the exclusive product of the West, but rather derived partly from India and the Islamic world. The deployment of the terms 'modern' and 'traditional', and their mapping onto 'western' and 'Indian' respectively, was in part a matter of strategy – when, for example, liberal reformers sought a change in government educational policy in the 1830s.

In chapter one the origins of the colonial secular education commitment are examined. It is shown that the categories of 'religion' and the 'secular' were in widespread use in colonial discourses over state education in India, as in Britain, by the middle part of the nineteenth century. As Talal Asad's anthropological enquiries remind us, however, the meaning of each of these categories has in the modern period been fluid rather than fixed.[77] Broadly conceived, the term 'secular' was mobilized in discussions of colonial public instruction to denote education without religious content. On occasion, the adverb 'exclusively' (or 'purely') was added to reinforce that education divorced of religion was being signified.[78] However, exactly what was meant by 'secular' education varied. Some British officials contended, for example, that teaching the Qur'an in government schools could be a 'secular' pursuit so long as studying Arabic language and literature, rather than learning Islamic prescripts, was its goal, while others strongly disagreed. The teaching of Muslim law in government colleges, meanwhile, was considered by most British administrators to be consistent with the secular education commitment, on account of the pressing demand for Muslim law officers to serve in colonial courts – a revealing example of the manipulation of the parameters defining the 'religious' and the 'secular' to suit temporal exigencies.

The deployment of the category 'secular' could be ideological as well as strategic, such as when those seeking the exclusion of Arabic and Sanscrit instruction from government institutions claimed that while European education could be divided into religious and secular components, oriental learning was entirely and irredeemably about (false) religion.[79] This study documents the ways in which the categories of 'religion' and the 'secular' were deployed and modified by parties seeking to uphold or overturn the colonial secular education commitment. The flexibility of those categories prompts us to remember that Muslim and British parties contesting the restrictions imposed on religious teaching in state education were not 'anti-secular'. Rather, through their discourses and negotiations the meanings of 'secularism' and the 'secular' were enquired into and changed.

In the course of the study, the question of power is not considered explicitly at length. This is not to suggest that power was unimportant to the exercise of colonial governmentality and the development of state educational provisions. Instead, the study begins with the understanding that relations of power underpinned all of the exchanges considered; contestation over colonial public instruction involved the playing out of multiple power relationships in public and private forums. As Foucault noted in his later work, to trace a history of government in a particular space and time inevitably sheds light on diverse relationships of power.[80] The extent to which Muslim elites were able to influence the development of government education suggests that in colonial India those relationships were not so heavily weighted in favour of European over Indian parties as might previously have been thought.

The organization of the book is loosely chronological and geographical. Chapter one explores the origins of the colonial secular education commitment and its development up to 1860. After charting the emergence of a distinction between the religious and the secular in colonial educational discourse, it establishes why the British government of India resolved in March 1835 to patronize secular education alone. The foundation of an extensive state educational system with Wood's dispatch, and the confirmation of its provisions following the Indian Rebellion are then considered. Before and after the Rebellion, as the government system of public instruction expanded, the colonial secular education commitment was confirmed. Simultaneously, however, religious identity was inscribed into government educational provisions, anticipating later contestation of the separation of education into religious and secular parts.

Chapter two considers in detail the process by which the Government of India developed a set of educational provisions specifically for Muslim subjects. It focuses on the career of Lord Mayo, viceroy of India between 1869 and 1872, and reveals for the first time that the inscription of Muslim identity into colonial education during his premiership was critically shaped by British experiences of the failings of education without religion in an alternative colonial context: nineteenth-century Ireland. From Ireland, an alternative conception of the relationship between state and religion was imported to India, informing the development of colonial educational provisions aimed at Muslims alone. A consequence of the reforms initiated by Mayo's administration was the articulation of demands for the abandonment of the colonial commitment to provide only secular instruction; as state education was revised to accommodate Muslim requirements, the religious neutrality, or secularism, of the colonial state was rethought.

Chapters three, four and five concentrate on the responses to the colonial secular education commitment of Muslim parties across northern India. In chapter three the attempts of European administrators and educationalists to remove Islamic teachings from the curriculum of the Calcutta Madrasa – a government institution for the instruction of Bengali Muslims – are examined. After the Indian Rebellion, these attempts were opposed by Muslim elites engaging with government via the emergent institutions of Bengal civil society. Muslims from across Bengal argued before representatives of the colonial state for the necessity of secular government-prescribed lessons being combined with religious education, and by 1875 had won significant concessions engendering the revival of Islamic religious instruction in the province.

Chapter four shifts attention to the Punjab, revealing how concerns for the provision of religious instruction provoked the withdrawal of the colonial state from the direct provision of education in favour of private agencies. Inspired by the foundation of the MAO College at Aligarh in the neighbouring NWP, Punjabi Muslims joined forces with an influential European critic of colonial education, Gottlieb Leitner, to argue for the reconciliation of religious and secular instruction in the colonial educational system. Unwilling to permit the teaching of religion in government-managed schools, British officials confronted with this demand sanctioned the reallocation of state funding to privately managed institutions in which religious and secular instruction might be combined. Muslim associations took over responsibilities for pedagogy previously claimed by the colonial state.

Chapter five considers the culmination of Muslim opposition to the separation of religion from colonial education in the campaign for a Muslim university. Concentrated on the MEC, an organisation headed by Muslim leaders at Aligarh, it reveals how Muslim elites in the NWP, Bengal and the Punjab, and also further afield in Bombay and Madras, were brought together in the final years of the nineteenth century in an influential movement against secular colonial education. The refusal of the Government of India to accede to appeals for the establishment of a Muslim university forced Muslim parties to interrogate their position as a minority religious community. In the first decade of the twentieth century, secularism in India was redefined by Muslims seeking the accommodation of a plurality of religions within the Indian state and nation.

1 SECULAR EDUCATION AND RELIGIOUS IDENTITY

The development of a national system of education in England in the first half of the nineteenth century was consistently checked by religious divisions and a mistrust of state involvement in the educational domain. In 1820 a bill for the establishment of national schools was dropped by parliament as unsatisfactory to both Anglican and Nonconformist parties. When Lord Melbourne's second Whig government attempted to extend state education at the close of the 1830s, the result was a compromise with the Established Church in response to which many Nonconformists turned towards the voluntary establishment of denominational schools. Amid often-acrimonious religious discord, however, all but a very small number – among them Secularists, Radicals and Chartists – rejected the possibility of establishing an Englisheducational system devoid of religious teaching. After 1840 attempts to expand the role of the state in education floundered on denominational grounds, yet majority factions united in their rejection of a secular solution. The Newcastle Commission on education observed in 1858 that the possibility of introducing a secular system of public instruction to England had gained no widespread support.[1] How then should the determination of British administrators in India to exclude religious teaching from government schools and colleges, and ensure the exclusive state patronage of secular education, be explained? In light of prevailing metropolitan opposition to education without religion it is clear that simply gesturing towards European post-Enlightenment notions of secularism is insufficient to explain the colonial secular education commitment. A better starting point might be the insight that prior to 1857 India served as a testing ground for liberal ideas and governmental practices untried and unpalatable in Britain.[2] The question remains, however: why secular education?

This chapter outlines the origins of the colonial secular education commitment and its development up to 1860. It begins by tracing the emergence of a distinction between religious and secular instruction in colonial discourse on education, and the embedding of that distinction into state educational provisions in a period culminating with Lord William Bentinck's February 1835 decision that the colonial state would sponsor secular education alone. Attention then shifts to the moment that was seminal in the establishment of an extensive system of public instruction in the territories of British India: Charles Wood's education dispatch of 1854. It is shown how, with the inauguration of a network of colonial schools and colleges, the principle of the exclusive state patronage of secular education was confirmed and new measures set in place by which, with the growth of government-sponsored instruction, the secular education commitment would be upheld. The chapter closes by considering the impact of the Indian Rebellion of 1857–8 on the colonial educational project, revealing how, after the transfer of sovereignty from the East Indian Company to the Crown, the secular education commitment was affirmed. The post-Rebellion colonial state would continue to structure its educational provisions around a distinction between religious and secular instruction, and patronize secular education alone.

Between the years 1830 and 1860 the establishment of a modern Indian educational system was accompanied by the institutionalization of the state non-patronage of religious education. Concurrently, however, religious identity was inscribed into government educational provisions. In the early nineteenth century, a growing number of East India Company administrators, who were committed to the transformation of India through education, envisaged the development of a system of public instruction composed of schools and colleges attended by members of all religious communities together. The vision of an Indian educational system organized independently of religious affiliation was not, however, achieved. For reasons which the chapter makes clear, the extension of colonial public instruction after 1830 involved the directing of educational provisions towards specific religious constituencies, building upon governmental practices inherited from an earlier generation of Company officials. Confirmation of the exclusive state patronage of secular instruction proceeded alongside the incorporation of religious identity into government education, setting in place institutional provisions through which the separation of education into religious and secular components would later be contested.

The Origins of the Colonial Secular Education Commitment

To account for the origins of the colonial secular education commitment, two interrelated decisions made by British authorities in early nineteenth-century India must be explained: the resolve not to devote state funds to the teaching of Christianity; and the determination to terminate the patronage of Hindu and Muslim religious teaching in government institutions – a part of colonial pedagogical arrangements from 1780. In existing scholarship, attempts have been made to explain each of these decisions. The termination of support for Hindu and Muslim religious instruction has been explained as part of the 1830s shift in colonial educational policy away from the encouragement of 'oriental' learning towards the promotion of western education and the English language in India, inspired by evangelical and utilitarian calls for reform.[3] The decision of the government to avoid patronizing Christian instruction has been accounted for by a prevalent British fear that the state promotion of Christianity would provoke a hostile Indian reaction, and a growing colonial perception of the potential of secular western education to effect moral and intellectual improvement among Indian subjects.[4]

Two contributions to a topic otherwise largely neglected in scholarship on South Asia should be noted. In her influential study of the role played by English literature in the colonial subjugation of India, Gauri Viswanathan argues that the British decision to avoid patronizing the teaching of Christianity was taken in deference to Indian religious feelings by officials concerned not to give the impression of a state attempt at proselytism. She suggests that the study of English literature, emphasized in colonial educational provisions, was invested with responsibilities including the inculcation of morality reserved in Britain for religious instruction. The advantage of English literature, which emerged as a subject of study first in a colonial context, was that it could be taught without an obvious compromise of the religious neutrality of the colonial state.[5] Latterly, Nandini Chatterjee has attempted to explain the origins of the colonial secular education commitment, suggesting that the removal of religious teaching from government institutions was synchronous with the offering of state support for private educational initiatives, opening up the field of education for missionary and, later, Indian parties.[6]

Both Viswanathan and Chatterjee make important points relevant to a correct understanding of the origins of the secular education commitment. Viswanathan rightly identifies the pervasive British concern that sponsoring the teaching of Christianity would provoke Indian opposition. Her study cogently traces the development of a European understanding that secular western education might be employed to transform its Indian recipients and even to disseminate Christianity, though the attention it bestows on missionary parties and the role of English literature means that major government interventions and wider pedagogical debates on secular instruction are overlooked. Chatterjee accurately identifies the influence of Christian and utilitarian parties urging the abandonment of state support for the Hindu and Muslim religions, and is correct to suggest that a consequence of the colonial secular education commitment was the growth of private educational agencies. Her claim to have historicized secular government education in India cannot, however, be substantiated. After noting the significance of arguments founded on utility to the case for secular education in the 1830s, Chatterjee races forward to explain the provisions of Wood's dispatch of 1854, offering no account and displaying no awareness of the religious-secular distinction confirmed in government education in 1835. Neither the origins nor development of the colonial commitment to secular education are satisfactorily explained in a study overlooking the fact that the principle of the exclusive state patronage of secular education was confirmed two decades before Wood's significant contribution.

If the inauguration of the Government of India's commitment to sponsor only secular education is to be fully understood, it is necessary to consider together explanations of the state non-patronage of Christianity and the cessation of its support for Hindu and Muslim religious instruction. When these two developments are viewed alongside each other it becomes clear that invested in administrative debates on colonial education by the early 1830s were competing conceptions of the most suitable relationship between religion and state in India. The governor generalship of Lord William Bentinck (1828–35) is conventionally considered the period during which colonial disputation over the objects of government education – between advocates of the continued state patronage of oriental learning ('orientalists') and of its replacement in India by western education and the English language ('anglicists') – reached a climax, provoking Bentinck to resolve in March 1835 that 'the great object of the British Government ought to be the promotion of European literature and science among the natives of India'.[7] Unnoticed in existing research is that this debate was structured around differing interpretations of the religious neutrality, or secularism, of the colonial state.[8] In 1835 a victory, though not a final triumph, was won by those European parties seeking the separation of the colonial state from religion in the educational domain.

From the final decades of the eighteenth century the educational policy of the East India Company had included the preservation of institutions for the teaching of Arabic, Persian and Sanscrit subjects. In 1780 the Calcutta Madrasa had been founded: a government college for the study of an Arabic and Persian curriculum including the Qur'an, Hadith and Muslim law; a state-sponsored institution for the receipt of a Sanscrit education was opened at Benares in 1791. The government's patronage of oriental learning in distinctly Muslim and Hindu institutions was consistent with the prevailing sympathy of colonial administrators in this earlier period for Indian history, culture and languages, and reflected the efforts of the Company to ensure continuity with pre-British forms of rule. To this end, Hindu and Muslim law was administered in colonial courts, while the business of government was conducted through the medium of Persian. Until 1830 European officials trained at the College of Fort William in Calcutta were required to gain proficiency in Persian along with one or more vernacular Indian languages.

That the East India Company's support of oriental learning at the Calcutta Madrasa and Sanscrit College was increasingly assailed by evangelical and utilitarian parties in Britain is well known. A powerful influence at the Company's headquarters in London – and well represented in the House of Commons – were evangelicals including, most influentially, Henry Martyn and Charles Grant, who argued for the depravity of the Hindu and Muslim religious systems encountered in India, and put the case that the support of oriental education, intimately related to Hinduism and Islam, was incompatible with the duties of a Christian government.[9] By the 1820s evangelical proponents of reform had been joined by a growing lobby denouncing the Company's support of Indian religions on the grounds of utility. The heightened influence of utilitarian ideas on the formation of East India Company policy is best captured by the court of directors' assertion of 1824 that the great object of government education 'should not have been to teach Hindoo learning, or Mahomedan learning, but useful learning'.[10] Composed by James Mill, a champion of utilitarian reform, the court's dispatch continued that with the establishment of the Calcutta Madrasa and Sanscrit College, the East India Company had bound itself 'to teach a great deal of what was frivolous, not a little of what was purely mischievous, and a small remainder indeed in which utility was in any way concerned'.[11]

Concurrent with condemnation of the Company's support of oriental learning was the emergence of proposals for the widespread introduction of western education to India. In the view of Grant and other evangelicals the dissemination of western ideas among the Indian population would be sure to expose the errors and superstitions contained within the Hindu and Muslim religions, paving the way for the advance of Christian truth.[12] Proponents of utilitarian ideas shared with their evangelical contemporaries the belief that Hinduism and Islam would be undermined by contact with western thought. For some it was indispensable that western education include the overt teaching of Christian precepts, but as early as the first decade of the nineteenth century the possibility had been raised that western scientific and literary subjects might be taught to Indian subjects, effecting their moral and intellectual improvement and encouraging a receptivity to Christian ideas without direct instruction in Christianity.[13] In 1813 the territories of the East India Company were opened up to European missionaries, precipitating the entry of missionary organizations into the Indian educational scene; the foundation of a college at Serampore (near Calcutta) by William Carey and other Baptist missionaries followed in 1818.[14] The anticipated boon for Christian religious instruction was qualified, however, by the Company's decision that no government funding would be awarded to missionary parties.[15] Justified in terms of government religious neutrality, this decision should be considered significant as an early example of the concept's application to denote not the state support of multiple religions, but its distancing from religious activity and belief.

In Bengal a distinction between the 'religious' and the 'secular' appears to have made its first appearance in educational discourse when in 1816 a group of Hindu gentlemen in Calcutta, among them Gopimohan Deb and Rhadhakanta Deb, approached the chief justice of the Calcutta High Court, Edward Hyde East, soliciting government assistance for the foundation of an institution in which they could acquire an English education. It is likely that the Hindu party sought the acquaintance of their community with western knowledge and ideas in part so that attacks on their religious customs and beliefs, including those made by the English-educated Rammohun Roy, could be responded to. In consultation with Hyde East, however, the party made clear that the teaching of Christianity to the sons of Hindu elites could not be tolerated.[16] The result was the foundation of the Hindu College, an institution offering Indian subjects western scientific and literary instruction – the first of its kind in Bengal.[17] The teaching of Christianity was avoided – a course welcomed by officials concerned to avoid the appearance of a government attempt at proselytism. The opening of the Hindu College in May 1817 was accompanied by the establishment of the Calcutta School Book Society, an organization with European and Indian members seeking to publish textbooks for use in the college and other institutions. In the society's rules the principle of excluding religion from public education was codified with the stipulation that no religious books would be printed.[18] The suggestion has been made that Hindu parties in Calcutta agreed to participate in the work of the society on the condition that it refrained from publishing works on religion.[19] To separate the study of science, mathematics and other subjects from religious faith was, additionally, a course consistent with the growth of positivist ideas in Bengal. After the appointment of Henry Derozio as teacher in 1828, the Hindu College developed into the centre of positivism and free thought in Calcutta – the wellspring of the movement of radical thinkers in the metropolis that became known as 'Young Bengal'.[20]

In 1823 the General Committee of Public Instruction (GCPI) was founded at Calcutta, as a new body of European officials to oversee the educational activities of government. The Calcutta Madrasa, Sanscrit College and Hindu College were brought under its control and new government institutions were founded at Agra and Delhi in which, it was hoped, western scientific subjects would be gradually added to oriental courses of study. These developments were contentious. If the western subjects introduced to state institutions did not include Christianity, and yet oriental curricula were taught in which Hindu and Muslim religious content was permitted, the argument followed, the colonial state was patronizing false Indian religions, but refusing support for Christian truth.[21] Both the continued sponsoring of Muslim and Hindu learning and the teaching of western lessons devoid of Christian content were lambasted by European critics. From England appeals were made that the government of India introduce Christian teaching to its colleges, while in India European missionaries were vocal in opposition to government policy.[22] One of the most high-profile critics was Alexander Duff, a member of the General Assembly of the Church of Scotland who arrived in Calcutta in May 1830 to found the General Assembly Institution – a missionary college in which English literature and science were taught alongside Christian lessons.[23] Convinced that western education ought not to be dissociated from Christianity, Duff was an outspoken critic of the Hindu College's secular western course and sought to develop the General Assembly Institution as an interdenominational Christian alternative. The state sponsoring of Hindu and Muslim religious learning he regarded with abhorrence.[24]

When Charles Trevelyan arrived at Calcutta in 1833 the stage was set for a decisive contribution to debates over the government patronage or non-patronage of Hindu, Muslim and Christian religious teaching. A prize-winning Persian scholar of the College of Fort William, Trevelyan, as we have noted, was nevertheless convinced of the necessity of disseminating western knowledge and the English language among Indian subjects. In April 1829, while stationed at Delhi, he had unveiled radical plans for the establishment of a comprehensive Indian educational system comprised of local schools, district colleges and an English-style university for the teaching of western subjects to Indians of all religions conjointly.[25] Taking after evangelical reformers such as Charles Grant, Trevelyan believed the advance of western learning necessary for the moral and intellectual regeneration of the people of India, raising their position on a scale of civilizational progress. Through the acquisition of western knowledge and ideas, he envisaged, Indian subjects would be elevated from degradation to relative civilization.[26]

Two features of Trevelyan's educational thought should be especially noted. The first is his determination that the government sponsoring of oriental learning must be stopped. In Trevelyan's view, Arabic and Sanscrit systems of learning were inseparable from the religions of Islam and Hinduism respectively, and accounted above all else for the degradation and stagnation of India. The state support of Arabic and Sanscrit teaching he considered a bar to the moral and intellectual improvement of Indian peoples. The second is his conviction of the possibilities of effecting that improvement through secular western instruction. Motivated in part by the belief that the teaching of Christianity would provoke an Indian reaction against government education, Trevelyan was convinced that secular western scientific and literary training could be employed to dissolve the Hindu and Muslim religions and reshape the Indian character. The object of this transformation would be the development of an anglicized Indian identity founded on the English language, literature and law – and ultimately Christianity. Trevelyan celebrated the graduates of the Hindu College – liberated from the religious errors of their countrymen, anglicized in tastes and opinion and converted into loyal subjects of government – as specimens of the desired product of state education, imperfect only insofar as they had not yet openly embraced Christianity.[27] In his view the Indian subject educated in a secular western course would over time inevitably seek a religion consistent with his new found intellectual proficiency and turn towards the Christian faith.[28]

In early 1833 Trevelyan was appointed to the GCPI and became the leading proponent, among its members, of the termination of government support for oriental learning in favour of the exclusive promotion of western education.

He did so with a clearly formulated conception of the ideal relationship between religion and state in the educational field. Trevelyan brought together arguments for the government sponsorship of secular western education and the cessation of state funding for Hindu and Muslim learning to propose the complete separation of the colonial state from religious instruction, termed in his correspondence the 'entire neutrality' of government with regard to religious education.[29] No state funding would be devoted to religious instruction, and the government of India would offer public encouragement to no form of religious teaching. For Trevelyan the object of colonial education remained to 'shake Hindooism and Mahommedanism to the centre and firmly establish our language, our learning and ultimately our religion in India'.[30] This, he believed, would be best achieved by the formal and absolute separation of the state from religious instruction.

The division of the GCPI into hostile 'anglicist' and 'orientalist' camps was provoked in the final months of 1834 by the introduction of proposals to force the study of western subjects on the holders of scholarships at the Calcutta Madrasa.[31] What followed has been often noted. To break the deadlock in the committee, up stepped Thomas Babington Macaulay, law member of Bentinck's council, with his sweeping condemnation of Indian learning and unequivocal endorsements: the printing of Arabic and Sanscrit books would be terminated, the award of stipends for the study of oriental subjects would be discontinued and the Calcutta Madrasa and other institutions of oriental education would be closed. According to Macaulay, the funds saved by these measures would be put to use promoting the study of western science and literature through the medium of English at institutions maintained by government.[32] On close inspection, however, it becomes clear that Macaulay's minute, so often repeated in colonial lore and postcolonial scholarship, was in fact little more than a restatement of Trevelyan's educational plans.[33] Like Trevelyan, Macaulay emphasized the great benefits to be obtained by the anglicization of Indian subjects – both for the stability of British rule and the condition of India. Macaulay was persuaded to endorse Trevelyan's programme for the separation of the colonial state from religious education, framing his argument by reference to the necessary 'neutrality' of government in religious matters.[34] Advocating the abolition of state support for oriental learning and the government non-patronage of the teaching of Christianity, he lent his rhetorical backing to the secular education commitment.

The arguments advanced by members of the GCPI opposed to the abandonment of government support for oriental education were extensive. The 'orientalists' put the case that while instruction in western subjects might be gradually introduced to government institutions, this ought not to be done at the expense of Arabic, Persian and Sanscrit studies; indeed, the best way of reconciling Indians to the study of western subjects would be their teaching alongside courses of oriental instruction.[35] To this it was added that the East India Company had for over five decades committed itself to the support of oriental learning; to revoke that support would marginalize Indian elites and create political danger for government. Underlying 'orientalist' arguments was a conception of the role and responsibilities of the government of India opposed to that expounded by Trevelyan and Macaulay. On grounds of principle and prudence, it was advanced, the East India Company ought to respond to the requirements of the Hindu and Muslim constituencies under its rule; support for oriental learning should there-fore be maintained. To explain the duty of government to continue supporting oriental instruction, 'orientalists' stressed the religious significance of Arabic and Sanscrit learning and advocated the continued state patronage of institutions in which Islamic and Hindu subjects were taught.[36]

When Lord William Bentinck resolved in March 1835 that government edu-cational efforts would be concentrated on the promotion of European subjects, the impasse in the GCPI over the objects of colonial education was brought to an end. Overlooked in existing research is that in that same month the gov-ernor general was moved to pronounce decisively in favour of the government non-patronage of religious instruction; under Bentinck's direction, the colonial secular education commitment was announced as the policy of state. That this decision would be reached was not inevitable. A statesman committed to utili-tarian and evangelical ideas of reform, Bentinck had had under consideration as late as April 1834 the possibility of government support for missionary schools and colleges.[37] In his private capacity he patronized missionary schools including the General Assembly Institution at Calcutta.[38] How, then, is his final decision in favour of secular instruction to be explained? The governor general had always taken a keen interest in the progress of students schooled in secular western ideas at the Hindu College, making regular visits to the institution.[39] His impression of the successes of the college may have informed a perception of the benefits to be derived from extending secular education more widely. Undoubtedly, a fur-ther major influence on Bentinck was Trevelyan, who in a series of letters in the final months of 1834 explained in detail to the governor general the advantages of separating the colonial state from religious education and committing govern-ment funds to sponsor secular western lessons alone.[40]

In January 1835 Bentinck was approached by a deputation requesting the financial support of the colonial state for the General Assembly Institution. In reply he explained that the school was 'not of the description for which the Government has any Funds available, or can otherwise extend assistance from the public revenue'.[41] The rationale behind this decision was explained several weeks later when Bentinck issued a parting address to a group of missionaries in Calcutta. The British government of India, he disclosed, had long pledged itself to 'strict neutrality' in religious matters – a necessary foundation for the perpetuation of its rule.[42] While in future the government would direct its attention towards the promotion of western education, the instruction sponsored would be exclusively secular. In government-managed institutions only secular subjects would be taught, while the state support of missionary schools and colleges imparting religious instruction would be avoided.[43] The high point of liberal reform – when the dissemination of western knowledge and ideas was first elevated as the 'great object' of state-sponsored colonial pedagogy – was therefore also the point at which the principle of the exclusive state patronage of secular instruction was confirmed.

Wood's Education Dispatch

In July 1854 the decision was taken to establish a far-reaching state educational system in the territories of British India. Universities would be founded to complement a network of schools and colleges supported from public revenues. Scholarships would be awarded on the basis of merit to allow talented pupils to pass from lower level schools into colleges where they would study for university degrees. Institutions would be established to train teachers and school books would be printed at government expense. This set of practices was to be overseen by public officials staffing new departments of education in each of India's three presidencies – the first colonial administrators with responsibility solely for public instruction. The principal aim of the system would be to inculcate knowledge of the arts, sciences, philosophy and literature of Europe.[44]

After 1835 responsibility for government educational initiatives had continued to rest on committees or councils of education in Calcutta, Madras and Bombay. In Bengal the GCPI and its successor from 1841, the Council of Education, had overseen the foundation and development of new institutions for the imparting of western scientific and literary instruction. Most higher level government schools and colleges taught a standard curriculum, including literature, philosophy, history, geography and mathematics – primarily through the English medium.[45] The incentive to study English was dramatically increased in 1844 when it was resolved that preference in competition for public employment would be given to candidates competent in the language. Accompanying government efforts to encourage the learning of English were a series of schemes to extend vernacular education. James Thomason, lieutenant governor of the NWP, oversaw the establishment of a system of state vernacular schools in upper India from 1845. The success of his efforts provoked demands for similar vernacular education schemes in lower Bengal, with the support of Lord Dalhousie. The governor general possessed an enthusiasm for extending western education in India comparable to that of his predecessor, William Bentinck.[46]

The design of a colonial system of education would take place, however, not in India under Dalhousie's direction, but in England. By the early 1850s a perception had taken root in the metropolis that the East India Company ought to be doing more for the western education of India. Following the renewal of the Company's charter in 1853 it was resolved to extend government-sponsored instruction. As president of the Company's board of control, Charles Wood was responsible for devising and dispatching extensive and ultimately influential plans for the establishment of an Indian educational system. Wood's dispatch may in part be considered the advancement towards realisation of 'anglicist' plans for the western education of India.[47] The dispatch affirmed the primary object of government education to be the imparting of western knowledge, adding that a sacred duty of Britain as an imperial power lay in the education of Indian people and their consequent moral and intellectual improvement.[48] In several significant ways, however, the pedagogical vision advanced by 'anglicists' in the 1830s was revised. The dispatch emphasized the importance of Indian vernacular media to the popular dissemination of western knowledge, abandoning the idea that western learning would gradually filter down from English-speaking Indian elites to the population at large in favour of the instruction of a wider section of the population in local languages. The importance of providing elementary and practical instruction in subjects such as arithmetic and agriculture was stressed, and educating Indian women was announced a government object.[49]

Two closely related educational provisions introduced to India by Wood's dispatch are particularly important to this study. Both were borrowed from England where they had been advanced and adopted as answers to the frequently vexed question of how to incorporate a plurality of religious denominations into the educational arrangements of a modern polity. Charles Wood considered these provisions to be solutions to the problem of how to extend colonial education while maintaining the government's secular education commitment and ensuring the religious neutrality of the state. Significantly, however, both provisions departed from the idealized educational arrangements advanced by Charles Trevelyan and others in the 1830s, by confirming in the Indian educational system the presence of institutions founded for distinct religious constituencies and attended exclusively by members of one religious group. I refer specifically to the introduction of the grant-in-aid system, and the establishment of examining universities, to which privately-managed colleges could affiliate. Celebrated in 1854 as a great advance in colonial plans for the advance of western learning, these measures would encourage the survival and strengthening of Indian religions alongside colonial public instruction, and pave the way for the later reorganization of Indian education according to religious identity.

Almost immediately, Bentinck's February 1835 announcement of the exclusive state patronage of secular education had come under come attack from British figures in India and at home. From Edinburgh, where he had recently returned, Alexander Duff argued that to impart western knowledge without Christianity would be to raise a nation of infidels – blank as regards morality or religious truth.[50] Henry Carre Tucker proposed in 1843 that the Bible be introduced as a class book in government schools in the NWP; his suggestion was repeated by Henry Marion Durand at Moulmein three years on.[51] The greatest British agitation in the 1840s came from Madras, where the governor – the Marquis of Tweeddale – was convinced by a party of European missionaries and residents to compose a minute praying for the introduction of the Bible as a class book in government schools and colleges.[52] The court of directors rejected the proposal, arguing that it was imprudent for government to introduce to its institutions 'any branch of study which can in any way interfere with the religious feelings and opinions of the people'.[53] Demands for the teaching of Christianity peaked when the renewal of the East India Company's charter was brought before parliament. In May 1852 a joint meeting was held in London of members of the Church Missionary Society, the Society for Promoting Christian Knowledge and the Society for the Propagation of the Gospel in Foreign Parts, three organizations instrumental to missionary education in India. Among the resolutions decided on was that teaching of the Holy Scriptures ought to be permitted in schools supported by the colonial state.[54]

In spite of this clamour, however, the parliamentary enquiries of 1852–3 reveal that the secular education commitment had gained widespread support among colonial officials. Almost all Company administrators submitting evidence to parliament rejected appeals for the introduction of Christian teaching to government schools and colleges, arguing that education in institutions under state management should remain exclusively secular. Take for example William Wilberforce Bird, a member of the Bengal Civil Service for almost forty years, who in 1835 had sided with Trevelyan, Macaulay and the 'anglicist' party in the GCPI. A firm supporter of the advance of western education in India, Bird was nevertheless adamant that government schools and colleges should continue to avoid teaching Christianity. In his view secular western education was achieving beneficial ends in elevating the moral standard in India. Moreover the government propagation of Christianity in its schools would, he feared, provoke Indian opposition, leading to 'catastrophes of a very serious description'.[55] The success of colonial pedagogy and the stability of British government in India were held to depend on the state sponsorship of secular education alone. Francis Horsley Robinson, who had served in the NWP, suggested to parliament that the introduction of Christian teaching to government schools would confirm Indian suspicions of an official intention to convert all to Christianity; such would be extremely dangerous to government, exciting the 'religious patriotism' of Hindus and Muslims in opposition to British rule.[56] Thomas Erskine Perry, formerly a member of the Bombay Board of Education, and Frederick Halliday, later to become lieutenant governor of Bengal, stressed before parliament the indispensability of the secular education commitment being preserved.[57]

With the parliamentary enquiries of 1852–3 an alternative proposal was first widely expounded by which religious instruction and western education might be reconciled in schools and colleges supported by the colonial state: the award of grants-in-aid. Following the failure of attempts to establish state-adminis-tered schools in England in 1820 a consensus had emerged that the government could better assist in the development of education by aiding the efforts of pri-vate societies attached to various religious denominations than by direct action in the educational field. Two rival religious societies dominated voluntary edu-cational provisions: the 'National Society for Promoting the Education of the Poor in the Principles of the Established Church' and the 'British and Foreign School Society'. The Anglican religious instruction in schools of the former was countered by the non-denominational teaching offered by the latter. In 1833 a sum of public money was for the first time allocated by the government for the building of primary schools, to be shared between the two organizations. Grants would be awarded for the building of new schools where either of the societies was able to meet half of the cost through voluntary contributions. The system of awarding grants to privately-managed schools was extended in 1839 and 1846 through increases to the parliamentary grant. A team of inspectors was appointed to monitor the condition of schools in receipt of state aid under the direction of a newly appointed committee of privy councillors. Each of the committee's attempts to increase its influence over the schools – principally via inspection and the training of teachers – was contested, particularly by members of the Estab-lished Church. Some Voluntaryists, among them a number of Congregationalists and Baptists, rejected the principle of state assistance in education outright. By the early 1850s, however, the grant-in-aid system had found considerable accept-ance across a broad spectrum of opinion in England, no doubt in part as a lesser evil to the development of a national system of education under exclusive state control. Grants were received by the Wesleyan Methodist Education Committee and Catholic Poor School Committee in addition to the older two societies.[58]

The operation of the grant-in-aid system in England raised the possibility of a distinction between the 'religious' and the 'secular' that was particularly attractive to officials concerned with government education in India. In Eng-land this distinction was not clearly defined. Among the fiercest battles fought between the committee of privy councillors and representatives of the Angli-can Church was that concerning the possible introduction of a clause granting freedom of conscience to pupils in schools receiving government grants. Some metropolitan observers critiqued the very idea of separating out education into religious and secular parts.[59] Emerging from the discussion over rules govern-ing the award of grants-in-aid in England, however, was the idea that the state might monitor and reward the secular efficiency of privately managed insti-tutions while abstaining from interference in any religious instruction that they imparted. This idea was latched upon by those seeking the extension of government-sponsored education, and above all the award of state funding to institutions maintained by Christian societies in India.

The introduction of the grant-in-aid system to India was favoured for several key reasons. Some observers made the persuasive case that it was unrealistic for the vast population of India to be educated in government-managed schools and colleges: far more would be achieved via the state support of institutions under private control.[60] To this was added the argument that grants-in-aid would stimulate Indian interest in education, raising private funds and fostering a highly desirable 'spirit of reliance'.[61] In much of the evidence submitted to the parliamentary enquiries of 1852–3 these arguments of principle and political economy were combined. The most prevalent argument for the introduction of the grant-in-aid system, however, was that it would permit government support for Christian missionary institutions without compromising the colonial secular education commitment and religious neutrality of government. The colonial state, it was argued, might award financial aid to any school in India teaching secular western subjects to a particular standard; the religious affiliation of the school's managers and any religious instruction imparted would be of no concern to the inspectors appointed to determine standards of secular education.[62] Alongside the colonial administrators putting this case, a number of missionaries advocating the introduction of grants-in-aid adopted the language of 'secular education' and 'religious neutrality' at this juncture. John Clark Marshman, formerly of the Baptist mission at Serampore, claimed that the award of grants-in-aid would extend government-sponsored education and reconcile religious and secular instruction while preserving the 'religious neutrality' of government.[63]

Perhaps the most influential proponent of the grant-in-aid system for India was Charles Trevelyan, recommended to Charles Wood as an authority on Indian education when he turned his attention to the writing of an education dispatch in late 1853.[64] Trevelyan had surprised contemporaries by not returning to India after 1838, instead finding employment as an assistant secretary at the Treasury. After fifteen years at home, however, he had lost none of his zeal for the education of India: his parliamentary evidence of June 1853 restated a liberal vision of the anglicization and Christianization of India through western education in preparation for eventual self-rule. Trevelyan remained convinced that English education would introduce new moral and intellectual standards to India, as a result of which the Hindu and Muslim religions would over time give way to Christianity. Until that point was reached, however, the preservation of the colonial secular education commitment was indispensable. In his evidence to parliament, Trevelyan described the 'religious neutrality' of the government's educational provisions as its 'great security' and 'the great cause of our success in enlightening the Natives'.[65] To depart from this principle and patronize the teaching of Christianity, he argued, would provoke opposition to colonial education and be 'of the greatest possible prejudice both to the progress of Christianity and to the continuance of our dominion in India'.[66] Avoiding state patronage of the teaching of Christianity was the only course by which Christianity could be safely and effectually promoted: 'if that principle of neutrality were once departed from ... the prospects of the evangelization of the people of India would be very seriously damaged'.[67] At the root of Trevelyan's support for the secular education commitment was a perception of the inevitable Indian opposition that would accompany the state propagation of Christianity – violent Muslim rebellion sparked by the state-sponsored teaching of Christianity was a possibility he particularly feared.[68] Where Trevelyan's educational thought had changed over the preceding two decades was in his belief that state support could be offered to Christian missionary institutions in a way consistent with the religious neutrality of the state. Like many of his contemporaries, Trevelyan argued that the award of grants-in-aid in return for the secular proficiency of a school would encourage the more extensive provision of western scientific and literary training, while permitting the British government to patronize institutions teaching Christianity without a compromise of its commitment to sponsor secular education alone. Trevelyan stressed the importance of making the rules governing the award of grants-in-aid known to Indian parties: that grants would be awarded solely for secular education, and irrespective of religious affiliation. In this way, he argued, Indian faith in government religious neutrality would be preserved.[69]

The following chapters show how in the later nineteenth century the grant-in-aid system introduced to India by Wood's dispatch allowed for the foundation and maintenance of schools and colleges in which the teaching of Indian religions was combined with government-prescribed curricula. The award of grants-in-aid was a crucial institutional mechanism by which the religions of India were preserved and strengthened alongside the advance of colonial public instruction. How far was this consequence anticipated by Trevelyan and his contemporaries? In what ways did proponents of the grant-in-aid system engage with the ideas of the denominalization of Indian education and of support for Hindu and Muslim institutions within the colonial system? It would appear that many did not consider the possibility of Hindu and Muslim schools and colleges receiving government grants at all. The focus of discussions over the introduction of grants-in-aid to India remained – as in English education – the public support of institutions belonging to multiple Christian denominations. Among those who gave the question thought, most were dismissive of the idea that the grant-in-aid system would mean the extensive patronage of Hindu and Muslim schools; widely it was assumed that most Indian institutions would fail to qualify for grants on account of the deficiencies of their secular courses of instruction.[70] So firmly convinced was Charles Trevelyan that western education would lead Indian students to embrace a higher level of morality and abandon their religions in favour of Christianity that he was untroubled by the possible short-term state patronage of institutions in which Hinduism or Islam were taught.[71] Other British observers were more accurate in anticipating the denominalization of education to accompany importing of the grant-in-aid system. Charles Hay Cameron, formerly president of the Bengal Council of Education, cautioned a select committee of the House of Lords that an inevitable consequence of grants-in-aid would be the patronizing of Hindu and Muslim schools. He, more than most, foresaw that grants-in-aid might work to strengthen a plurality of religious identities alongside the dissemination of western learning.[72]

Charles Wood consulted John Clark Marshman, Charles Trevelyan and others before determining that grant-in-aids would be introduced to India. Wood viewed the grant system as a pragmatic way of extending western education with the support of European and Indian private agencies. More important to him, however, was the possibility presented by grants-in-aid of preserving the colonial secular education commitment, while rapidly extending government-sponsored instruction. Wood was adamant that the government of India must continue to sponsor secular education alone: his letters recorded that the greatest danger to British rule in India lay in the possibility of a 'national-religious movement' incited by the state-sponsored teaching of Christianity.[73] Wood's papers betray his conviction that for the continued security of colonial government, however, it was the perception of state neutrality in religious matters – not simply the abstract fact – which mattered. Privately he noted that while grants-in-aid might be theoretically available to any institution, their awarding exclusively to Christian colleges and schools would inevitably create the impression of government-sponsored proselytism. The introduction of grants-in-aid necessarily entailed supporting Hindu and Muslim institutions, in order that the appearance of government religious neutrality and the stability of colonial rule might be preserved.[74]

That Wood viewed as essential the government sponsorship of secular education alone, and sought to strengthen the claim of the colonial state to religious neutrality, is confirmed by the measures which he put in place for the establishment of universities in India. In 1826 a radical change to university education in England had been heralded by the foundation of the 'London University'. Unlike the historic universities of Oxford and Cambridge, which imposed religious tests as late as 1871, the 'London University' was a non-denominational institution to which students would be admitted irrespective of their religious affiliation. The 'University' aimed at providing a self-consciously 'modern' scientific and literary education and permitted students to study for degrees without residing on its premises. In contrast to Oxford and Cambridge, it offered no religious education and played no part in the religious upbringing of students. In an Anglican reaction led by the Reverend Dr George D'Oyly, rector of Lambeth, with the support of the duke of Wellington, then prime minister, King's College was opened in 1831. Though the institution shared with the 'London University' the aim of imparting a more 'modern' education than that available at Oxford and Cambridge, a fundamental part of its programme would be instruction in the doctrines of the Established Church. By the early 1830s rival Anglican and non-denominational claims existed on higher education in the metropolis, provoking the chartering of the University of London in 1836 – an examining body to which King's College and the 'London University' (renamed University College) were affiliated. The colleges retained responsibility for teaching students, while the university examined their proficiency and awarded degrees. No religious subjects were examined; the religious divisions characterizing the debate over university education were overcome.[75]

The idea of establishing universities in India was of course not new at the time of Wood's dispatch. As we have seen, Charles Trevelyan proposed the foundation of an Indian university teaching western scientific and literary subjects as early as 1829, while more concrete proposals had taken shape in the Bengal Council of Education under the direction of Charles Hay Cameron in 1845. Charles Wood's vital contribution to Indian higher education plans was to determine that the model of the University of London would be copied. By 1853 the university had expanded greatly with the affiliation of almost thirty additional colleges for the teaching of the arts and law and sixty-eight medical schools from across Great Britain and Ireland, examined by the federal centre.[76] The university's supplemental charter of 1849 had made possible the affiliation of teaching institutions based anywhere within the formal British Empire and East India Company's territories. A significant proportion of these colleges were denominational institutions, teaching the catechism of a particular creed alongside the examined secular course. Wood considered the model of the University of London best suited to Indian university education. In January 1854 he wrote to Lord Elphinstone, governor of Bombay, suggesting that the simplest educational measure to effect in India would be the foundation of a university of the London type, with teaching colleges affiliated to an examining head institution.[77] The considerations informing this suggestion were several. To grant colleges responsibility for teaching university courses was consistent with Wood's attempt to extend private agency in education via the award of grants-in-aid. The size of India made the federal model of widely dispersed teaching colleges an attractive course for the greatest possible extension of higher education. Above all, however, Wood sought to copy the University of London design in order to avoid religious difficulties in Indian higher education. To Frederick Halliday he explained:

> We have taken for the model of our Indian University, the London University, because its framework is quite independent of any form of religious belief, which is indispensable in India. ... [Y]our Colleges may be Christian, Mahometan, or Hindoo, or admitting all if you can manage it (which we clearly cannot do here [in England]); but leaving all religious instruction (if any) to the Colleges, the University is to be open alike to all comers from any of the affiliated Institutions.[78]

As with the University of London, an Indian university would examine secular subjects alone; religious instruction would be imparted only in affiliated colleges under private management. For Wood, copying the University of London model meant strengthening the government's commitment to secular education and reinforcing the religious neutrality of the colonial state.

In July 1854 Wood's dispatch was sent to India. Among its provisions were the award of grants-in-aid to institutions under private management in return for proficient secular western instruction and the foundation of universities upon the University of London model in each of India's three presidencies. The exclusive imparting of 'secular' education in institutions under government management was confirmed – the first employment of the term in colonial educational policy.[79] The dispatch facilitated the rapid expansion of colonial education on the subcontinent; simultaneously, it preserved the British claim, founded on a distinction between religious and secular education, of the religious neutrality of government in the educational domain. In order to preserve that claim, however, Charles Wood introduced a university system which, coupled with the award of grants-in-aid, encouraged the foundation and preservation of institutions exclusively for members of one religious constituency. As Wood envisaged, Hindu, Muslim and Christian institutions were later established under government patronage and affiliated to the Indian universities. Upon first viewing, Charles Trevelyan declared himself delighted with Wood's dispatch, believing it the fulfilment of long-held wishes to see colonial public instruction extended.[80] Like many others he was unaware of the role the dispatch would come to play in strengthening heterogeneous Indian religious identities alongside the dissemination of new knowledge and ideas. As we shall see, its provisions provided a foundation for later nineteenth-century Indian negotiations of colonial pedagogy and the extension of Muslim education in Bengal, the NWP and the Punjab.

The Indian Rebellion and its Aftermath

The task of implementing the provisions of Wood's dispatch fell on officials in India. First in Bengal and the NWP, and soon after in Bombay, Madras and the Punjab, departments of education composed of a director and school inspectors began their operations. Grants-in-aid were awarded to institutions under European management – principally missionary schools and colleges – and in January 1857 the universities of Calcutta, Madras and Bombay were established. Just several months later, however, word spread of a sepoy rebellion at Meerut and the march of the mutineers on Delhi. The Indian Rebellion had begun.

The Rebellion is often interpreted as an ideological turning point in the colonial project, after which liberal explanations of the British imperial role – which were centred on the transformation and improvement of Indian peoples – were usurped by more conservative, paternalist justifications for colonial rule. Widely it is held that the opposition to British domination manifested in 1857–8 led observers to question the possibility and desirability of inculcating change on the subcontinent, engendering a revision of the aims and responsibilities of colonial government based on a new emphasis on Indian difference.[81] However, the resolve of British administrators to continue with the colonial educational project after 1858 suggests that the Rebellion marked less of an ideological rupture than is often posited: in the aftermath of its suppression, the British commitment to the moral and intellectual regeneration of India through public instruction was affirmed. To be sure, the Rebellion raised questions about colonial pedagogical plans. Lord Ellenborough, president of the East India Company's board of control, was among those arguing in early 1858 that colonial public instruction had provoked the uprisings and ought to be curtailed.[82] For a larger number of British officials, however, the Rebellion served as a reminder of the continued importance of colonial education. As Charles Trevelyan pointed out, western-educated Indian subjects had almost unanimously remained loyal to the British in 1857: the Trevelyan-Macaulay hypothesis of a link between western education and support for British rule appeared to have been upheld.[83] In England, missionary parties constituted a powerful lobby pressing for the continuation of colonial public instruction; Frederick Halliday was among the most high-profile officials in India urging government educational activities forward.[84] Once the dust of the Rebellion had settled, the idea of abandoning colonial pedagogical efforts was dismissed. An April 1859 dispatch confirmed that the Government of India remained committed to raising the moral, intellectual and material condition of Indian people through the improvement and extension of public instruction.[85]

If colonial education was to be advanced, however, two major issues affecting the religious neutrality of the state would have to be settled. The first concerned the award of grants-in-aid. In the view of Ellenborough and others, the awarding of grants to missionary schools and colleges explained above all else why Indians associated government education with Christianity and felt averse to state-sponsored public instruction. Ellenborough suggested that Indian peoples attached little significance to the distinction in grant-in-aid rules between religious and secular education; regardless of the stipulation that grants be awarded solely for the secular instruction imparted in a school, government support of missionary institutions was widely considered to be the state propagation of Christianity. To affirm the religious neutrality of the state, he argued, grants-in-aid to missionary schools had to be stopped.[86] Coterminous with this suggestion, a second, antagonistic proposal was gathering support: that the teaching of Christianity be introduced to schools and colleges under the management of government. In January 1858 a memorial was drafted by members of the Church Missionary Society in London calling for the abandonment of the principle of religious neutrality observed by the British government in India. It suggested that the catastrophes of the Rebellion were a 'divine judgement' on the policy of neutrality hitherto pursued; in future, the government should actively promote Christianity by introducing Bible teaching to its colleges and schools.[87] The campaign for the teaching of Christianity in government institutions found influential supporters including John Lawrence, chief commissioner of the Punjab.[88]

For a period of two years after the Rebellion, colonial educational provisions were subjected to rigorous scrutiny. Both the exclusion of religious teaching from government schools and colleges and the award of grants-in-aid to missionary institutions came in for criticism across a broad range of British opinion in India and England. The provisions of Wood's dispatch were assailed for their promotion and neglect of Christianity and their usurping and upholding of the principle of religious neutrality. Opposition to the plan of terminating government grants for missionary institutions was led in India by Frederick Halliday, lieutenant governor of Bengal, who insisted that the award of aid to missionary schools in return for their secular proficiency was compatible with the religious neutrality of the state.[89] In April 1859 the newly organized Indian home government sought to allay fears that the grant-in-aid system would be disbanded, noting that the imperative of government religious neutrality had not been compromised by its operation.[90] Ultimately, the decision to retain the provisions of the 1854 dispatch and render them the foundation of government public instruction in the post-Rebellion period was taken by Wood himself. Appointed secretary of state for India in June 1859, amid continued clamour for the introduction of Christian teaching to government schools, Wood wrote to Lord Canning (governor general), Lord Elphinstone (governor of Bombay) and Charles Trevelyan, who had recently returned to India as governor of Madras, asking each for his opinion of the subject.[91] Trevelyan was in his element. In December 1857, with the Rebellion ongoing, he had insisted in the *Times* that it was imperative to continue excluding religious teaching from Indian government schools while supporting missionary and other private institutions through the award of grants-in-aid.[92] In letters to Wood in July and August of 1859 this position was reiterated: to patronize Christian teaching directly would provoke violent Indian opposition; the award of grants-in-aid was consistent with the religious neutrality of government.[93]

Returning to Indian office after a four-year absence, Wood had expressed a conviction that his 1854 dispatch outlined the 'true ground' on which education in India should be based.[94] As a result of his correspondence with Trevelyan, coupled with an awareness of the opinions of Halliday and others in Bengal, this conviction was confirmed. And so in the post-Rebellion period the provisions of the 1854 dispatch were approved. In government schools and colleges only secular lessons would be taught, while government funding would be awarded to private institutions solely in return for the secular education which they offered.

Religious instruction would be no concern of the colonial state. In July 1860 a petition was presented in the House of Lords calling for Christian teaching in Indian government schools, but by this point Wood's mind was made up.[95] Though very few missionary institutions were awarded grants-in-aid in the early 1860s, the Indian Rebellion had left no lasting structural impact on colonial educational provisions, which continued to be organized around a distinction between religious and secular instruction.

What must finally be noted, however, is that this confirmation of the colonial secular education commitment – issued shortly after Queen Victoria's November 1858 proclamation that the British government would avoid interfering in Indian religious customs and beliefs – was accompanied by further moves to incorporate religious identity into state educational provisions.[96] In the view of many British figures, responsibility for the outbreak and escalation of the Indian Rebellion lay with Muslims in the Company's territories. Observers pointed to the convergence of rebellious elements around the figurehead of the nominal Mughal Emperor in Delhi and the kingdom of Awadh at Lucknow as proof of Muslim leadership in revolt. European accounts explained the Rebellion as a religious response to British rule, emphasizing perceived doctrinal tenets of Islam enjoining Muslims to rebel.[97] Before 1857 colonial administrators had periodically noted what they perceived as the reluctance of Indian Muslims to receive instruction in government institutions. The perception of Muslim responsibility for the Rebellion, coupled with the belief that Indian subjects educated in the colonial system would be loyal to government, now rendered the instruction of Muslims a major concern. 'What shall we do with the Musulmans?' asked one anonymous pamphlet published at Calcutta in June 1858.[98] The author admonished European officials and missionaries for neglecting the education of Muslims and suggested that by this failure the calamities of the Rebellion had been invited upon their heads. '[T]he Mussulman is a stranger in the land (as well as a danger)', recorded another short publication: 'One may pause to notice the proud contempt with which the Mussulman everywhere stands apart from Government Education'.[99] Charles Trevelyan drew a contrast between the English-educated Hindu government servant in lower Bengal and his backward Muslim counterpart in upper India – the one faithful to government and the other permanently disposed to rebel.[100]

The city of Patna in Bihar, once a seat of administration for the Nawabs of Bengal, was approximately one-quarter Muslim in 1857.[101] From as early as 1835, when the first attempt was made to establish a government school, British administrators had lamented the reluctance of its inhabitants to accept colonial public instruction. The city's commissioner, William Tayler, concluded in 1856 that Patna's elites failed to distinguish between English education and Christianity and consequently rejected both.[102] When the Indian Rebellion began, suspicion fell immediately on Patna's Muslim population. A state of martial law was imposed and a series of pre-emptive arrests of Muslim leaders were made. Tayler recorded his belief in a Muslim 'crusade' against the British government to re-establish the temporal superiority of Islam.[103] The culpability of Muslims from Patna in the Rebellion was never proven – some British officials rejected Tayler's concerns outright – but in the aftermath of the uprisings the city was selected by the government of Bengal as a priority site for inducing Muslim entry into the colonial educational system. To this end, the foundation of an Arabic and Persian class specifically for Muslims at the Patna government school was proposed. For the Bengal director of public instruction, William Atkinson, Patna's Muslims would, with the incentive of learning the Arabic and Persian languages, enter the school, where they would also receive instruction in a regular government course.[104]

The formation of a Muslim class at Patna's government school should be considered an important event in the development of separate Muslim provisions within the colonial educational system, a precursor to later India-wide governmental initiatives encouraging Muslim subjects to embrace colonial pedagogy.[105] After the Indian Rebellion the commitment to secular education announced in 1835 and embedded in colonial public instruction by Wood's dispatch was confirmed, but the process of developing state educational provisions for distinct religious constituencies – a practice of government from the late eighteenth century – was given fresh momentum. By 1860 the institutional arrangements were in place through which religious groups would later contest the secular education commitment.

2 EDUCATION, RELIGION AND STATE IN IRELAND AND INDIA

The development of colonial educational provisions specifically for Indian Muslims was accelerated in August 1871 when a resolution was passed by the Government of India noting with regret the deficit of Muslims participating in state education.[1] Building on the precedent set at Patna in 1860, the widespread teaching of Arabic and Persian was proposed to induce Muslim entrance into government schools, alongside the appointment of Muslim teachers and use in schools of the vernacular language best suited to local Muslims. The award of grants-in-aid for the maintenance of Muslim institutions in the colonial system was also recommended. The recognition by central government of a Muslim educational 'problem' – identified by British observers after the Indian Rebellion – was a critical development in colonial policy, provoking India-wide administrative discourses on Muslim education and the further embedding of Muslim identity into colonial public instruction.

In chapters three and four the contribution of Muslim parties concerned with reshaping colonial education to the composition of the Government of India's August 1871 resolution is considered. It is shown that from the late 1860s the deficiencies of government-sponsored instruction – in particular the absence of religious education – were of major concern to Muslim elites formulating opinion and engaging with colonial authorities through emergent public institutions across northern India. This chapter concentrates on the official actor responsible for the government's resolution: the Viceroy of India between 1869 and 1872, Lord Mayo. It reveals that Mayo's decision to reform state education for Muslim parties was crucially shaped by his experiences of the politics and government of an alternative colonial context where experiments with the separation of religion from education had been attempted: nineteenth-century Ireland. The Government of India's August 1871 resolution was decisively influenced by Mayo's identification of India's Muslim minority with the Anglican community in Ireland; by his personal aversion to the separation of religion from education; and by an understanding of the responsibilities of government to respond to the requirements of multiple religious constituencies fashioned by his Irish career. Mayo sought the development of a system of public instruction in India attuned to the demands of heterogeneous religious groups. His resolution engendered significant debate over the future of the colonial secular education commitment and the nature of Indian secularism.

The role played by Lord Mayo in pioneering the reform of government education for Muslim parties has passed unnoticed in existing research on account of the dominant influence on subsequent historiography of William Wilson Hunter's *The Indian Musalmans* (1871).[2] The thesis advanced by Hunter, a Bengal civil servant, in his influential treatise is well known. Published shortly after the conclusion of the final state trial of Wahabi leaders accused of sedition against the government, Hunter's text popularized in colonial discourse the question of whether or not Indian Muslims were bound by their religion to rebel against foreign rule. The conclusion he arrived at is that no rebellion could be undertaken against the British consistent with Islamic law, so long as Muslim civil and religious rights were fully protected by the colonial state. This contention was followed, however, by the documenting of a series of Muslim grievances with government which, it was inferred, could provoke rebellion if unchecked. The effect of his text despite, or rather because of, its professedly sympathetic outlining of the damaging consequences of colonial rule for Indian Muslims, was to present every Muslim as a potential opponent of government. Hunter conjoined Wahabi conspiracy and Muslim discontent, elevating the idea of Muslim disaffection through his exposition of the 'wrongs of the Muhammadans under British rule'.[3] Foremost among these 'wrongs' was the neglect of Muslim interests in colonial education. 'The truth is', he recorded, 'that our system of public instruction ... is opposed to the traditions, unsuited to the requirements, and hateful to the religion, of the Musalmans'.[4] For Hunter the reform of state education was required to ensure the fidelity of Muslims to government.

To explain the timing of the Government of India's August resolution – passed so soon after the close of the Wahabi trials – the concerns expressed in *Indian Musalmans* to conciliate Muslims to British rule and encourage their participation in state education were undoubtedly significant. A first draft of the resolution was penned in May 1871 with the final trial of suspected Wahabi conspirators ongoing; its privately disclosed object was to produce a positive effect 'on the feelings of the Mahomedan population at this moment'.[5] What must be clarified, however, is that William Wilson Hunter played no part in the resolution's composition. Contrary to what is often assumed, the question of the reform of government educational policy was settled in August 1871 prior to Hunter's contribution, so often regurgitated in scholarship.[6] Moreover there is little evidence to support the claim made in Hunter's diary, and first publicized in F. H. Skrine's biography, that Hunter was requested to write *Indian Musalmans* by Lord Mayo.[7] Notes passed between Mayo and members of his council indicate that, far from requesting the text to be written, the viceroy had under consideration its censuring in the final months of 1871.[8]

This chapter moves beyond notions of loyalty, disaffection and the reconciliation of Muslims to British rule popularized by *Indian Musalmans*, to consider the contribution to the formation of the Government of India's August resolution of ideas on secular education, religious identity and the relationship between religion and state – developed by Lord Mayo and imported to India from Ireland in 1869. That it was Mayo, rather than Hunter, who played the leading role in engineering the reform of state education for Muslims was recognized by a handful of contemporaries. Soon after Mayo's death in February 1872 E. C. Bayley, secretary to the Government of India, noted:

> In regard to the special question of the encouragement of education among the Mahomedan community, it is, I believe not generally known that Lord Mayo took the active and leading part. It is perhaps no longer any breach of confidence to say that he himself first drew attention to this subject, and that the resolution of Government in which it was recently discussed, and to which I have alluded, proceeded word for word from his pen; nor need I, perhaps hesitate to add that in other more general measures, intended for the benefit of the Mahomedans he took an equal interest, and that this portion of the community have lost in him not only a most powerful but a most sincere friend.[9]

Bayley's observations are confirmed by a survey of Mayo's papers. During the summer of 1871 Mayo personally composed three separate drafts of a note on Muslim education, each slightly amended, before the government resolution of 7 August.[10] The viceroy brought the question of Muslim education before his council and personally devised reforms of colonial public instruction deriving in the first instance from his knowledge and experiences of Ireland.

Recent years have witnessed a proliferation of literature on the two-way transfer of knowledge and ideas between Ireland and India under British rule, as attempts are made to map the complex networks and exchanges termed by one scholar the 'webs of empire'.[11] A majority of this literature has concentrated on the migration and translation of nationalist ideas between the two territories and a smaller number of studies on the transfer of knowledge and techniques of government.[12] The role of several imperial administrators influential in Ireland and India – including Charles Trevelyan – has received attention, but Lord Mayo has been entirely overlooked in existing studies, a remarkable omission in light of the prominent role that he played in Irish politics and government during the 1850s and 1860s, and his subsequent ascension to the Indian viceroyalty.[13] Mayo was born in 1822, the eldest son of an Irish Protestant peer, Robert Bourke.[14] Educated at Trinity College, Dublin he entered parliament in 1847, representing the Irish constituencies of Kildare and Coleraine. Mayo was one of the leading figures in the Irish Conservative Party and served as Chief Secretary for Ireland during Lord Derby's governments of 1852 and 1858–9. In June 1866 he became Chief Secretary for a third time, holding the post under Derby and then Disraeli before his departure for India in November 1868. During his parliamentary career, spanning twenty-one years in government and opposition, Mayo spoke consistently on Irish issues and acted for a period as de facto leader of the Conservative Party in Ireland, and of the Irish Conservatives in the House of Commons.[15] As an Irish politician and statesman he straddled the divide between London and Dublin and was immersed in political debates in both England and Ireland. His career is suggestive of the transfers of ideas and practices between not two but three major sites – or 'overlapping territories' – in the British imperial world: England, Ireland and India.[16] To consider those transfers is to contribute towards an important reimagining of the spatial parameters of empire.

Principal developments in colonial government under Mayo drew directly from his Irish experiences. To explain the genesis of new governmental techniques and strategies during Mayo's viceroyalty, a career immersed in the politics and government of Ireland must take centre stage. Innovations encouraged by Mayo in India – including the commitment of government to the relief of famine, the undertaking of public works projects, the development of state railways and reform of tenancy-occupier agreements on land – borrowed directly from Irish experiences. That the construction of roads, railways and canals would contribute to the relief of famine and simultaneously extend the civil power and military capacity of government was a lesson that Mayo had learnt in Ireland during recurring incidences of famine and rural unrest. Mayo's Irish career shaped Indian policy in other unacknowledged areas, including prison reform, agricultural development and the suppression of 'criminal' groups. Thom's *Almanac* in Ireland – 'that most wonderful repertoire of information respecting any country that is annually published' – served for the viceroy as the model for an *Imperial Gazetteer* of India, prompting the establishment of an Indian department of statistics.[17]

In the reform of colonial education and historical development of Indian secularism the impact of Mayo's Irish career on India was perhaps most strongly felt. Later, Mayo's attempts to charter a Catholic university in Ireland and endow the Irish Catholic Church are examined – endeavours revealing his personal opposition to the separation of religion from education, and his understanding of the responsibility of government to support the religious constituencies under its rule. The opening section below highlights that in addition to these motivations, Mayo's resolution on Muslim education was determined by his identification of an affinity between Indian Muslims and Anglicans in Ireland based upon their shared rejection of exclusively secular education and the resistance of both to the receipt of instruction in institutions dominated by another religious group.

An 'Extraordinary Similarity'

Upon its foundation in 1831 the Irish system of education was characterized by restrictions on religious instruction and the attempt to school children of different denominations conjointly. Control over schooling was vested in an interdenominational national board with responsibility for managing applications from private parties seeking to establish new schools. Institutions successful in obtaining the board's funds committed to imparting secular moral and literary instruction to children of all religious denominations together; religious instruction was confined to just one or two sessions each week on a separate, denominational basis.[18] Following soon after Catholic emancipation in 1829, the introduction of these rules sought to assuage concerns over the dominant role of Protestant societies in the provision of education in Ireland: in the national system, the threat of proselytism through education was removed. As in India, however, British authorities departed from metropolitan practice by imposing restrictions on religious instruction and engineering a degree of state control over education that swiftly proved unpopular to many.

Irish Anglican opposition to the national system, growing through the 1830s and 1840s, centred on the control exercised by the board at the expense of the Established Church and the confining of religious instruction to specified times. In 1839 the Church Education Society was founded – a body committed to the establishment of schools outside of the national system in which religious instruction would be imparted without restraint. Substantial subscriptions to the Society enabled it to fund privately almost 2,000 schools by 1850.[19] As a result of Anglican withdrawal, however, the national system became dominated by Catholic schools. Lord Mayo entered the House of Commons in November 1847. In that parliamentary year, a motion introduced to the house by George Alexander Hamilton, an Irish Conservative MP, called for the presentation of an address to Queen Victoria explaining that a very large proportion of Anglicans in Ireland held conscientious objections to the existing operation of the Irish system of education, which 'negatived the great principle of all Protestant churches ... the free use of the Holy Scriptures'.[20] Hamilton urged that state funding be awarded to schools of the Church Education Society 'to extend the blessings of Scriptural education in Ireland'.[21]

In the decade that followed, increased political support was gained for the idea that the Irish system stood in need of reform. Hamilton's motion was reintroduced to parliament in its 1849 and 1850 sessions and supported each time by more than 100 (predominately Tory) MPs.[22] Anglicans advocating change advanced two major reasons in its favour: that the national system, dominated by Catholic schools, had in practical terms ceased to be an interdenominational one and that the principle of interdenominational education was abhorrent, or else fundamentally unsuited to Ireland, requiring as it did the separation of religious and secular instruction. To determine Lord Mayo's feelings on the subject we must turn to his first major speech on education, delivered when the question of reform of the national system was again put before parliament in April 1853. Mayo had voted in favour of the award of state funding to Church Education Society schools in June 1850.[23] Three years on he explained why: the Irish system was in practice not interdenominational but overwhelmingly Catholic.[24]

Mayo produced statistics showing that of 491,927 children in national schools in March 1852, 424,917 were Catholics, 40,618 Presbyterians and just 24,684 Anglicans. Out of 4,705 schools, 2,778 were controlled by the Catholic prelacy and just 147 by the Established Church. Seeking to prove decisively that no interdenominational system existed, he added that just eight schools in Ireland were under the joint management of Catholic and Anglican clergy.[25]

Shortly after the foundation of the national system in 1831 the rules governing religious instruction had been tweaked by the stipulation that scriptural extracts might be used for moral instruction during regular school hours, as long as no objection was raised by the parent or guardian of a pupil.[26] The effect of that concession, Mayo held, had been to encourage the participation of the majority denomination – the Roman Catholic – in national education while checking the involvement of minority denominations, and particularly of members of the Established Church. In many national schools, Mayo suggested, Catholic catechism was being freely taught.[27] In contrast to many of his peers in the Irish Conservative Party, Mayo did not denounce the principle of interdenominational education outright. He did, however, call for the revision of rules governing religious instruction to permit the inclusion of schools of the Established Church in the national system.[28] During Mayo's second tenure as chief secretary, negotiations in Ireland between representatives of the Established Church, the Catholic Church and the national board produced a potential compromise solution: that a limited form of state aid would be granted to those schools seeking to opt out of national board restrictions on religious teaching.[29] Mayo considered resigning from government when Lord Derby stalled on bringing the proposal before the cabinet in early 1859.[30]

It was as chief secretary for a third time that an opportunity was presented to Mayo to resolve Anglican educational grievances. As one of the most senior Irish Conservative politicians by 1866, Mayo's influence over the determination of policy was far greater by this stage than it had been in either 1852 or 1858–9. In the summer of 1867 he proposed the establishment of a royal commission to consider the question of Irish education. Speaking in the House of Commons, Mayo noted the great secular benefits that had been conferred to Ireland by its national system: the rules of that system now required revision so that religious instruction might form a larger portion of education in schools, and a wider section of population – read members of the Established Church – might benefit from national instruction.[31] Before his departure for India, Mayo followed the proceedings of the royal commission closely. Among its final recommendations was that the denominational character of a great number of national schools be recognized: in areas where two or more schools existed – one Catholic and the other Protestant – religious instruction would be permitted without restriction.[32]

The extent to which the position of Muslims in relation to state education in India was for Mayo analogous with that of Anglicans and national education in

Ireland is revealed in several sources. In his *Memories*, O. T. Burne, private secretary to Mayo during his viceroyalty, details Mayo's preparations for Indian office in London in the final months of 1868, which included his perusal of recent reports and statistics on India.[33] It is very likely that Mayo's reading included the most recent comprehensive survey of government education – A. M. Monteath's 'Note on the State of Education in India' – in which it was recorded that in all but the most basic government schools the proportion of Muslims was lower than in the population at large. '[I]t is unquestionable', Monteath observed, 'that the Hindoos, as a race, take more readily to our system of education [than the Muslims]'.[34] Was it at this point that Mayo began to realize similarities between the positions of Irish Anglicans and Indian Muslims – powerful or once powerful minorities excluded by religious convictions from their national educational systems? Burne notes Mayo's surprise at learning of the tremendous size of the Muslim population of India and suggests that this realization informed his growing conception of the responsibility of the Indian government towards its Muslim subjects.[35] In India, reform of Muslim educational provisions was urged on Mayo by officials including E. C. Bayley and James O'Kinealy – the latter chief prosecuting officer during the Wahabi trials. They argued that Muslims rejected entry into government schools because the instruction offered was devoid of religious content and the majority of students and teachers were not Muslim.[36] Mayo would have immediately recognized a likeness between these arguments and explanations of the unwillingness of Anglicans to participate in the national system in Ireland. An additional parallel enabled Mayo to understand why Muslims did not send their sons to Christian missionary schools and colleges either: just as Irish Anglicans refused to participate in schools teaching Catholic doctrine, Muslims rejected institutions offering 'false' religious instruction.

Drafting his resolution on Muslim education, Mayo made explicit reference to these analogies: 'I cannot avoid noticing', he recorded, 'the extraordinary similarity which appears to exist between the position of this [Muslim education] question and that of national education in Ireland'.[37] In an Irish context, Mayo continued, a system of education established according to the principle of interdenominationalism had been practically denominalised, with three-quarters of national schools under the direct management and patronage of the Catholic Church. He asserted,

> The consequence is that, while the Presbyterian and Roman Catholic children are admitted to the full benefits of the immense grant which is annually voted by Parliament for national education in Ireland, a portion of the members of the Church of England [the Anglican church in Ireland] refuse on religious grounds to participate therein.
>
> The Mahomedans of India appear to have taken the same line that a certain proportion of the extreme Protestant party took in Ireland, and have consequently, to a great extent, placed themselves out of the Government educational pale.[38]

The Catholic University Question and Religious Endowments

If the Government of India's resolution on Muslim education is to be fully understood, Mayo's recognition of an affinity between the educational problems faced by Muslims in India and Anglicans in Ireland must be combined with an appreciation of his personal opposition to the separation of religion from education, and the conception held by the viceroy of the correct relationship between a government and the religious constituencies under its rule. These factors are revealed with great lucidity by Mayo's attempts to meet demands for the chartering and endowment of a Catholic university in Ireland.

During the nineteenth century what T. W. Moody termed the 'Irish university question' centred on the demands of Catholics and Presbyterians for degree-level education recognized and sponsored by the British state.[39] The demand for a Catholic university had grown from the final decade of the eighteenth century. In 1793 Trinity College, Dublin – bastion of the Anglican establishment and then the only university in Ireland – had been opened to other denominations with the abolition of religious testing, though fellowships, professorships, scholarships and prizes continued to be held exclusively by Anglicans. Two years later a government grant was awarded for the foundation of Maynooth College, an institution under the management of the Catholic Church which developed into a seminary for the training of clergy. Seeking to consolidate Catholic support, Peel's Conservative government of 1841–6 increased the annual grant to Maynooth amid widespread protests in England at the endowment of 'Popery', and proposed the establishment of three new university colleges in Ireland. The resulting institutions at Cork, Galway and Belfast operated according to the same principles that had informed the foundation of the national school system: a wholly secular education was taught to members of all denominations conjointly.

The intention of Peel's government in founding the Queen's colleges, as they became known, had been to reconcile not only Catholic laity but also the Catholic Church to university provisions. However, the stipulation that the colleges would impart only secular instruction provoked the opposition of the Catholic hierarchy; led by the Archbishop of Tuam, members of the Catholic prelacy demanded changes to the institutions' organization and course of studies – including the appointment of Catholic professors of history, logic, metaphysics and moral philosophy, and of salaried Catholic chaplains to superintend religious instruction. Peel's refusal to grant these concessions prompted three papal rescripts against the colleges, and a condemnatory decree from the national synod of the Catholic Church. By the time that the Queen's college system was completed in 1850, with the inauguration of the Queen's University as an examining body to which the colleges would affiliate, Catholic clergy and prelacy had united in opposition to the 'Godless' university arrangements. Mayo's predecessor as chief secretary in 1866, the Irish Liberal Chichester Fortescue concisely summarized Catholic objections to university provisions – which remained unchanged sixteen years on – when he recorded that the only options available for lay degree-level education in Ireland were the Queen's colleges, with their provisions solely for secular instruction, and Trinity College, in which only Anglican religious instruction was offered.[40]

As chief secretary from June 1866 Mayo played the leading role in his government's attempt to resolve Catholic university grievances. In early 1868 he composed a memorandum, intended for consideration by the Conservative cabinet, in which he outlined his proposals for the chartering of a Catholic university.[41] Mayo had just returned from Ireland, where he had held negotiations with representatives of the Catholic prelacy and senior figures at Trinity and the Queen's colleges. Before his visit he favoured the incorporation of these existing institutions into a single degree-awarding university, to which other denominational institutions – including a Catholic college – could affiliate. That proposal, he held, would answer the demand for a Catholic institution of higher education and place all students on an equal footing in the competition for university degrees.[42] However, the scheme for a single university was abandoned when Mayo was confronted with the opposition of Trinity College leaders. The alternative – to charter an independent Catholic university – he announced in parliament in March 1868.[43]

Mayo's Catholic university plan might be explained as a piece of political calculation, the outcome of an aspiration to attract Catholic support for his government. That political advantage could be derived from meeting the demands of religious constituencies in Ireland, Mayo was of course aware.[44] The plan might also be considered a defensive manoeuvre to protect Trinity College's Anglican character, threatened by demands for the opening up of scholarships and fellowships to all.[45] Throughout his involvement in the politics of Irish higher education, Mayo was concerned to safeguard Trinity as a characteristically Anglican institution, albeit with non-Anglican students admitted. There is, however, far more to an explanation of Mayo's proposals than this. Advocating the establishment of a Catholic university, Mayo adopted a position at odds with that of most of his British and Irish Conservative contemporaries, for whom the state recognition and endowment of a Catholic institution could not be countenanced. Such a position can only be explained by Mayo's genuine sympathy for the university demand, which in correspondence with the attorney general for Ireland he described as 'very reasonable'.[46]

Emerging clearly from the study of Mayo's third term as chief secretary is his personal dislike of the divorce of religion from education. In exchanges over the future of Trinity College, Mayo contended that there were three types of education then in operation in Ireland: the 'denominational', the 'united' and the 'mixed'.[47] The 'denominational', he argued, were those institutions in which students, teachers and governors were exclusively of one denomination, whose catechism was taught. The college at Maynooth provided an example. 'United' institutions, in contrast, were those including the Queen's colleges attended by members of all denominations, in which only secular instruction was offered. Mayo rejected this type of institution, contending that 'a purely secular University education did not at present commend itself to the feelings of any great class [in Ireland]'.[48] For Mayo, 'mixed' educational institutions, combining the inter-denominational principle with religious instruction, provided the best blueprint for the future of Irish university education. Open to students of all persuasions for more than seven decades, Trinity College was one such institution, and a chartered Catholic university would be another.[49]

Announcing to parliament his government's intention of chartering a Catholic university, Mayo noted the opposition of most Irish Catholics to instruction in Trinity College or the Queen's colleges, before asking his predominantly Protestant colleagues:

> Are these objections unreasonable? I ask this House to consider whether there are not many among us who would have the same objection to send their sons to Universities where the Roman Catholic religion alone was taught, or where all religious instruction was studiously omitted?[50]

In raising these questions Mayo betrayed his own aversion to education without religion, while presenting prevailing Catholic opinion to the floor. Catholic rejection of state higher education on the grounds that it did not cater for religious requirements was a further analogy surely on Mayo's mind as he drafted his resolution on Muslim education: it cannot have escaped the viceroy's memory that Irish Catholics – like Indian Muslims and Irish Anglicans – had widely rejected purely secular instruction. With this recognition, Mayo's individual disapprobation of exclusively secular pedagogy was reinforced.

The plan to charter a Catholic university additionally highlights Mayo's particular understanding of the role of government in relation to the religious constituencies under its rule. Mayo was not a noted intellectual figure and did not publish books or pamphlets on the important issues of his day. His correspondence, however, leaves no doubt about his conviction that the foundation of a Catholic university was the correct, 'just' course for government to pursue.[51] On grounds of equity, Mayo believed, a Catholic institution with comparable privileges to Trinity College should be recognized and endowed. For Mayo a governmental responsibility lay in responding to the requirements of multiple religious groups, which inevitably meant a repositioning of the state in relation to the religions of its subjects. The effect of chartering a Catholic university would have been to lend the sanction and financial resources of government to an additional non-Anglican institution – a further movement away from the idea of the 'Protestant Constitution' in Ireland.

When contemporaneous debates over the position of the Irish Established Church are examined, Mayo's conception of the relationship of government to religious constituencies and the extent to which he was prepared to countenance the state support of multiple religions are confirmed. The anomalous position of the Established Church had long been raised as a grievance by non-Anglicans in Ireland. From the late seventeenth century an annual state grant, the *Regium Donum*, had been awarded to the Presbyterian Church; the training of Catholic clergy at Maynooth had been funded by government since 1795. Those grants, however, were greatly exceeded by the annual stipend awarded to the Established Church – the church of a minority. In 1864 a new Irish National Association was founded in Dublin with disestablishment of the Church of Ireland one of its foremost aims.[52] In parliament a series of resolutions introduced by the Irish Liberal MP John Gray called for settlement of the Irish Church question on the basis of 'the principle of perfect religious equality between all sections of Her Majesty's subjects'.[53] William Gladstone offered his support for Gray's campaign, and soon after repositioned the Liberal Party as a vehicle for the political interests of Nonconformists and Catholics in the Union.

The initial response of Mayo to criticisms of the position of the Established Church during his third spell as chief secretary was to highlight the inconsistencies of the line of argument adopted by Gladstone and others. If, as Gladstone had argued, the position of the Irish Church was indefensible because it was a church of the minority, what about the national churches of England and Scotland? If an endowed church was only acceptable where that church belonged to the majority, did it not follow that state support for the English and Scottish churches would also have to be removed?[54] In pursuing this line of argument, however, Mayo was not denying that change to religious endowments was necessary but paving the way for an alternative course of reform: the increased state endowment of the other churches of Ireland. In May 1867 he announced that he would be 'very glad to see the clergy of the Roman Catholic Church in the enjoyment of incomes larger than they enjoy at present'.[55] Just as the state had supported Maynooth College and provided for the Presbyterian Church, it ought in future to assist churches other than the Anglican in Ireland. State funding for the Catholic and Presbyterian churches should be increased, redressing grievances at the privileged position of the Established Church.[56]

A similar conviction informed this plan as had motivated Mayo's Catholic university scheme. Increasing the annual stipend of the Catholic and Presbyterian churches was a defensive measure insofar as it offered a way of safeguarding the revenues of the Established Church. Attempting to sell the idea to members of his party, Mayo introduced his policy in these terms, noting that the raising of endowments to other Irish churches provided the surest way of protecting the Church of Ireland.[57] Mayo's proposal was not primarily the product of this calculation, however, but of his conception of the responsibility of government to respond justly to diverse religious constituencies, and offer state support with impartiality. Rejecting church disestablishment, Mayo articulated a sincere belief in the errors of the separation of state from religion. Every church in Ireland, he argued, would derive benefit from state support: the separation of the state from the churches was a solution to the debate over religious endowments equally unsuited to all.[58] To increase religious endowments, however, was a controversial course for a Conservative minister to advocate. Shortly after announcing the plan, Mayo was forced to deny in parliament that he had proposed an 'immediate and large' increase in the state award to Catholic and Presbyterian churches.[59] In private, however, he was to grow increasingly frustrated with the opposition of members of his party to an endowments policy. He recorded,

> I desire to continue the policy for Ireland which every statesman, Whig and Tory, not blinded by bigotry, from Pitt to Peel, has tried to promote ... But since the day that Pitt was forced to abandon emancipation and endowment of the Roman Catholic clergy as a portion of his Union scheme, the most powerful minster has never been able to advance more than a very short step at a time.[60]

Writing to Disraeli from India, Mayo later recorded that his endowment plan would have secured peace in Ireland, and expressed regret that so few contemporaries had offered their support.[61] A long-standing colleague and friend, Disraeli was one of a small number in the Conservative government to support Mayo's proposals in 1868 and had earlier played an active role in negotiations towards the chartering of a Catholic university.

Mayo's policies in the period 1866–8 are largely omitted from histories of the British government of Ireland and of Irish politics at Westminster. Where the attempt of the Conservative government to formulate policy sympathetic to Catholic interests is noted, it is usually considered a calculated bid for political gain headed by Disraeli.[62] However, attempts to charter a Catholic university and reform religious endowments reveal Mayo as a far-sighted statesman with a conception of the relationship between state and religion very different to most Conservative contemporaries. Mayo's attempts to set a new course for the Conservative Party on Ireland ultimately came to nothing. Just six days after his announcement of the government's intention of chartering a Catholic university, in an address on the state of Ireland in which the possibility of increasing endowments to non-Anglican churches was also raised, Gladstone trumped Mayo's offer with his declaration that the Church of Ireland 'as a State Church, must cease to exist'.[63] Between March and November of 1868 Gladstone was able to expose divisions in the Conservative Party over the endowments policy; the Conservative Party adopted an increasingly defensive position and fought the general election of November 1868 on the simple platform of opposition to disestablishment. In that same month, Mayo departed for India and landed at Bombay in December to be told that the Conservative government had been forced out.[64] After Gladstone's decisive electoral victory, a bill on church disestablishment was introduced to parliament and passed the following year.

The Meanings of Secularism

The lasting impact of Mayo's attempts to charter a Catholic university and steer his party towards the support of multiple religious endowments was felt not in Ireland, but in India. Mayo arrived on the subcontinent with a conception of government based upon principle – that a governmental responsibility lay in responding to the requirements of religious constituencies – and pragmatism – that the interests of government would be best served by such responses – which predetermined his likely course of action when the need for reform of Muslim educational provisions was pressed upon him in 1871. This, in addition to Mayo's personal dislike of purely secular education and his identification of an affinity between Indian Muslims and Irish Anglicans encountering state education, explains his August resolution. On account of his Irish experiences, Mayo saw no contradiction in a colonial administration professing neutrality between Indian religious communities while intervening to promote the interests of a specific religious group. In his view, reforming state education for Indian Muslims was a just response to the requirements of a particular religious constituency and a prudent measure for encouraging its support of government.

The effect of Mayo's Irish proposals – had they been implemented – would have been to extend the state patronage of institutions belonging to diverse religious constituencies, and commit public funding to the support of a plurality of faiths (denominations). His August resolution promised something similar: grants-in-aid would be more extensively awarded for the foundation of Muslim schools in the government system and Muslim requirements would be recognized in state-managed institutions. In light of all we have learnt, it is perhaps surprising that Mayo stopped short of recommending a complete abandonment of the colonial secular education commitment in favour of the unfettered teaching of Christianity, Islam and other religions in government schools. His aversion to the separation of religion from pedagogy, and his recognition of affinities between Ireland and India made this an attractive course. In the event, however, Mayo was advised by members of his close circle that sponsoring the teaching of religion in government schools would be unwise: to teach Christianity in state-managed institutions would incite Indian opposition, while the teaching of Hinduism or Islam would provoke an outcry among sections of the British population in India and at home.[65] Perhaps reluctantly, Mayo pencilled into the final draft of his resolution that any encouragement of Muslim education would have to take place 'without infringing the fundamental principles of our educational system': the colonial commitment to sponsor only secular education would be maintained.[66] Mayo was aware of the significance of the Arabic language to a Muslim's religion: by encouraging the widespread teaching of Arabic in government schools his resolution equipped Muslim students with an important tool for the observance of Islam.[67] For the reconciliation of secular instruction and a comprehensive Islamic education, however, Muslim parties would have to found schools of their own and apply for government grants. In keeping with existing grant-in-aid rules, funding would be awarded solely for the secular proficiency of institutions, yet, Mayo knew, Muslim-managed schools would very likely offer religious instruction alongside their prescribed secular course.

The establishment in the Indian educational system of Muslim institutions teaching both Islamic subjects and secular lessons was a consequence of great lasting significance of Mayo's resolution. As we shall see in the following chapter, the enactment of his recommendations by provincial administrations engendered the widespread denominalization of government-sponsored public instruction. This result too was anticipated by his Irish career. Throughout his involvement in the politics of education in Ireland Mayo had professed his opposition to educational denominationalism. When critics in the 1850s and 1860s denounced the principle of interdenominationalism outright, Mayo disagreed, contending that the conjoint instruction of members of different denominations remained worth aspiring to.[68] Mayo's commitment to the interdenominational principle was problematic, however, when it conflicted with his desire to see the reconciliation of religious and secular instruction. His aversion to the separation of religion from education steered him towards denominational solutions in spite of his sympathy for the interdenominational ideal. As we have noted, Mayo advocated the foundation of what he termed 'mixed' educational institutions – those such as Trinity College offering religious instruction, but open to members of all denominations. The problem with such institutions, however, is clear: a 'mixed' school or college offering the religious instruction of just one denomination would be attended overwhelmingly by members of that group, as Mayo himself conceded. His Catholic university, theoretically open to all, would in practice have been Catholic in its management and teaching staff, have taught only Catholic theology and have been attended almost exclusively by Catholics.[69] As chief secretary for Ireland Mayo proposed a movement towards the denominalisation of national schooling with his encouragement of a relaxation of rules governing religious instruction, while advancing plans for the foundation of a 'mixed' university which would in practice have been denominational. His resolution on Muslim education had a similar denominalizing effect.

In the months following the resolution's publication, as provincial administrations began discussing and implementing its terms, the attention of British observers was turned to the relationship between religion and state in India once again. The encouragement of Muslim education in the colonial system and the nature of Indian secularism were subjects finely intertwined. It is in the popularization of discourse on this topic that William Wilson Hunter assumes significance. Published one month after the resolution, his *Indian Musalmans* repeated the case previously made to Mayo by his advisers that Muslim parties widely rejected colonial education because of its purely secular character: 'our system of Public Instruction makes no provision for the religious education of the Muhammadan youth'.[70] In addition to the redress of wider grievances, Hunter argued that reconciling Muslims to British rule required reform of colonial education provisions to permit the more widespread imparting of religious and secular lessons together. The distribution of *Indian Musalmans* in Britain turned metropolitan attention to the subject. In Cambridge the prize-winning essayist Henry Courthope Bowen paraphrased Hunter with his contention that colonial schools were unattractive to Indian Muslims because no religious instruction was imparted.[71] A comparison was naturally made with Ireland, where the separation of religion from education had been seen to fail. Reviewing *Indian Musalmans*, an editorial in the *Spectator* noted that Muslims refused instruction in colonial 'Godless Colleges';[72] the phrase had been coined by Robert Inglis and popularised by Daniel O'Connell in denouncement of the secular prescriptions of the Queen's colleges in Ireland after 1845.[73] Muslim rejections of purely secular education were often commented upon favourably in Britain, and were likened to Christian aversion to education without religion in both Irish and English contexts.

    The policy recommendations in *Indian Musalmans* reiterated Mayo's resolution. Alongside the appointment of Muslim instructors and teaching of Arabic and Persian in government schools, Hunter proposed the extensive award of grants-in-aid to Muslims for the foundation of schools in which religious and secular education might be combined.[74] Like the viceroy he stopped short of recommending the introduction of religious classes to government-managed institutions, finding in the relaxation of grant-in-aid rules an alternative means for overcoming Muslim opposition to education without religion. Hunter concurred with Mayo that the colonial secular education commitment should be maintained. Others disagreed, however. Among the most high-profile respondents to the debate popularized by Hunter's text was William Gifford Palgrave – a member of the British diplomatic service stationed at Trebizond in the Ottoman Empire, who had entered public view after publishing an account of his travels through Palestine and Syria to Nejed in 1862–3, one of the first European chronicles of Wahabism on the Arabian Peninsula.[75] In February 1872 Palgrave published an article in *Fraser's Magazine*, 'The Mahometan Revival', in which he posited that the British government of India might learn a series of lessons from Ottoman rulers in governing its Muslim subjects.[76]

From the final decade of the eighteenth century, governors in the Ottoman Empire had sought to reform civil and military administration upon European lines.[77] During the reigns of Sultan Abdulmecid I (1839–61) and Sultan Abdulaziz (1861–76), state bureaucracy had been rationalized, a modern system of imperial finance established and power devolved to new provincial assemblies. French-style civil and criminal codes were introduced, and in 1856 the *Islahat Fermani* (Reform Edict) guaranteed the legal equality of all citizens, irrespective of their religion. The creation of a common Ottoman citizenship followed in 1869. Accompanying these innovations was the development of a secular educational system from school to university level; government institutions imparted secular lessons derived from textbooks printed by a new Academy of Learning.[78] For Palgrave a problem had emerged in the Ottoman Empire when it was realized after 1846 that the majority of Muslims would not accept secular, European instruction. In resolution of this difficulty, he contended, Ottoman administrators had tacitly permitted – and in places actively encouraged – the denominalization and religification of the new secular schools. Over a period of twenty-five years, schools founded under official patronage had throughout Ottoman territories been practically converted into religious institutions: the European curriculum, with its emphasis on the French language, history, mathematics and the natural sciences, had been replaced by a traditional Muslim syllabus, centered on the Turkish, Persian and Arabic languages, grammar, logic and a thorough religious education.[79] Palgrave's advice for the Government of India was that it should emulate its Ottoman counterpart by sanctioning the imparting of Islamic instruction in state-sponsored institutions. This, he argued, would appease 'the most important, because the most dangerous, element in our Indian Empire'.[80]

The most advanced treatise on the colonial secular education commitment developed following Mayo's resolution, was that of Alfred Lyall, commissioner in Berar and later lieutenant governor of the NWP. In 1872 Lyall submitted an article to the *Theological Review*, in which he responded to *Indian Musalmans* and Palgrave's development of Hunter's recommendations for reform.[81] Lyall refuted the charge made by Hunter that the colonial educational system had been ruinous for Indian Muslims, and added that the progress of India under British rule dictated that Muslims become acquainted with western scientific and literary thought: 'we cannot stand still, or shut out the rush of light and air which have followed our throwing open the windows of the West, because at first it chills and dazes the conservative Mahomedan'.[82] In spite of this assertion, however, Lyall followed Hunter and Palgrave by endorsing the revision of government educational provisions to accommodate Muslim needs: in his view the Indian universities ought to award degrees in Islamic subjects including theology and philosophy, which should be taught in state institutions. 'To those Mahomedans who cling to their own classics, and who adhere to the kind of training afforded by the study of Arabic theology and philosophy, every facility and even encouragement should be given.'[83]

The rationale behind this assertion was revealed in a further article written by Lyall in 1872. In 'Our Religious Policy in India'[84] Lyall argued that the stability of colonial rule would be greatly enhanced if the government was to respond more effectively to the requirements of religious constituencies. He added that the process of managing the demands of diverse religious groups would be better carried out if the colonial commitment to the separation of state from religion was renounced. For Lyall the refusal of government to endow the religions of India had been a mistake: great political benefits could be obtained by the state support of multiple religions. Lyall, therefore, proposed a redefinition of the 'religious neutrality' or secularism of the colonial state which, he argued, should mean not the formal separation of state from religion, but the public support of a plurality of faiths.[85] The award of state endowments to religious institutions, and the introduction to government schools of instruction in a diversity of creeds, were proposals suggested by Lyall that derived from and sought to establish this alternative conception of Indian secularism.

Lord Mayo brought to India a conception of government centred on the idea of responding to the needs of diverse religious constituencies that decisively influenced his resolution on Muslim education in August 1871. In Ireland the policies deriving from this conception promised the state endowment of multiple religions, but in his reshaping of government educational provisions for Indian Muslims Mayo felt bound to uphold the colonial secular education commitment. Lyall, in contrast, built upon the interventions of Hunter, Palgrave and others to argue publicly for the abandonment of that commitment and a redefinition of the relationship between religion and state. In the aftermath of Mayo's resolution, the nature of Indian secularism was rethought.

3 THE CALCUTTA MADRASA AND MUSLIM EDUCATION IN BENGAL

With Mayo's resolution a series of new governmental practices was sanctioned for the encouragement of Muslim participation in the colonial system of public instruction. The colonial secular education commitment was preserved but debate was raised among British figures about its worth, in which proposals were made for the introduction of religious teaching to government institutions and the definition of a new relationship between Indian religions and the colonial state. The efficacy of both the exclusion of religion from government education and the preservation of a distance between state and religion were called into question by commentators seeking a stronger foundation for the British government of India.

The following two chapters concern the engagement of Muslim parties with government on the subject of education in the years before and after the resolution. Focused on emergent public spheres in Bengal, the North-Western Provinces (hereafter NWP) and the Punjab, the chapters examine the significant, previously unnoticed role played by Muslim individuals and associations shaping colonial educational provisions during a two-decade period from 1865, as restrictions on the teaching of religion in state institutions were probed and responded to. Uncovering Muslim negotiations of the colonial commitment to secular education, the chapters reveal the impact of Muslim-British exchanges on evolving understandings of the relationship between religion and state. Chapter four concentrates on the Punjab, exploring the ways in which Muslim elites inspired by the success of the Muhammadan Anglo-Oriental College (hereafter MAO College) at Aligarh lobbied for the wider teaching of Islamic subjects in state-sponsored schools and colleges, provoking the withdrawal of the colonial state from the management of higher level institutions in favour of the more extensive award of grants-in-aid. The focus of this chapter is the Calcutta Madrasa and Bengal. The first government institution in northern India established specifically for Muslims, the Madrasa was the subject of the earliest engagement with colonial authorities of Muslim parties concerned for the reconciliation of religious and secular instruction in the Indian educational system.

In chapter one it was noted that the colonial state's support of the Calcutta Madrasa – an institution teaching Islamic subjects including the Qur'an, Hadith and Muslim law – was increasingly assailed during the first four decades of the nineteenth century by reformers convinced that the object of colonial pedagogy should be the introduction to India of European scientific and literary knowledge, and the English language. The determination of British officials to avoid teaching Christianity in state-sponsored schools rendered the Madrasa and Sanscrit College at Benares, with their instruction in religious subjects, an obvious target of evangelical and utilitarian critique. The first part of this chapter returns to the 1830s to document how, in the face of liberal opposition, the survival of the Madrasa as a state-sponsored Muslim institution was made possible only by the exclusion of what administrators considered the religious elements of its course; the attempt was made to bring the Madrasa into line with the secular education commitment of the colonial state. After 1850 this attempt was extended; as section two reveals, reforms of the Madrasa's curriculum introduced by successive European principals sought the introduction of western scientific and literary subjects and the development of a philological Arabic programme devoid of Islamic elements.

The third and final parts of this chapter consider Muslim responses to colonial efforts to refashion the Madrasa, and the revisions of government educational policy that they inspired. Engaging with the colonial state, Muslim elites from across Bengal argued for the indispensability of instruction in government-prescribed subjects being combined with teaching of the religion of Islam. Their negotiations with British authorities impacted substantially on the development of state education in the province, triggering the establishment of further Muslim-specific pedagogical provisions including a network of madrasas in which Islamic subjects were taught.

A Madrasa without Islam?

For reformers in the 1830s the Calcutta Madrasa was an anomaly. An institution maintained by the colonial state, it departed from the liberal educational ideal by imparting instruction to Muslim students alone. At the Madrasa an Arabic and Persian curriculum was taught which, it was held, was incapable of effecting the moral and intellectual improvement desired for India. Moreover the Madrasa's course included subjects intimately related to the religion of Islam at a time when the exclusion of religious teaching from other government institutions was settled upon. In the view of many it was imperative – both on point of principle and for the best allocation of the government of India's educational resources – that government support of the Madrasa be ceased. For the colonial state to continue patronizing the institution was inconsistent with liberal plans.

The Madrasa had been established in 1780 in response to the appeal of a delegation of Muslims to Governor General Warren Hastings for the foundation of an institution for the study of Islamic law and other subjects of a madrasa curriculum.[1] Initially supported by Hastings in a private capacity, it would be brought under the patronage of the East India Company in 1785. It was under Hasting's stewardship that the Company had embraced an 'orientalist' approach to government, determining to govern Bengal according to the dictates of Hindu and Muslim law. The foundation of an institution to teach Muslim law and the Islamic sciences was in keeping with that approach, allowing for the conciliation of Muslim elites to British rule and the simultaneous training of Muslim candidates for public office. The *dars-i-nizami* curriculum prevailing in many of the learned Muslim institutions of the period was adopted as the basis of the Madrasa's course of study – its emphasis on the rational sciences was considered suitable for those aspiring to posts in government.[2] The object of the Madrasa, Hastings recorded, was to qualify for public office Muslim candidates possessing 'a considerable degree of erudition in the Persian and Arabic languages, and in the complicated system of laws, founded on the tenets of their religion'.[3] A code of regulations dictating the subjects to be taught in the Madrasa was introduced by government in 1791. The Madrasa curriculum would include the study of commentaries on the Qur'an, Hadith, theology, and natural philosophy, in addition to law, geometry, astronomy, logic, grammar, rhetoric and arithmetic.[4]

For more than three decades, the course of study at the Madrasa remained substantially unchanged, with management of the institution in the hands of a series of Muslim principals subject to only nominal government control. This situation was altered when, amid growing utilitarian and evangelical calls for reform, a European secretary was appointed.[5] Matthew Lumsden had served as professor of Persian and Arabic at the College of Fort William in Calcutta. Transferring to the Madrasa in March 1822 he was convinced of the benefits to be obtained by the introduction of instruction in western subjects. To government he argued that the Madrasa's Arabic curriculum was incomparable to a European education in its intellectual results: while the Madrasa served a useful purpose in preparing Muslim law officers for public employment, its course of study was incapable of effecting more general improvement.[6] Two major questions confronted Lumsden as he set about planning the introduction of western knowledge to the Madrasa. Precisely which subjects would be taught? And in which language(s) would instruction be imparted? Lumsden argued that teaching European science was a priority. The effect of western scientific knowledge, he posited, would be to counter in the minds of Muslim pupils the errors contained in the false sciences of a traditional madrasa course. The Madrasa should teach geography, natural history, chemistry, mathematics and medicine upon western lines, encouraging in recipients 'a sincere disposition to enquire after truth'.[7] On the question of introducing the English language, or else conveying western knowledge through the Arabic and Persian media, Lumsden hedged his bets. In early 1823 he procured the services of Maulvi Abdur Rahim, one of a small number of Muslims in Calcutta to have acquired a working knowledge of the English language, and began the translation of European scientific works into Arabic and Persian for use at the Madrasa.[8] The following year English language classes were introduced. This innovation was undertaken with a degree of caution. Lumsden made the study of English voluntary for students, noting in explanation that many Muslims associated the English language with Christianity and would interpret its forcing upon them as an attempt at proselytism. A financial incentive was nevertheless offered to students to attend English classes in the shape of a small stipend.[9]

Between the years 1825 and 1830 the model established by Lumsden for the gradual introduction of western subjects to the Madrasa was largely uncontested. The study of English was encouraged by Lumsden's successor as secretary, Captain Ruddell, who also sought the translation of European scientific texts into Arabic and Persian.[10] In 1830 100 students attended English classes where they were also introduced to geography, history and western natural philosophy.[11] The task of translating European works into Arabic, Sanscrit and Persian was brought under the supervision of John Tytler, head of the GCPI's educational press. Translators at the Madrasa including Abdur Rahim worked under Tytler's direction producing Arabic translations of European works on anatomy, mathematics, algebra and surveying in addition to Arabic and Persian copies of *Aesop's Fables*.[12] In 1827 the Madrasa was moved to a new site facing on to Wellesley Square in a neighbourhood populated by higher class Muslims in Calcutta. The Madrasa's graduates found employment as public officials, *qazis* and teachers in private Muslim institutions.[13]

It was this gradual approach to the introduction of western knowledge at the Madrasa – the teaching of western subjects through the English, Arabic and Persian languages, alongside continued instruction in the regular subjects of a madrasa curriculum – which a class of colonial administrators represented by Charles Trevelyan increasingly assailed. Trevelyan was convinced that the translation of English texts into Arabic and Persian would fail to disseminate western knowledge in India: English was the natural medium for this process.[14] From 1833 his campaign to concentrate colonial educational efforts on the dissemination of western knowledge through the English medium was accompanied by a sustained critique of Arabic and Sanscrit learning. In public Trevelyan argued that the Calcutta Madrasa did nothing but bribe Muslims by means of excessive stipendiary support 'to imbibe systems of error, which we all know have been exploded, and their falsehood demonstrated ages ago'.[15] In the GCPI he described the Madrasa as an almshouse for the support of irrelevant Arabic superstition.[16] The Madrasa not only failed to impart 'useful' western instruction: as a Muslim institution teaching Islamic subjects its preservation was

positively pernicious to liberal plans for the development of a common angli-
cised Indian identity through colonial education. Trevelyan cautioned:

> To whatever extent ... we encourage Mahammadan learning we raise up a class of peo-
> ple who are, from feeling and principle, the despisers of our learning and the enemies
> of our rule. There are no persons in India who so thoroughly hate us and who are so
> determinedly opposed to the introduction of European improvements as the finished
> bigots who are turned out by us at so heavy an expense at the Mahammadan College.[17]

In April 1834 Trevelyan and the other 'anglicists' in the GCPI backed a resolution that stipendiary support should be offered to Madrasa students only if
they studied English alongside an Arabic course.[18] The Madrasa, they argued,
should teach European subjects through the English medium or else be closed.
The opposition was immediate: headed by H. T. Prinsep, the 'orientalist' party
argued that such a measure would convert the Madrasa into an English seminary,
breaching the trust of the Muslim community for whom it had been founded.[19]
The escalation of this dispute into a debate about the aims of colonial educational policy paved the way for Thomas Babington Macaulay's infamous minute,
followed swiftly by William Bentinck's announcement that the overriding aim
of colonial public instruction should be the promotion of European literature
and science. Within two weeks of Bentinck's verdict the GCPI began establishing a series of new English language government schools in Bengal.[20] The
Trevelyan-Macaulay plan to terminate government support for all Arabic and
Sanscrit learning was not, however, acted upon. In the aftermath of Macaulay's
minute, members of Bentinck's council cautioned that closing the Madrasa and
Sanscrit College would be a policy mistake, alienating higher class Indians whose
support should be conciliated. Lieutenant Colonel William Morison added that
the Sanscrit and Arabic languages were for Hindus and Muslims the repositories
of their sacred learning; to supplant them with English would be interpreted by
members of both communities as an assault on their religion.[21]

The case that it would be to the political advantage of government to maintain
its support of the Madrasa was dramatically strengthened in February 1835 when
a petition was submitted against abolition by Muslim residents of Calcutta. The
circumstances surrounding the petition remain unclear: Macaulay accused H. T.
Prinsep of deliberately leaking news of the government's intention to abolish the
Madrasa, and of encouraging the institution's Muslim teaching staff to instigate
opposition while Prinsep – for his part – thought that J. R. Colvin, a supporter of
the Trevelyan-Macaulay scheme, had inavertedly let slip the government's plan.[22]
This notwithstanding, the petition is a striking early example of Muslim negotiation of colonial public instruction. With just over eight thousand signatories, it
argued that the Calcutta Madrasa was venerated by Muslims in Bengal and beyond
on account of its role in training Muslim candidates for public service, and above

all because of its teaching of Islamic subjects. To abolish the Madrasa, it added, would give rise to the impression of a government object 'to eradicate the literature and religious system of Islam' and convert Muslim subjects to the religion of their rulers.[23] In minutes either side of the petition H. T. Prinsep did his best to talk up the peril in which government might find itself should Muslims in Bengal become convinced of an official intention to propagate Christianity.[24]

The influence of the petition on Bentinck's administration is clear. Initially Bentinck had recorded his 'entire concurrence' with the views expressed by Macaulay in his minute, thereby endorsing the Madrasa's abolition.[25] Bentinck's resolution of 7 March was initially drafted by Macaulay and contained nothing to contradict this plan. Only later was the crucial line pencilled in (in a separate hand) that '[i]t is not the intention of his L[ordshi]p in C[ounci]l to abolish any college or school of native learning while the native population shall appear to be inclined to avail themselves of the advantages which it affords'.[26] In the resolution's final version this amendment stood: the Madrasa would not be abolished for as long as its retention was desired by the Muslim community.[27] Two days later Bentinck replied to the Muslim petitioners directly, offering the assurance that 'the Government has no intention to abolish the Institution in the prosperity of which they profess so warm an interest'.[28] His response contained the promise that the Madrasa would remain an institution offering instruction 'in the language and literature of Arabia and in the laws, morality and science of the Mohammedan faith'.[29]

Bentinck's successor as governor general, Lord Auckland, oversaw a series of further retreats from the Trevelyan-Macaulay plan to terminate all government support for oriental learning. In 1836, in response to a second Muslim petition, the award of scholarships to Madrasa students recommenced; the state-sponsored printing of Arabic and Sanscrit books was reinstituted soon after.[30] Once again, concerns to conciliate the support of Indian elites and satisfy British supporters of oriental learning informed the revision of government policy. When it is recognized that the main question dividing 'orientalists' from 'anglicists' in the 1830s was not the encouragement of English education – indeed almost all officials favoured the introduction of the English language to government institutions to some degree – but the continued state support of Arabic and Sanscrit learning, it becomes evident that the idea of a resounding 'anglicist' triumph in colonial educational debates should be qualified. The continued government funding of Arabic and Sanscrit education through the preservation of the Calcutta Madrasa and Sanscrit College, the award of scholarships and the printing of books, was confirmed by Auckland in November 1839.[31]

Before the survival of the Madrasa is celebrated, however, the changes introduced to its Arabic course under Auckland's direction must be noted. The governor general's revival of state support for Arabic learning was accompanied by the removal of what officials considered the religious elements of the Madrasa's curriculum – extending a process begun in the previous decade by Matthew Lumsden. From 1823 Lumsden's introduction of European science to students of the Madrasa through the English, Arabic and Persian media had been undertaken alongside a wider revision of the Madrasa's Arabic curriculum. Lumsden regarded with disdain the Arabic course taught prior to his appointment as secretary – too great a proportion of the Madrasa's teaching was devoted to the Qur'an, Hadith and philosophy, and also to traditional Arabic sciences such as astronomy, barren of useful results.[32] Lumsden relegated the study of the Qur'an, Hadith and other religious subjects to voluntary classes outside of regular school hours. In their place he established a new Arabic curriculum centred on the teaching of language and literature.[33]

British critics were not slow to comment on the inconsistency of William Bentinck's final educational resolutions. Just weeks after announcing that the government would patronize only secular education, the governor general had been forced into a retreat from plans to abolish the Calcutta Madrasa – instead promising that a thorough Muslim religious education would continue to be offered in an institution supported from public funds. For many observers the colonial state had denied support for the spread of Christian truth, while endowing the perpetuation of religious error.[34] Auckland's response was to advance the marginalization of the religious teaching at the Madrasa begun by Lumsden. From 1836 the formal teaching and examination of religious subjects – bracketed under the heading 'Theology' in government reports – was stopped. Among the subjects of a traditional madrasa curriculum associated by administrators with religion, only Muslim law continued to be taught, in order to train candidates for public office.[35] Announcing the continued government support of Arabic learning in November 1839, Auckland described the principal object of the Madrasa to be the qualification of Muslim law officers to serve in colonial courts before confirming that other religious subjects would form no part of its curriculum. No longer would the Madrasa be an institution for the receipt of a comprehensive Islamic education.[36]

Philology and Religion

The reforms of the Madrasa's curriculum carried out in the 1820s and 1830s were extended from 1850, when the Bengal Council of Education resolved that a full-time European principal would be appointed in place of the part-time secretary. During the intervening decade, members of the council had grown increasingly frustrated with the failure of the Madrasa to impart instruction in western subjects. Aloys Sprenger took up the position of principal with the task of reorganizing the institution and raising it to 'usefulness'.[37]

A proficient Arabic, Persian, Turkish and Urdu scholar, the Austrian-born Sprenger had trained in Vienna and Paris before departing for India in 1843.[38]

Sprenger began his Indian career as a Company assistant surgeon before replacing the Frenchman Felix Boutros as principal of the government college at Delhi in March 1845, a position held until he departed for Lucknow to work on a catalogue of the royal libraries of Awadh in December 1847. F. J. Mouat, secretary to the Council of Education, recorded that by the time of his appointment to the Calcutta Madrasa Sprenger was the 'most eminent' Arabic scholar in India, a view with which it would appear he concurred.[39] In recent research that has focused on his time as principal at Delhi, Sprenger is presented as talented, argumentative and egotistical.[40] On departure from India in 1856 he took with him a large collection of oriental manuscripts accumulated with the aid of a network of Indian maulvis. The integrity of his character had, however, been called into question following a long-running dispute over pay.

In spite of his Arabic proficiency Sprenger held little sympathy for the course of study pursued in the Arabic department of the Madrasa prior to his appointment. Soon after assuming office he recorded that the Madrasa's Arabic curriculum acted to keep up 'antiquated prejudices', to give sanction to superstition and to encourage purely dialectical pursuits.[41] The specific target of Sprenger's condemnation were the traditional Arabic sciences – among them dialectics and metaphysics. These, he suggested, were full of ideas long proven false in Europe, and incapable of effecting intellectual improvement. For the principal, the Madrasa's course was analogous to that pursued in Europe during the Middle Ages. The effect of its teaching was to render recipients hostile to true, western science and incapable of appreciating art, beauty, equity and morality. A year after joining the Madrasa, Sprenger published a *Life of Mohammad* in which Islam was denounced as a false religion that had introduced nothing original to man's understanding of the world; the chief characteristics of Muhammad were described as his 'cunning' and 'bloody fanaticism'.[42] The great object of Sprenger's Madrasa would be 'to lead the Mussulmans from the absurd substilities of dialectics and metaphysics, to the study of the sciences of experience' – western science – and thereby 'mould the Mahomedan mind in a modernized form'.[43] For Sprenger the result of new education would be abandonment of the false religion of Islam. The diffusion of western ideas, he believed, would introduce a 'spirit of liberality' working against 'oriental and Mohammadan' thought.[44]

To understand the reforms that Sprenger attempted at the Madrasa, his tenure as principal of the Delhi College must be considered. Under the direction of Felix Boutros, the Delhi College of the early 1840s acquired a reputation, reinforced by recent scholarship, as a location for cross-cultural communication and exchange between European and Indian Muslim parties – a foremost institution in the pre-1857 cultural flourishing often termed the 'Delhi Renaissance'.[45] Within the college's walls pupils studied in English and oriental departments. In both the Urdu medium was employed, encouraging dialogue between scholars of eastern and western learning. With the addition of European texts to the curriculum of the oriental department the college's two branches were brought increasingly close together. Boutros oversaw the foundation of the Delhi Vernacular Translation Society, responsible for translating European works on medicine, law, science, history, philosophy and political economy into Urdu for teaching at the college.[46] A student in the oriental department in 1844 might have studied translations of works on European philosophy, law, political economy, history and science in addition Arabic and Persian texts.[47] Sprenger succeeded Boutros with strong credentials to continue promoting Urdu language education. The previous year he had published articles in the *Friend of India* arguing the necessity of employing Indian vernacular media in the government system of education.[48] As principal, Sprenger brought the Vernacular Translation Society under his control and accelerated its work; an Urdu printing press was established at the college alongside a weekly Urdu journal for the popularization of western ideas.[49] The Austrian placed emphasis on the translation of western scientific texts – on medicine, surgery, magnetism, geometry and astronomy – into Urdu. Continuing Boutros's work he played a substantial role in the development of the Urdu language and dissemination of European learning in Delhi. The Delhi College fell into decline as an intellectual and literary centre after his departure for Awadh.

While Sprenger's role at the Delhi College has been the subject of recent research, very little attention has yet been paid to his principalship of the Calcutta Madrasa. The major transfer of ideas and educational initiatives between the two institutions has been overlooked. Sprenger's reforms in Calcutta borrowed heavily from his experiences at the Delhi College, while the Madrasa period casts revealing light on the motivations informing his earlier educational efforts. Consistent with his time at Delhi, Sprenger sought the introduction of western subjects to the Madrasa's course; once again it was the Urdu medium that he sought to develop for this purpose. For Sprenger, Urdu was the natural medium of instruction for sharif Muslims in Calcutta; the teaching of European science through the Urdu medium was a priority.[50] Some of the translations of European scientific works undertaken by the Delhi Vernacular Translation Society found their way into the Madrasa's curriculum.[51]

Among the questions confronting Sprenger in Calcutta was what to do with the Madrasa's existing Arabic course. Sprenger believed that the earlier the age at which western scientific knowledge was introduced to Madrasa students, the better chance it would have of usurping the errors and absurdities contained within Arabic scientific texts. Western science would be taught from the lowest classes upwards so that students might know empirical truths before becoming acquainted with the falsities of Arabic science.[52] The principal was not, however, content with this solution alone: the Madrasa's Arabic curriculum required reform. In Sprenger's view two major possibilities existed. The first was to teach

Arabic and western science alongside each other: Madrasa students would be taught to discern what little truths could be found in Arabic scientific texts – what was consistent with western scientific ideas – and to discard all else. Sprenger's model for an undertaking of this kind was the efforts of James Ballantyne in the Sanscrit department of the government college at Benares, where from 1846 western scientific subjects had been taught alongside an established Sanscrit course. In his recent study Michael S. Dodson has shown how at the Benares college Ballantyne presented western scientific and philosophical ideas as the development of basic truths contained within ancient Sanscrit texts.[53] The Sanscrit language and the authority of the college's Brahman pandits were employed by Ballantyne as he sought to steer members of the Sanscrit department towards western knowledge and Christianity. Some of the intricacies of Ballantyne's programme were lost on Sprenger, who summarized it as a process of exposing the errors of Sanscrit learning in the light of western knowledge: 'He [Ballantyne] takes what is valuable in the antiquated science, and refutes what is erroneous, and thus attacks the schoolmen on their own ground'.[54]

The second possibility was to terminate the teaching of Arabic science and encourage in its place the linguistic and philological study of Arabic. For Sprenger, Ballantyne's efforts at Benares departed from older attempts to engraft western knowledge onto Sanscrit learning by their unrestrained exposure and refutation of the errors of a regular Sanscrit course. However, the principal was doubtful of his chances of emulating Ballantyne's success at Calcutta, arguing that open refutation of the errors of Arabic science would be sure to provoke opposition on the part of the Madrasa's maulvis and the wider Muslim community. It was therefore the second option that he sought to adopt. In Sprenger's envisaged Madrasa curriculum students would be taught western science in Urdu, while also learning Arabic through the study of grammar, etymology, syntax and translations from and into Urdu. In advanced classes Arabic texts would be studied as literature in an intellectual exercise comparable to the study of Latin and Greek in the universities of Europe. Students would be trained to treat with scepticism the claim of Arabic texts to scientific accuracy.[55]

Sprenger's understanding of the possibility of teaching oriental texts for their philological value derived in part from his European orientalist training, but was more decisively inspired by two key precedents in India. The first was the example of Matthew Lumsden who, as we have seen, cultivated the linguistic and literary study of Arabic at the Madrasa in the 1820s. The second was his career at the Delhi College, where the philological study of Arabic had been promoted. Before 1843 the syllabus that was followed in the oriental department of the college was an abridged version of the *dars-i-nizami* – concentrated on the Arabic language, philosophy, logic and Muslim law. Sprenger's contribution to the reform of this curriculum was to encourage the study of Arabic texts as literature and introduce specific literary works, including the *Arabian Nights* and the *Kalila Dimna*, to the college's course.[56] The philological teaching of Arabic at the Madrasa was a continuation of his Delhi College programme. Like Matthew Lumsden, Sprenger considered the commencement of Arabic philological instruction part of a welcome secularization of more traditional courses of study. At Delhi the introduction of Arabic literature was accompanied by the removal of religious texts, including collections of Hadith, from the oriental department's curriculum; by 1846 religious books were being taught only as 'free lectures' outside of the regular college course.[57] At the Madrasa rules dating to 1840 prevented the formal teaching of 'Theology'; philological enquiry would replace the study of error-strewn Islamic scientific works and be a wholly secular pursuit. So convinced was Sprenger that the study of Arabic texts as literature would render their meaning secular, that he even advocated the reintroduction of the Qur'an as a class book at the Madrasa, to be taught philologically.[58]

When Sprenger's plans for reform of the Arabic curriculum of the Madrasa were put before the Council of Education in 1852 widespread support was offered for the idea that the philological study of Arabic should be encouraged. To teach Arabic texts as literature, it was recognized, would allow instruction in the Arabic sciences to be terminated: Muslims would enter the Madrasa to acquire a linguistic and literary Arabic training and while there would be introduced to 'useful' western education through the English and vernacular media.[59] Members of the council also appreciated that the philological teaching of Arabic would permit a further distancing of the colonial state from religious education through the development of a more thoroughly secularized Madrasa course.[60] However, precisely what constituted secular education was contested. As in the 1830s administrators accepted that Muslim law would continue to be taught, on account of the continued demand in the colonial judicial system for officers knowledgeable of *shari'at*. One council member raised the question of whether or not the commitment to impart only secular education was compromised as a result: could a distinction really be maintained between Muslim law and religion?[61] More controversial was Sprenger's proposal to teach the Qur'an as a literary text. While several officials supported the idea, arguing that it was perfectly compatible with the secular education commitment, others disagreed and contended that to reintroduce the Qur'an to classes – even as a work as literature – was an objectionable plan certain 'to give some colour to an accusation that we ... teach false religion'.[62] The parameters of the religious-secular distinction in government education remained hazy and subject to debate.

In August 1853 the Council of Education resolved that the Madrasa would be divided into separate Anglo-Persian and Arabic parts. Consistent with Sprenger's plan, students would enter the Madrasa aged 9 or 10 and study the English and Persian languages with either Urdu or Bengali. Western subjects, including science, would be taught in both the English and vernacular media. Aged 15 or 16 a student would decide whether to progress to the senior, Arabic department or to attend the new Presidency College in Calcutta, where a higher level western education could be obtained. In the Arabic department, traditional Islamic sciences would no longer be taught, with the solitary exception of logic; language, literature and law would be the basis of the Arabic curriculum. After lengthy deliberations it was determined that the Qur'an would not be reintroduced to the Madrasa and taught as a work of literature. Instruction in western scientific subjects would be imparted through the Urdu medium.[63] His proposals broadly accepted, Sprenger was given licence by the council to make specific Arabic department reforms. The introduction of a compulsory class on western natural philosophy was among his first acts, followed by the exclusion of Arabic texts on physical science.[64] Maulvi Sadididuddin, formerly of the Delhi College, was appointed to teach Arabic language and literature.[65] Alongside these curricula changes Sprenger took further decisions aimed at reducing the Madrasa's religious character. Prior to his arrival, the Madrasa was used as a place of congregation for Muslims each Friday to perform prayers and hear a sermon delivered by the institution's *amin*, Hafiz Ahmad Kabir; corpses were regularly brought to the Madrasa to have funeral rites performed by one of the Arabic department's maulvis. The principal imposed a ban on students attending religious ceremonies during class hours.[66]

The task of effecting wider changes in the Madrasa's Arabic department fell on Sprenger's successor as principal: William Nassau Lees. Just six months after the sanction of the Bengal government was granted to Sprenger's proposed reforms, the Austrian returned to Europe on medical leave. Lees took over as officiating principal and remained in control, save for a nine-month period when Sprenger returned to India in 1856. Lees had arrived in India as a member of the Bengal army in 1846 before acquiring a reputation as an Arabic and Persian scholar. From March 1854 he acted on the instructions of the Council of Education to continue the programme of Madrasa reform that Sprenger had begun. Lees concurred with Sprenger in believing instruction in western science, coupled with the linguistic and philological teaching of Arabic, the correct course to pursue in the Madrasa's Arabic department. The new principal described his object as the conversion of that department from a madrasa into an Arabic College for the study of language and literature, alongside the subjects of a regular government curriculum.[67] Lees believed his task to be the regeneration of Indian Muslims. Under his direction, entry into the Madrasa's Arabic department continued to follow preparatory instruction in English and western science in its Anglo-Persian branch.

Lees's tenure as principal reveals him as an enthusiast for Arabic and Persian literature, poetry and history. At the Madrasa he completed a biography of the Persian poet Jami and from 1856 republished Arabic and Persian manuscripts using his private printing press.[68] Lees made immediate changes to the syllabus in the Madrasa's Arabic department, removing more Arabic scientific texts and introducing new class books on law and literature.[69] Classes in western natural philosophy were continued, and history and geography lessons commenced. Like Sprenger, Lees was not opposed to teaching the Qur'an for its linguistic and philological value and made a case for this to government: the Qur'an, he argued, was elegant and beautiful, the basis of Arabic grammar and the most important work of Arabic literature; its introduction as a class book need not mean the teaching of religion.[70] Once again, however, the proposal was vetoed by government; Frederick Halliday had by this stage assumed the position of lieutenant governor and insisted that to reintroduce the Qur'an to Madrasa lessons would be contrary to the principles of colonial education, and an affront to most British people.[71] The Qur'an would be available in the Madrasa's library for students to consult freely, just as the Bible was available in the libraries of other government institutions – but excluded from all classes.

When the Indian Rebellion broke out in 1857 the Madrasa reforms continued by Lees were endangered by Halliday's opposition to the continued government sponsoring of Arabic education. The lieutenant governor was convinced of Muslim responsibility for the 1857 uprisings. In a manner reminiscent of Charles Trevelyan he related Muslim opposition to British rule to the continued teaching of Arabic subjects at the Madrasa and, overlooking the recent introduction of western lessons through the Urdu medium, recorded:

> [T]o encourage Arabic and nothing else but Arabic (which is what we are now doing in the Arabic Department of the Mahommedan College,) is to foster against ourselves the old Mahommedan hostility, and to prolong, at our own expense, and to our own continual disadvantage, the bitter sentiments of religious and political hatred of which we have but lately reaped some of the natural fruit. ... [T]he Mahommedan College has produced and is producing *extensive political evil*. It is in fact a nursery of disaffection. And ... it can never be otherwise in an exclusive School of Mahommedan Learning. ... [T]he sedulous dissemination of this exclusive learning by the Government itself has in it something suicidal.[72]

Halliday believed that attempts to reform the Arabic department of the Madrasa were destined to fail. In an extensive minute he argued that the Madrasa's Muslim teachers retained favour for a traditional Arabic course concentrated on antiquated science and the religion of Islam. It was hardly to be anticipated that they would embrace the philological study of Arabic. What then should be done? For Halliday, the Anglo-Persian department of the Madrasa was playing an important role in introducing the English language to upper class Muslims and leading them away from their 'religious bigotry'.[73] The Arabic branch, however, should be closed; the teaching of Arabic literature, Halliday argued, might be carried on in other institutions affiliated to the Calcutta University, where it would be a truly philological pursuit.

Support for this proposal was most notably forthcoming from W. G. Young, director of public instruction in Bengal. Young fleshed out a plan to add one or more professors of Arabic literature to the staff of the Presidency College and shut the Madrasa's Arabic side, with the support of members of the non-official British community in Calcutta.[74] When Halliday's scheme was forwarded to the Government of India, however, it was almost unanimously rejected by members of Lord Canning's executive council. Cecil Beadon, secretary to the Indian government, took issue with Halliday's suggestion of a link between the Madrasa's teaching and Muslim opposition in 1857. The idea that the Madrasa was producing extensive political evil, he argued, was entirely devoid of proof: not one Muslim educated at the Madrasa was known to have been involved in the Indian Rebellion, while the college's maulvis had come out in support of government during the uprisings.[75] As in the 1830s, members of government expressed a concern that the termination of state support for Arabic learning at the Madrasa would create a Muslim impression – to be carefully avoided – of a government attempt to undermine their religion. The belief was restated that, as at Patna after the Rebellion, the best chance of reconciling Muslims to western education lay in the teaching of western subjects alongside an Arabic course. Consistent with his policy of conciliation following the uprisings' suppression, Canning resolved that the Madrasa be preserved as an institution for the study of Arabic subjects.[76] The exclusion of religious elements from the Madrasa's curriculum would, however, be continued: in the course of administrative deliberations after the Rebellion no suggestion was made to reintroduce the Qur'an and Hadith in the Arabic department. Nor was recommencing the teaching of Arabic sciences proposed: there would be no return to instruction in what were considered the antiquated scientific ideas held by most Indian maulvis.[77] In Cecil Beadon's view the secularization of the Madrasa's curriculum was a wise and necessary course: the colonial state could not patronize the teaching of Islam.[78] Arabic department reforms tending towards the exclusive teaching of the Arabic language, literature and Muslim law would be advanced.

For some European observers Arabic learning was inseparable from Islam: the attempt to teach a secular Arabic course at the Madrasa was therefore theoretically unsound, in spite of the exclusion of the Qur'an and other religious books from its course. This suggestion was intimated by Charles Trevelyan and Alexander Duff – among others – after 1853.[79] In 1860, however, William Nassau Lees was given a mandate by the Government of India to continue reforming the Madrasa's Arabic department aiming – through the cultivation of a philological Arabic course – to secularize its curriculum. Through the reports that Lees submitted periodically to government it is possible to chart his progress. In June 1860 a new syllabus was announced in which, as expected, the study of the Arabic language, Arabic literature and Muslim law was emphasized.[80]

Logic and rhetoric completed the course, simplified further by the exclusion of algebra and arithmetic. Lees introduced what he considered new pedagogical techniques founded on a distinction between memorization and understanding. No longer were passages of textbooks to be committed to memory and recited: they would have to be understood.[81] Proficiency in Arabic would be gained through composition and translation – from Arabic into Urdu and Persian and back again – to be practised alongside older methods for the study of grammar and rhetoric. In the annual examinations sat by students during Lees's principalship, half of all marks were awarded for competency in 'Literature': extracts of Arabic poetry and prose were translated into Urdu and Persian, and one piece of prose from Urdu into Arabic; questions were answered on a chosen Arabic historical text. The remaining marks were split evenly between Muslim law and logic/rhetoric.[82] By the close of 1862 the Arabic department had expanded to include 115 students considered by Lees to be making satisfactory progress in a philological Arabic course. The study of history as a critical western discipline was also regarded as a success. Lees cited the assistance offered to the Asiatic Society's writing of a history of Muslim India as proof of the curricular innovation embraced by the Madrasa's teaching staff.[83]

There is compelling evidence, however, to suggest that Muslim parties did not entirely share Lees's optimism about the ongoing project of Madrasa reform. In 1823 Matthew Lumsden's attempt to promote the philological study of Arabic had provoked the opposition of Maulvi Abdul Majid and other members of the Madrasa's staff who argued that it must continue to offer instruction in religious subjects including the Qur'an, Hadith and Muslim law.[84] From 1850 attempts to reform the Arabic department provoked similar responses from students and staff. In reaction to Aloys Sprenger's curriculum changes, a protest resulting in the expulsion of a large number of students was staged. The government enquiry into the 'disturbance' of April 1851 concluded that student opposition had been provoked by Sprenger's removal of certain textbooks on Arabic science from the Madrasa course and his insistence that all students attend the Urdu language class on western natural philosophy.[85] A petition signed by 102 rebellious students prayed for a return to the Arabic syllabus pursued prior to Sprenger's arrival, and a reorganization of the timetable so that religious observances might be carried out during the school day. Officials in the Council of Education were convinced that members of the teaching staff including Ajeeb Ahmad, brother-in-law of Hafiz Ahmad Kabir, had sided with students in opposing Sprenger's reforms.[86] The head professor of the Arabic department, Maulvi Muhammad Wajih, certainly held great reservations about reform. In 1860 Wajih responded to Lees's announcement of a new Arabic curriculum with an appeal to government that the ancient constitution of the Madrasa was being destroyed: no longer was the religious upbringing of students provided for.[87] Two further teachers in the Arabic department, Maulvi

Khadim and Maulvi Ilahadad Hossain, shared his view.[88] To ascertain Muslim responses to changes at the Madrasa beyond the perimeters of the institution the emergence of a Muslim public sphere in Bengal must now be considered.

Muslim Civil Society in Bengal

The foundation of civil institutions in nineteenth-century Bengal was stimulated by the ending of restrictions on press freedom in 1835 and the growing number of non-official Britons residing in the province. As the seat of government and the centre of trade, Calcutta was the natural location for the development of a vibrant public sphere populated by clubs, societies and newspapers that brought together particular subsections of the city's population and represented their interests. Some of the earliest associations in Calcutta – such as the Landholders' Society (1838) and Bengal British India Society (1843) – admitted both European and Indian members. Others like the Calcutta Trade Association (1830) and Bengal Chamber of Commerce (1853) aimed exclusively to promote the interests of Europeans. The British Indian Association (1851) was the most successful early society formed solely by Indian elites. Largely composed of Hindu landowners, it appealed for political concessions, including Indian representation in government.[89]

The Muslim public sphere possessed of most vitality before the Indian Rebellion was at Delhi. With the introduction of lithography, the publication of printed texts in Persian and Urdu made possible a new economy of information. During the 1830s two regular Urdu newspapers, the *Delhi Akbar* and the *Sayyid al-Akbar*, were established. Their form and content was heavily influenced by the Persian newsletter, via which information had been transmitted during the Mughal period.[90] At the Delhi College several Urdu journals were founded, including the *Qiran al-Saʾadain* – initiated by Aloys Sprenger – and the *Khairkhwah-ye-Hind*.[91] In her recent research Margrit Pernau suggests that only after 1857 did Indian newspapers gain a wide enough audience to influence groups outside of the traditional reach of written public discussion in Delhi: the formulation of Muslim public opinion before the Rebellion remained confined to 'semi-private' gatherings.[92] This notwithstanding, the expansion of the lithographic press and the interaction of Muslim literati with European figures suggests a dynamic public sphere for exchange through the media of Persian, English and Urdu. Studies of the development of Muslim civil society in Bengal have concentrated on the final three decades of the nineteenth century, emphasizing the impact of improved means of communication, education and printing in fostering consciousness of religious identity.[93] There is significant reason to think, however, that Bengali Muslim civil institutions were flourishing much earlier, particularly in Calcutta. In 1822 the Persian *Jam-i Jahan Numa* newspaper was founded in the city; it was joined soon after by the *Dorbeen*. The raising of over eight thousand signatures on the petition against the abolition of the Calcutta Madrasa in February 1835 suggests an extensive, rapid network of communication between Muslim parties.

The first modern-style Muslim association in Calcutta, the Anjuman-i-Islam, was founded in 1855.[94] With its successor, the Mahomedan Literary Society (MLS), it was the leading Muslim organization in Calcutta between 1855 and 1875. Both the Anjuman and MLS were founded by individuals intimately associated with the Calcutta Madrasa, and both were bodied by members of a sharif Muslim class literate in Persian and Urdu. While the Anjuman has been little noticed in research, a tendency has been exhibited to dismiss the MLS as an elitist organization, unimportant to the history of Muslim Bengal. Members of the MLS have been portrayed as elites subservient to the British government and concerned only to preserve their social and political status under colonial rule.[95] The following will serve as a corrective to this view, which does justice neither to the complexities of Muslim–British engagement, or to the multifarious motivations informing the actions of sharif Muslims. Though the Anjuman-i-Islam and MLS were undoubtedly elitist in composition, their members acted with more than a concern for self-preservation, and ultimately played a pivotal role in reshaping colonial educational provisions, with profound implications for Bengali Muslims. By the late 1860s multiple Muslim associations inspired by the MLS had been founded in Bengal; Muslim participation in public discourse had multiplied to such an extent as to problematize the notion of a clear distinction between sharif and non-sharif groups.

The first meeting of the Anjuman-i-Islam was held on 6 May 1855 at the residence of Maulvi Muhammad Mazhar – a teacher of Arabic at the Madrasa. Presiding over it was Abdul Bari, *qazi* of Calcutta, and speaking at length, Abdur Rauf, editor of the *Dorbeen*. The declared intention of the Anjuman was to promote the 'general welfare' of the Muslim community of India.[96] In July 1855 a managing committee was appointed and a code of rules framed. 200 pamphlets were printed and circulated that reported the proceedings of the Anjuman's preliminary meetings, alongside 600 copies of its rules.[97] By the autumn of 1855 the Anjuman could claim 126 members, 85 of whom resided in Calcutta and the others in wider Bengal. Additional branches of the Anjuman were established at Sylhet and Midnapore, where support had been most forthcoming. Several important features of the Anjuman should be highlighted. The nominal leader was Maulvi Fazlur Rahman Khan, the chief *qazi* of Calcutta. Exerting influence beneath him were vice presidents Abdul Bari and Muhammad Wajih, the latter of whom was also head professor of Arabic at the Madrasa. Muhammad Mazhar was chosen as secretary. From the outset the Anjuman acted as a political organization and represented Muslim interests in government. In July 1855 it appealed against the government of Bengal's decision that all candidates to the position of *vakeel* in British *sudder* and *zillah* courts should be required to speak English, which it argued unfairly discriminated against Muslims, and obtained a reversal of the decision.[98] It launched an enquiry into allegations of discrimination against Muslims seeking public employment and protested against the regulation that prisoners in Bengal jails be shaved every fortnight.[99]

In many respects the Anjuman-i-Islam was similar to other associations in Calcutta civil society founded in the 1850s. Conducting its monthly meetings in Persian and Urdu, it submitted petitions to government in English, confidently employing several different media. Like other indigenous associations, the Anjuman modelled its form on that of an English club or society, publishing regular reports of proceedings, codifying rules of procedure and asking for subscriptions from members. The Anjuman shared its minutes and proceedings with other organizations – including the British Indian Association – and on occasion joined in common cause with other bodies.[100] The idea that the Anjuman resembled a modern, European association should, however, be partially qualified. With one very notable exception meetings of the Anjuman took place not in public venues but in the residences of various members in Calcutta – a fact resonant with Pernau's contention that Muslim public opinion was formed at Delhi prior to 1857 in the 'semi-private' sphere. The one attempt to hold a truly public meeting of the Anjuman was abandoned when an estimated 12,000 Muslims descended on the Calcutta town hall. Their cause of protest was a concern that the government intended to convert all Muslim subjects to Christianity.[101]

The Anjuman-i-Islam lasted just several years before ceasing its activities soon after the Indian Rebellion. Among its final acts was to offer congratulations to Queen Victoria upon the transfer of sovereignty to the Crown in November 1858.[102] By this time, however, the Anjuman had commenced on a path particularly important to this study. In October 1855 one of its members, Nawab Abdul Latif, had proposed that it undertake enquiries into the progress of Muslim education in Bengal to ascertain why Muslim parties were reluctant to accept education in government institutions and to propose reforms of colonial public instruction.[103] That Latif stressed the importance of education on members of the Anjuman should come as no surprise. During the 1840s he had excelled as one of just two holders of a government scholarship to study at the Calcutta Madrasa and, after completing a Persian, Arabic and English education, remained to teach English in the Madrasa's Arabic department before accepting the position of deputy magistrate in the Alipore district of Calcutta in 1849.[104] Latif was the first Muslim in Bengal to evince a public concern for the participation of his co-religionists in the Indian educational system. In August 1853 he announced a competition for the best Persian essay written by a Muslim on the subject of Muslim responses to western learning: 'How far would the inculcation of European Sciences through the medium of the English Language, benefit Mahomedan students in the present circumstances of India, and what are the most practicable and unobjectionable means of imparting such instruction?'[105] With the support of the Council of Education the competition was publicized in the *Calcutta Gazette* and judged by a panel including Maulvi Fazlur Rahman Khan and Qazi Abdul Bari. The prize of Rs. 100 was awarded by Latif personally. Respected for his proficiency in English and successes as a deputy magistrate, Latif had been approached by the council to assist its ongoing enquiries about reform of the Madrasa and later claimed to have been influential in its 1853 separation into Anglo-Persian and Arabic departments.[106]

Several major aspects of Latif's educational thought must be stressed. It is clear that Latif was concerned by what he perceived as the reluctance of Muslims in Bengal to acquire a colonial education at the Madrasa and more widely. His initiation of the essay competition and attempt to direct the Anjuman towards the subject of education betray an anxiety to reconcile Muslims to instruction in European science and the English language. Latif was convinced that knowledge of English was indispensable to Muslim temporal progress: English, he noted, was increasingly the language of commerce and of the courts, and essential to advancement under British rule.[107] This sentiment was shared by Maulvi Muhammad Ali, a second teacher of English at the Madrasa, who published a collection of articles on the subject in 1858.[108] For Latif, however, Muslim study of English could not come at the expense of Arabic and Persian learning. Latif was convinced that while proficiency in the English language was necessary for a Muslim's worldly position, the Persian language remained indispensable to his social standing and knowledge of Arabic was essential to his religion.[109] Latif rejected plans to terminate the study of Arabic at the Madrasa, instead advocating the conjoint teaching of English and Arabic in government institutions.[110] In this way, he perceived, Muslim faith might be preserved alongside the acquirement of western learning.

In April 1863 Latif founded the MLS, an organization with the declared intention of 'promoting the educational progress of the Mahomedans'.[111] Leadership was taken up by the same individuals who had earlier directed the Anjuman-i-Islam: Muhammad Wajih was elected president, and Abdul Bari second in command. Latif assumed the influential position of secretary. The MLS proclaimed itself a non-political body concerned simply for Muslim educational advancement and the betterment of relations between different communities in India. It received the support and encouragement of the Bengal government, with Lieutenant Governor Cecil Beadon accepting the invitation to become a patron.[112] It is not difficult to discern ways in which the MLS encouraged the dissemination of new knowledge among elite Muslims, contributing to colonial plans for the refashioning of Muslim subjects through western learning. At weekly meetings members heard lectures on topics including commerce, agriculture and the arts. The value of specific western academic subjects such as history and geography was discussed. Perhaps most influential of all were the regular lectures given on scientific topics. In August 1863 members of the society received a lecture on electricity and the operation of the electric telegraph – imparted by the European assistant director-general of the government telegraph department, and translated into Urdu by Latif.[113] A special meeting of the MLS was held at the Calcutta Medical College, where the principle of combustion was discussed, while lectures on chemistry and physical science were also given. The MLS held an annual grand conversazione at the Calcutta town hall to which members of all communities were invited and where exhibitions were displayed on scientific subjects.[114] By 1867 the society had expanded to include 500 members; in this year Abdul Latif was honoured by the Bengal government for his services to the promotion of education.[115] Once again, however, it would be erroneous to suggest that Latif was concerned solely for the advance of western education among his co-religionists. In January 1868 he spoke before the Bengal Social Science Association and repeated his contention that it was indispensable for government to provide facilities for Muslim boys to study English and Arabic conjointly – only through Arabic might a person know Islam.[116]

In July 1869 a new committee was appointed to consider the condition and future of the Calcutta Madrasa. Latif was appointed to represent Muslim interests alongside two European members. Significant about the enquiries is that, unlike in an earlier period when reform of the Madrasa had been enquired into by government, the views of Muslim parties were extensively sought. Between August and November 1869 Muslim individuals and associations submitted opinions to government on the Madrasa's future and the wider question of Muslim education in Bengal. At the front of the queue to influence government policy was the MLS. Following behind it, however, Muslims from across Bengal engaged with government. The proceedings of the Madrasa reform committee provide a major insight into the extent and nature of Muslim civil society at the close of the 1860s. Its records permit an understanding of the concerns of Muslim parties engaging with colonial authorities on the subject of education. For most of the 1860s the Madrasa had remained under the control of William Nassau Lees. His reports suggest that the Anglo-Persian department enjoyed modest success in imparting an English, Persian and vernacular education to pupils who went on to the Presidency College to sit for university degrees.[117] In the Arabic department Lees had continued to cultivate a philological course while campaigning for the Madrasa's affiliation to the Calcutta University, and a greater recognition of Arabic literature in university degrees.[118] Increasingly, however, members of the Bengal administration had grown frustrated at Lees's principalship. The announcement of a new reform enquiry was occasioned by his departure to Europe on leave of absence amid accusations of his mismanagement of the institution.[119]

It is instructive to consider the professions, locations and written or spoken languages of Muslim respondents to the Madrasa reform enquiries of 1869, so as to build a fuller picture of the social composition and geographical extent of a Bengal Muslim public sphere engaging with the colonial state. Two methods existed by which individuals and associations brought views before the reform committee: through an appearance in person, often as the spokesman of a particular group; or through a written entry, in the form of a memorial, letter or petition. Unsurprisingly most personal representations before the committee were made by individuals resident in Calcutta or its environs. Those attending in person included twelve members of the Madrasa's staff and a number of former students, but extended beyond individuals with an evident connection to the institution. Two professors from the nearby Hooghly College appeared before the committee, in addition to a teacher from a privately-endowed madrasa at Sealdah in Calcutta. More widely, the committee was visited by Muslim gentlemen employed in a variety of public roles, at the Calcutta High Court or in the administrative apparatus of the Bengal and Indian governments.[120]

When the written submissions of Muslim respondents to the committee are considered, a far more extensive pattern of engagement is revealed. From as far west as Mirzapur (near Benares), and as far east as Chittagong, individuals and associations expressed a concern for the future of the Madrasa and laid out recommendations for its future. Opinions on the Madrasa were submitted by parties in urban centres including Burdwan, Barisal, Noakhali, Rangpur, Hooghly, Chittagong and Calcutta in Bengal, and Gaya, Bhagalpur, Muzaffarpur and Patna in Bihar, in addition to Mirzapur. In late August 1869 a special meeting of the MLS was convened before it submitted a memorial on reform.[121] Other *anjumans* presenting proposals included the Mahomedan Improvement Association of Mirzapur and the Scientific Society of Bihar at Muzaffarpur.[122] Through the English medium some Muslim government officials and educationalists forwarded their recommendations – among them Sayyid Amir Hossain, assistant to the European commissioner of Bhagalpur, and Muhammad Allahdad Khan, a senior scholar at the Bengal Presidency College.[123] A greater number of submissions were received in Persian and Urdu. In August 1869 government advertisements were placed in the *Dorbeen* soliciting opinions on the Madrasa's future. The responses that followed derived in part from individuals acting alone – such as Sayyid Serajooddeen Ahmad, a Bihar-based zamindar with responsibility for overseeing a local, endowed madrasa – but more often from a collectivity representing a particular locality.[124] From Gaya, for instance, Waris Ali (a deputy magistrate) headed a group of forty-seven of the town's inhabitants who provided their counsel in an Urdu memorial; separate memorials were submitted in Persian and Urdu by Muslim gentlemen in Patna.[125]

It is evident from the responses received by the committee that the future of the Madrasa was widely discussed by Muslim parties in Bengal civil society. Civil society was the location for the formation of Muslim public opinion through discussion and debate and, via the drafting of memorials and petitions, its articulation to government. Opinion was expressed by formally constituted *anjumans* and by sharif Muslims of particular towns and cities coming together in one-off meetings and temporary ensembles. The speed with which news of the government's intention to reform the Madrasa was translated into public meetings and responses in August and September of 1869 indicates a developed economy of information between *ashraf* in multiple locations, operating via the Persian and Urdu languages in written and spoken form. It is also suggests shared Muslim concerns with regard to the Madrasa, confirmed in what follows.

Among those Muslims submitting recommendations for the Madrasa, near-unanimity was expressed that the study of English must be encouraged. The assertion of Maulvi Muhammad Ilahdad, professor in the Arabic department, was typical: 'Mahomedans are anxious to get into the service of Government, and the only way is through a knowledge of English'.[126] Other teachers at the Madrasa concurred and were supported by members of the MLS, including Abdul Bari.[127] Striking, however, was the consensus that the study of Arabic must continue alongside the acquisition of proficiency in English. Consistent with Latif's representations to government earlier in the decade, Muslims responding to the Madrasa committee insisted on the continued teaching of Arabic. A petition by the Madrasa's students was just one of many submissions urging this course. '[A]mong the Mussulmans', it read, 'those who have a knowledge of English only are despised and hated ... but if they know English in addition to their knowledge of Arabic, they are much praised and respected by their co-religionists': English should be encouraged at the Madrasa, but not at the expense of Arabic instruction.[128]

The great question to be answered was what subjects should be included in the Arabic curriculum. It would appear that some respondents to the committee subscribed to the view that to prioritize the teaching of Arabic language and literature had been the correct course to pursue: the approach of Aloys Sprenger and William Nassau Lees was partially endorsed. For as long as each student learnt the Arabic language, noted one of the Madrasa's teachers, a relationship to his religion would be maintained.[129] To this was added a stress on maintaining the Madrasa's teaching of Muslim law. For a larger proportion of respondents, however, the Arabic course taught at the Madrasa stood in need of major reform. A number of witnesses and petitions pointed out that the Madrasa's reputation as a seat of Arabic learning had fallen among Muslims over the past two decades on account of the exclusion of many of the subjects of a regular madrasa curriculum and the near-exclusive emphasis placed on the Arabic language, Arabic literature and Muslim law. From several different quarters the suggestion was made that in the Madrasa's Arabic department too much 'pointless' Arabic literature was taught.[130]

Recent scholarship has unearthed no instances of Muslim opposition to the exclusion of religious books and introduction of Arabic literary texts to the course of studies at the Delhi College under Felix Boutros and Aloys Sprenger in the

1840s.[131] Two decades on, in discourses over the future of the Calcutta Madrasa, opposition of that nature is precisely what can be identified. In Calcutta and wider Bengal, Muslim parties announced their disfavour for an Arabic course at the Madrasa that concentrated on the philological and proposed alternative curricula involving a wider range of subjects. Some Muslims knowledgeable of the colonial secular education commitment proposed new Arabic syllabi that took that commitment into account. Muhammad Mazhar, for example, argued that it was quite possible to abandon the Arabic course encouraged over the past two decades and reintroduce texts from a traditional madrasa curriculum without directly teaching Islam; portions of works containing religious doctrine and instructions on observances might be read by students at home.[132] In 1868 Nawab Abdul Latif had hinted at his favour for the reintroduction of religious instruction to the Madrasa when he noted that the institution had been most popular among Muslims when religious subjects were freely taught. To the Muslim community, he added, the Madrasa was 'more than a mere school of literature and science'.[133] When the MLS came to propose a new Madrasa curriculum the following year, however, it accepted that religious teaching could not be imparted in a government-managed institution. The MLS's proposed Arabic course of studies was a significant departure from the curriculum pursued under William Nassau Lees – with arithmetic, geometry, algebra and philosophy reintroduced and moral philosophy taught for the first time; no proposal was put forward, however, for the reintroduction of texts excluded from the Madrasa on account of their religious content.[134]

A far greater number of proposals for extending the Arabic department's course did include the readmittance of religious teaching. Respondents to the committee made a powerful case for reconstituting the Madrasa as a seminary offering a complete Islamic education alongside a government-prescribed course. It is not ascertainable how far those recommending the teaching of religious subjects were aware of the government's secular education commitment and deliberately sought its abandonment. What is beyond doubt, however, is that in Calcutta and locations throughout Bengal, Muslim parties desired a Madrasa teaching Islam. Closest to the Madrasa were the students in its Arabic department, who together submitted a Persian petition stressing that their syllabus must be extended to include religious texts.[135] Murhumut Hossain studied at the Madrasa before finding employment as a pleader at the Calcutta High Court. In his view it was imperative for a Madrasa pupil to receive religious instruction: 'without a full and perfect knowledge of one's own religion he is nothing'.[136] Stressing the necessity of religious education, a further memorandum dwelt at length on the dangerous consequences of 'irreligion' to be anticipated should generations of Muslims be raised at the Madrasa without a true knowledge of Islam.[137] Proposals for the reintroduction of religious teaching emphasized the need for instruction in the Qur'an and commentaries, Hadith and fiqh – in addition to Muslim law.[138]

By the end of 1860s William Nassau Lees had emerged as a champion of the teaching of Arabic language and literature in schools and colleges under the management of the colonial state, and of the extension of a philological Arabic course in Calcutta University degrees. With his argument that the teaching of Arabic language and literature was essential to the reconciliation of Muslims to government education, Lees pre-empted by several years one of the major provisions framed in Mayo's resolution.[139] However, dialogue over the future of the Calcutta Madrasa reveals that Muslim parties in Bengal civil society widely desired not just this, but something more: unfettered Islamic instruction in the state educational system. The final section of the chapter considers how, after the close of the Madrasa reform enquiries, these demands were partially satisfied.

Religious Education and Denominalization

In the emergent Muslim institutions of Bengal civil society religious faith played an important role. Proposing the continued teaching of Arabic and the reintroduction of instruction in Islamic subjects at the Calcutta Madrasa, Muslim parties were motivated by concerns about religion and asserted the significance of their faith in a growing public sphere. Concerns about religious matters coexisted with temporal anxieties, and shaped public expressions of the interests of an envisaged Muslim community. Assertions of the importance of religious education made faith a public concern and challenged the official distance between state and religion. The colonial secular education commitment was opposed by Muslim elites concerned for the future of the Madrasa.

Discussions of the Madrasa in 1869 frequently spilled over into consideration of the wider reform of Muslim education in Bengal. To encourage Muslim participation in the colonial educational system Muslim parties proposed the more extensive teaching of Arabic, Persian and Urdu in government schools, the appointment of Muslim teachers to existing institutions and the foundation of new state-managed schools exclusively for Muslims. The MLS stressed the necessity of appointing Muslim teachers and offering Arabic and Persian instruction in government schools.[140] Others insisted that Muslim pupils in state institutions should be instructed in the tenets of Islam.[141] The influence of the views of the MLS on Mayo's resolution is undoubted. Shortly before the resolution was drafted Mayo was visited by Nawab Abdul Latif who urged reform upon him.[142] The MLS had earlier won favour for its professions of loyalty to government during the 1870–1 Wahabi trials.

As we have seen, Mayo's resolution proposed a series of modifications of colonial pedagogy designed to encourage Muslim participation in the government system of public instruction while preserving the colonial secular education commitment. Where provincial administrations saw fit, the provision of instruction in the vernacular language best suited to Muslims would be encouraged; the Arabic and Persian languages would be taught in government schools and colleges and given greater recognition in university degrees. Muslim teachers would be appointed to government schools and grants-in-aid awarded so that Muslim parties could establish schools of their own. In Bengal, where the proportion of Muslims in government education was believed to be lowest, the resolution had major consequences. Its suggestions were adopted enthusiastically by the Scottish Liberal and Indian veteran, George Campbell, lieutenant governor from 1870. In September 1871 Campbell recorded that his views on the subject of Muslim education were 'in a great measure, identical' with Mayo's and instructed the Bengal education department to put the provisions of the resolution into effect.[143]

The administrative discussions that ensued are revealing of significant disagreement between British parties over the revision of government educational provisions to accommodate Muslim interests. Some influential administrators such as Charles Bernard, secretary to the Government of Bengal, joined Campbell in supporting Mayo's resolution, emphasizing the benefits of extending colonial public instruction among Muslim subjects for government and Muslims alike.[144] In the view of other officials, however, introducing educational provisions exclusively for Muslims was a policy with significant undesirable implications. For one, it was argued, the overt encouragement of Muslim education would publicly compromise the claim of the colonial state to impartiality between the different communities of the population of India. Proposals for the extension of vernacular education in languages spoken by Muslims, the granting of special fee concessions and scholarships to Muslim students, and the amendment of grant-in-aid rules for Muslim parties were criticized in these terms.[145] Moreover a number of the measures under discussion would, it was feared, inevitably mean the denominalization of government education in Bengal. In official deliberations over the extension of Muslim education the merits and demerits of educational denominationalism were assessed.

Chapters one and two revealed the extent to which, with the growth of the colonial system of public instruction, British administrators were prepared to incorporate religious identity into Indian education, and establish institutional arrangements for the instruction of distinct religious groups. Responding to Mayo's resolution, however, some officials in Bengal argued against the further inscription of Muslim identity into colonial education: the liberal ideal of schools and colleges imparting western instruction to members of all religious communities conjointly continued to claim administrative support. When George Campbell added to Mayo's resolution by proposing the foundation of Muslim-only government schools in Bengal, British disagreements on the subject were brought to the fore. Campbell believed that separate Muslim schools teaching Arabic and Persian alongside a regular government course would be most effective at reconciling Muslims to colonial education.[146] However, the opposition to his plan was intense. William Atkinson, director of public instruction, and James Sutcliffe, principal of the Presidency College in Calcutta, denounced the principle of denominational government schools outright.[147] Other officials in the education department recorded notes of dissent in which aversion to the principle of educational denominationalism and to the government establishment of Muslim institutions was combined.[148] Following lengthy deliberations, a compromise was struck whereby, as Mayo's resolution had proposed, special classes for the teaching of the Arabic and Persian languages would be added to existing government schools. No new Muslim-only state-funded institutions would be founded, but Arabic and Persian classes would be attended exclusively by Muslim pupils. The rationale behind this decision was explained candidly by Campbell:

> As a special concession to the Mahomedans, whenever there is a sufficient demand to justify the supply, there will be a special class to teach Mahomedans Arabic and Persian ... It is on the ground that it is a political object to encourage the Mahomedans – to bribe them as it were to accept the education which leads to their own advancement – that I would say, if you will come to our schools we will give your children the education in Arabic and in Persian which you require, provided that you will accept at the same time an English education and instruction in practical arts and sciences.[149]

During the course of 1872 Muslim teachers were added to government *zillah* schools throughout the eastern districts of Bengal. In the Muslim-only classes no religious subjects were taught and so, consistent with the terms of Mayo's resolution, the colonial secular education commitment was preserved. A further major step was taken, however, towards the denominalization of state education in Bengal.[150]

In December 1869 the committee responsible for reform of the Calcutta Madrasa resolved that the institution would remain divided into distinct Arabic and Anglo-Persian departments. In its view a responsibility of government lay in the continued provision of an Arabic course: the Madrasa would be a location for the study of Muslim law and the Arabic language for as long as demand existed. This reassurance was coupled, however, with confirmation of the exclusion of religious subjects from the Madrasa's curriculum. The Government of India, it was noted, 'repudiates' the teaching of religion in its schools and colleges: 'Mahomedans ... no more than Christians or Hindoos, have a right to expect that the Imperial Exchequer should provide funds for absolute instruction in the tenets or ceremonies of their religion'.[151] Soon after the close of reform enquiries a new managing council was appointed for the Madrasa consisting of three European and five Muslim members, among them Abdul Latif and Abdul Bari.[152] The council reintroduced certain Arabic texts excluded by William Nassau Lees, including the *Hidayat* for the teaching of Muslim law.[153] In accordance with government direction, however, the Qur'an, Hadith and other religious subjects remained absent from the Madrasa's course.

It would appear that Muslim appeals for the teaching of Islam in state-managed institutions remained unanswered. Both in the Madrasa and government *zillah* schools, instruction in the Arabic language would be offered to Muslim pupils but the provision of a religious education avoided. In one significant way, however, the reconciliation of religious instruction and a colonial education was made possible by the changes introduced in Bengal after Mayo's resolution. Notwithstanding its profession of 'non-interference' in Indian religion the colonial state had continued after 1858 to manage Hindu and Muslim religious endowments, among the largest of which in Bengal was that bequeathed by Muhammad Mohsin – a Shia landowner in the town of Hooghly, north of Calcutta – brought under the control of the East India Company in 1824. Originally used to maintain a small religious shrine and school, Mohsin's endowment had in 1836 been appropriated by the Bengal administration to fund the establishment of a government college at Hooghly with English and oriental departments attended by pupils of all religions.[154] Among Muslim parties concerned for the extension of education in the 1860s, an often-noted bone of contention was that an endowment intended to facilitate the education of Muslim boys was being used to support an institution in which Hindu and Christian students were preponderant. By 1871 the Hooghly College was attended by in excess of 500 Hindu and Christian boys and just 162 Muslims. While the oriental department was by this point reserved exclusively for Muslim students – of which there were 54 – Muslim participation in the English branch of the institution was dwarfed by that of pupils of other religious affiliations.[155]

As early as 1861 Nawab Abdul Latif had publicly stressed the imperative of reapplying the Mohsin endowment to the exclusive benefit of Muslim education.[156] When Muslim parties were invited to engage with government on the question of reform of the Calcutta Madrasa the case was put that, consistent with the intentions of its founder, the Mohsin endowment must be redirected to support the education of Bengali Muslims.[157] When the managing council of the Madrasa, headed by Latif, advanced this suggestion again in June 1871 the Bengal government conceded: the Mohsin fund would be set free from its maintenance of the Hooghly College to further Muslim education more widely.[158] For British administrators a great advantage of redirecting the endowment was that Muslim participation in the colonial system of public instruction might be encouraged without the partisan award of state funding to the Muslim community. The endowment could be used to fund the subsidizing of fees and to award special scholarships to Muslim pupils in government schools without a compromise of the neutrality of the colonial state.[159]

Most significant for our purposes is that the Mohsin endowment was also redirected to the establishment of three new madrasas under government management at Dacca, Rajshahye and Chittagong. In July 1873 the decision was taken to add Rs. 50,000 to the educational budget of the Bengal government to maintain the Hooghly College as a regular government institution. The Mohsin endowment was reallocated to the support of Muslim students in existing government institutions, the preservation of the oriental department of the Hooghly College as a Muslim seminary and the foundation of the new madrasas.[160] The proceedings of the Government of Bengal suggest that the plan to found the madrasas originated with George Campbell; the lieutenant governor had embarked on a tour of eastern Bengal and brought under personal consideration the question of Muslim education in the eastern districts in 1872.[161] According to the plan he formulated, the new madrasas at Dacca, Chittagong and Rajshahye would teach the Arabic, Persian and English languages; each would be managed by government but placed under the control of a local supervisory committee of Muslim and European gentlemen responsible for determining exact courses of instruction.[162] At each madrasa – it was envisaged – the Arabic curriculum would concentrate on language, literature and law but, crucially, there would be no restriction on the provision of religious education. Maintained by a private endowment rather than state funds, each would be permitted to teach Islamic subjects alongside a course of secular western lessons.[163]

By 1875 the Calcutta Madrasa stood at the centre of a network of five government-managed institutions in Bengal exclusively for Muslim pupils in which western education was imparted adjacent to Arabic learning.[164] At only the Calcutta Madrasa was instruction in religious subjects avoided. Alongside the inauguration of separate Muslim classes within government *zillah* schools, the establishment of the madrasas was a major innovation moving the colonial system of public instruction towards denominationalism in Bengal. Encouraged by Mayo's resolution, both the institution of separate Muslim classes and foundation of the madrasas had been critically shaped by the negotiations of Muslim parties with government. Through the emergent institutions of civil society, Muslim individuals and associations concerned in the first instance for the Calcutta Madrasa asserted the importance of both religious community and faith to colonial education – securing significant revisions of the state educational system. Convictions of the importance of religion informed the negotiation of Muslim elites with colonial authorities in a period seminal to the development of a Bengal public sphere from which Islam would refuse to disappear.

4 RELIGIOUS EDUCATION AND STATE WITHDRAWAL IN THE PUNJAB

In October 1884 the government of the Punjab began a process of withdrawal from the management of colleges and higher level schools in its territories. In future, officials determined, institutions of secondary and further education would be established not under the direct administration of the colonial state, but only through the award of grants-in-aid. The gradual substitution of state-managed for aided institutions was declared a government object. Grants would also be more extensively given to lower level privately-managed schools.[1] The consequence of this new direction in colonial policy was the transformation of state educational provisions. At the start of the 1880s the grant-in-aid system had made little progress in the Punjab. Just three aided colleges and thirty-five secondary schools received government grants, compared to more than double that number in the neighbouring North-Western Provinces (hereafter NWP). Unlike in the other British Indian provinces, state-managed primary schools far outnumbered their aided counterparts. Not a single higher level institution under Indian management was awarded state funds.[2] For the Punjab administration to begin stimulating private educational agency in 1884 was a dramatic reversal of its existing practice. Through a major increase in grant-in-aid funding, Punjabi parties were encouraged for the first time to found schools and colleges within the colonial system.

The focus of this chapter is a two-decade period culminating in the Punjab government's U-turn. Concentrated on the emergent institutions of Punjab civil society, it reveals the extent to which shared Muslim and European concerns about the absence of religious instruction in state-managed colleges and schools provoked the withdrawal of the colonial state from direct educational provision in favour of private agencies. Between 1875 and 1885 it was in the Punjab that the exclusion of religion from colonial education was most vociferously contested. The lasting effect of demands for the reconciliation of religious and secular instruction was the replacement of government-managed colleges and schools in which, consistent with the colonial secular education commitment, only secular subjects could be taught, by grant-maintained institutions delivering religious education. Muslim, Hindu and Sikh parties capitalized on the change in government approach to establish state-sponsored institutions. As in Bengal after Mayo's resolution, the revision of colonial educational policy stimulated the denominalization of education.

The chapter consists of two main parts. The first examines the growth of opposition to the separation of religion from colonial education in the Punjab, centring on the most outspoken critic of government pedagogical provisions in the province – Gottlieb Leitner – head of the Punjab University College, and the influential association of Indian and European elites that he founded – the Anjuman-i-Punjab. The second considers the enquiries of the Indian Education Commission of 1882 – when Muslim negotiations decisively impacted on state educational policy – and investigates the responses of Punjabi Muslims to state withdrawal from the direct provision of education, as the Anjuman-i-Islam and Anjuman-i-Himayat-i-Islam entered the educational field. We begin, however, by returning to an event well documented in the historiography of nineteenth-century Muslim India: the foundation of the Muhammadan Anglo-Oriental College (hereafter MAO College) at Aligarh. The college served as a precedent for Punjabi Muslim parties seeking the establishment of Muslim institutions with the support of the colonial state.

The MAO College

In December 1870, Sayyid Ahmad Khan, a government judge at Benares in the NWP, founded a committee to consider the condition of Muslim education in India. The committee sought to ascertain why Indian Muslims did not accept the education offered in colonial schools and colleges and to suggest means for the removal of obstacles to Muslim participation in the state educational system. To this end, an essay competition was initiated. In the year up to December 1871 thirty-two essays were submitted to Sayyid Ahmad's 'Committee for the Better Diffusion and Advancement of Learning among the Muhammadans of India' by Muslim respondents across northern India.[3] The similarities between this and the essay competition organized by Nawab Abdul Latif on Muslim education in Bengal were more than coincidental. Sayyid Ahmad had visited Calcutta in 1863 and spoken before a meeting of the MLS on the subject of education. Thereafter he maintained correspondence with Latif and was periodically informed of MLS activities.[4]

The proceedings leading up to the establishment of the MAO College are well known.[5] Among the essays submitted to Sayyid Ahmad's committee a consensus was expressed that one reason stood out above all others in explanation of the small proportion of Muslims participating in the government system of education: the absence of religious instruction from state-managed schools and colleges. When the committee headed by Sayyid Ahmad sat to review the conclusions and recommendations of the essayists in December 1871, unanimous agreement was expressed that Muslim students required religious education in addition to a secular course of study.[6] Though some members of the committee argued for an appeal to government to admit religious teaching into schools and colleges under state management, it was a second course, favoured by Sayyid Ahmad, which the committee adopted: the establishment of an institution under Muslim control in which religious instruction and a state-prescribed secular curriculum would be combined. In April 1872, Sayyid Ahmad outlined his plan for a college in which Muslims might receive a western scientific and literary education – through either the English or Urdu medium – alongside religious instruction.[7] Coming so soon after Mayo's resolution, the proposal was welcomed enthusiastically by high-ranking British officials including William Muir, lieutenant governor of the NWP, and Lord Northbrook, Mayo's successor as viceroy.[8] The MAO College was opened in 1875 and became the first Muslim collegiate institution in northern India to receive government funding. Its curriculum combined a regular government course with basic religious lessons focused on daily observances.[9]

For most of the 1860s Sayyid Ahmad's public concern had been not the education of Muslims, but the advance of western learning among Indian subjects more widely. Shortly after returning from Calcutta in 1863 he had founded a Scientific Society at Ghazipur, where he was then stationed, with the declared object of publishing rare oriental manuscripts and translating European scientific and literary works into Indian languages. Participated in by Muslim, Hindu and European gentlemen, the society attempted the translation of European works into Urdu – no doubt inspired by the example of the Delhi Vernacular Translation Society.[10] Sayyid Ahmad's speech before the MLS in 1863 stressed the importance of western knowledge to Indian progress, but made no reference to the imperative of advancing education among Muslims specifically.[11] How then should his later determination to act on behalf a Muslim constituency be explained? One might be tempted to point towards Mayo's resolution as a stimulus for Sayyid Ahmad's burgeoning interest in the education of his co-religionists, yet his committee of enquiry was appointed eight months prior to the Government of India's public bestowal of attention on the subject in August 1871. It is likely that Sayyid Ahmad was aware of Bengali Muslim appeals to government for educational reform during the Calcutta Madrasa enquiries of 1869. To account for his determination to act on behalf of a Muslim constituency, however, Sayyid Ahmad's visit to England in 1869–70 must be considered. As David Lelyveld has shown, it was during this visit that Sayyid Ahmad determined to found a college for Indian Muslims. While in England, Sayyid Ahmad imbibed the Victorian doctrine of laissez-faire and became aware of the importance of religion to education and society in the metropolis.[12] Sayyid Ahmad's decision to establish a Muslim college derived from a realization of the possibility of acting independently of the state to reconcile religious and secular instruction. A concern for the strengthening of Islam in the colonial milieu – in addition to a growing perception of the low proportion of Muslims in the the government system – informed his resolve to act on behalf of his religious community.

The foundation of the MAO College anticipated events in the Punjab in several key ways. In the Punjab, as at Aligarh, the decision of Muslim elites to act publicly on behalf of their religious constituency would be motivated in part by concerns for the provision of religious education. Muslim elites negotiating with government through the institutions of Punjab civil society urged the reconciling of religious and secular education, and settled upon the foundation of new Muslim institutions as the most effective means for bringing that reconciliation about. Awarding grant-in-aid funding to a Muslim institution, colonial authorities embarked on a course that would prove increasingly attractive as British and Muslim concerns over the divorce of religion from education in state institutions grew.

Gottlieb Leitner and the Anjuman-i-Punjab

The Punjab differed from Bengal and the NWP as a territory brought formally under the control of the East India Company as late as 1849, at the close of the Second Anglo-Sikh War. Though a small number of missionaries operated in the Punjab prior to this date, it was only after annexation that official attempts to provide colonial education began. The Punjab government borrowed from its counterpart in the NWP by attempting to affiliate indigenous vernacular schools to newly founded government institutions in a hierarchical system known as '*halkabandi*' that prefigured the provisions of Wood's 1854 dispatch, after which the Punjab education department was formally constituted.[13] In chapter one it was noted that during the 1850s some of the most outspoken requests by European administrators for the teaching of Christianity in government schools were made by individuals in the Punjab, including John Lawrence, chief commissioner up to 1859. However, no exception was made to the colonial secular education commitment for this province: instruction in government-managed institutions would be exclusively secular, while privately-managed institutions would be supported by grants-in-aid, in return for proficient secular lessons. A decade on from the dispatch, all grants-in-aid awarded to higher level schools and colleges in the Punjab were received by institutions under European management; of the eighteen institutions receiving government grants, all but three belonged to Christian missionary organizations, while no Indian-managed institutions received state aid.[14] At a lower level, just a handful of indigenous vernacular schools were supported by government after the abandonment of the *halkabandi* scheme.[15] This situation was ripe for critique by Punjabi parties concerned for the religious education of their co-religionists.

In 1864 the first government college was founded in the Punjab – at Lahore. Gottlieb Leitner, a Hungarian-born, naturalized British citizen who had earlier taught at King's College London, was appointed principal and arrived in India in November of that year. In what follows, Leitner's educational thought and influence in the Punjab are considered in detail. It is first necessary, however, to introduce the association that he founded, which would come to play a key role in Punjab educational debates: the Anjuman-i-Punjab. Established in January 1865, the Anjuman-i-Punjab was the first modern-style association in the province, combining regular public meetings, paid-up members and a permanent committee of management. Bringing together Hindu, Muslim, Sikh and European members, it conducted its proceedings through the medium of Urdu. At the close of its first year, the Anjuman's membership numbered 255; a majority of members resided in Lahore, though Indian patrons – most of whom derived from a sharif government service and landowning class – could be found scattered around other locations in the Punjab, including at Bannu on the north-west frontier. With influential European supporters including Donald McLeod, lieutenant governor of the Punjab, and Lepel Griffin, assistant commissioner at Lahore, the Anjuman was the foremost institution of an emergent Punjab civil society before 1875.[16]

One of two declared intentions of the Anjuman-i-Punjab – decided upon at its first meeting – was the diffusion of 'useful' knowledge in the Punjab, and multifarious ways in which the association assisted in the advance of European learning among its members may be identified. Among the Anjuman's first actions was to found a public library in which English, Urdu and Hindi books and newspapers were made available. A principal concern of the Punjab government and education department at this juncture was the development of Urdu as a medium for the dissemination of western knowledge.[17] To this task the Anjuman contributed with the compilation of an Urdu dictionary and the foundation of two basic vernacular schools at Lahore. The translated European texts of Sayyid Ahmad's Scientific Society were added to the Anjuman's library.[18] Through its regular public lectures the Anjuman encouraged the spread of European scientific knowledge, and particularly an awareness of western medicine and physiology, among an elite Punjab group. Other topics discussed at early meetings – many of which reflected prevalent government and wider European concerns – included means for the encouragement of trade, the principles of health and hygiene, the necessity of female education and the evils of female infanticide, early marriage and the marrying of a second wife.[19]

However, members of the Anjuman also negotiated aspects of colonial educational provisions, with substantial success. The Anjuman's second declared aim was to revive 'oriental' learning in the Arabic, Persian and Sanscrit languages.[20] Though some European administrators including Donald McLeod lent support to this object, the encouragement of Arabic, Persian and Sanscrit studies departed of course from the overriding aim of colonial pedagogy to disseminate western knowledge through English and vernacular media. Within months of its foundation the Anjuman had declared its support for the establishment of a university in the Punjab combining the study of western and oriental subjects; it was subsequently influential in rallying the support of Punjabi elites for the university cause. By 1868 public subscriptions totalling almost Rs. 100,000 had been raised for a separate Punjab university in which the study of oriental subjects would be permitted.[21] In response to the campaign of the Anjuman-i-Punjab, Lahore Government College was the following year raised to the status of a university college with the capacity to award certificates for the attainment of a western scientific and literary education and the study of those Arabic, Persian and Sanscrit subjects considered consistent with the colonial secular education commitment.[22]

In recent years considerable research has been undertaken into the career of Gottlieb Leitner who, after the conversion of Lahore Government College into the Punjab University College, became its first registrar. Scholars have documented the role played by Leitner – a talented linguist and orientalist – in the Anjuman-i-Punjab's campaign for a university teaching Arabic, Persian and Sanscrit subjects, suggesting that the debate provoked by Leitner's ideas produced administrative divisions between the advocates of oriental and western learning comparable to those at Calcutta in 1835.[23] Leitner's favour for Arabic, Persian and Sanscrit learning has been explained by his orientalist education, his distance from other members of the British community in Lahore and his desire to protect Indian traditions and social hierarchies.[24] Other research has detailed Leitner's efforts to develop the Urdu language with the aid of Muslim scholars at Lahore.[25] Several attempts have been made to explain his educational philosophy, believed by one scholar to centre on the necessary 'adaptation' of European ideas to accompany their translation into vernacular media and dissemination in India.[26]

There is one major and ultimately influential aspect of Leitner's educational thought that until now has been entirely overlooked in research: his profound conviction that education ought not to be distanced from religion. Leitner played a critical role encouraging Punjabi Muslims to respond to the colonial secular education commitment and grew into the leading advocate of the withdrawal of the colonial state from the direct provision of education as a measure for the reconciliation of religious and secular instruction. For Leitner's first statement of the importance of religion to education we must turn to his publication at Lahore in 1870 of a pamphlet entitled *The Theory and Practice of Education with Special Reference to Education in India*. In this short text many of the ideas that became central to his increasingly forthright criticism of colonial educational provisions were entered into the public sphere. Leitner's basic contention in *Theory and Practice* was that governments in India had erred by not consulting members of the Indian population before determining the school and college courses to be offered in the colonial system of public instruction. To ignore the thoughts and feelings of the people of India, he argued, was to proceed by blind prescription – an unsound basis upon which to found an educational system.[27] Leitner used the basic premise that the content of education must be in harmony with the wishes of its recipients to argue for a scheme of higher education in the Punjab combining western and oriental subjects and, as far as possible, the English, vernacular and classical Indian languages. At the level of primary schooling, he suggested, a more basic and practical government curriculum was required – consistent with Indian preferences. In Leitner's pamphlet, however, one criticism was elevated above all others in explanation of the unsuitability of government education: the absence of religious instruction from state-managed schools and colleges. 'We shall never inaugurate a really popular, because truly national, system of education', he advanced, 'unless we give religious instruction in our primary schools'.[28] In a second short pamphlet published the following year, Leitner elaborated on this contention: education, he argued, must always derive from the character, laws and religion of a people; to disassociate religion from education was to remove the latter's indispensable foundation.[29]

To explain Leitner's belief in the importance of religion to education, his upbringing in the Ottoman Empire should be considered. Born in 1840 at Budapest, Leitner was relocated as a child to Constantinople where he became proficient in Arabic, Turkish and Greek and served during the Crimean War as chief interpreter to the British commissariat.[30] Either side of the war, Leitner studied Islamic theology and Muslim law, before departing for England to teach Arabic and Muslim law at King's College, London from 1859. It is very likely that Leitner's views on the importance of religion to education were shaped in part by his instruction at Constantinople. Unlike other orientalist scholars trained in the academies of Europe to study texts for their linguistic and philological value, Leitner approached the learning of Arabic as a process inseparable from the study of the religion and laws of Islam. At the Punjab University College he developed an Arabic curriculum prominently featuring Muslim law – the major Islamic subject that could be taught without a compromise of the colonial secular education commitment.[31]

Arguing against the exclusion of religion from colonial education, however, Leitner was primarily concerned not with the advanced study of an Arabic curriculum but the elementary instruction of Indian children. On close inspection it becomes evident that Leitner's desire to see religious education admitted into the colonial system of public instruction derived more from a concern with education as a moral force, than a desire that orientalist scholars study an Arabic course incorporating theological enquiry. Leitner's writings make clear his belief that education ought to cultivate morality as well as intellectual improvement; in his view the essential foundation of morality in India was religion.[32] The emphasis placed by Leitner on morality marks a significant departure in British discourse on secular education. When other European commentators such as Alfred Lyall and William Gifford Palgrave proposed abandoning the secular education commitment, their principal concern was pragmatic or strategic: the teaching of religious subjects was recommended as a measure for reconciling Indian subjects, particularly Muslims, to colonial education; the definition of a new relationship between religion and state was suggested as a measure for strengthening British rule. Leitner's distress over the deficiency of moral training in government education, in contrast, represents one of the first examples of a new discourse concentrated on the failings of colonial education to effect moral improvement. This discourse would play a critical role engendering criticism of the exclusively secular education imparted in schools and colleges managed by the colonial state.

The absence of religious instruction from state educational institutions was ideationally contingent on the notion, contained in Wood's dispatch, that secular western education was capable of effecting both moral and intellectual improvement among the population of India. For Gottlieb Leitner this idea was a fallacy: an effective moral training, he believed, required religious instruction. The nature and extent of Leitner's personal religious convictions are hard to gauge. Born of Jewish descent, he identified himself as an Anglican when applying for British citizenship in 1861, while his writings betray sympathies for Islam. Rather than explaining Leitner's conviction of the importance of religion to morality in India as a result of personal faith, it is most helpful to invoke a European context where, in spite of long-standing theorizations of the possibility of moral principles independent of religion, popular morality was still very widely held in the later nineteenth century to depend on religious belief.[33] It is probable that Leitner arrived in India with a firmly established view of the necessary popular basis of morality in religion, which informed his belief that at an elementary level religious education was required to counter the demoralizing effects of secular colonial instruction. Though it was Muslim religious education to which he devoted the greatest personal attention, Leitner also extolled the moral benefits of Hindu and Sikh religious teaching to counter the pernicious impact of secular government instruction.[34]

The most conspicuous British official in the early 1870s concurring with Leitner that, in the absence of religious teaching, education in state institutions was incapable of effecting moral improvement was Arthur Howell, a government secretary at Calcutta. As a member of the Government of India's Home Department, Howell was responsible for the periodic collation and publishing of statistical accounts on the progress of government education in India. In 1872 he made known his conviction that without religious instruction pupils in government schools and colleges were growing up unaware of basic moral obligations.[35] This, he cautioned, would be productive of great problems in Indian society. Howell denounced the exclusion of religious instruction from colonial institutions through a comparison with prevailing practice in Europe where, in spite of denominational divisions, he observed, the importance of religious teaching to national education was almost universally recognized. Convinced that the effect of advanced western instruction without religious lessons was to create Indian graduates devoid of religious belief, Howell was perhaps the first government administrator to argue publicly that if religious education could not be provided in government institutions, the colonial state ought to withdraw from the management of schools and colleges in favour of private agencies. Supported by grants-in-aid, private institutions combining religious and secular education would take the place of state-managed establishments, in which only secular lessons were taught.[36]

Leitner's initial recommendation for the reconciliation of religious and secular education in the Punjab was the addition of religious lessons to government schools and colleges. In *Theory and Practice* he argued that teachers of the Hindu, Muslim and Sikh religions should be attached to state institutions for the regular instruction of students – a proposal which, he noted, would mean the abandonment of the colonial secular education commitment.[37] Throughout the following decade Leitner advocated the imparting of religious instruction in Punjab government schools, and by the early 1880s was explicitly arguing for a redefinition of the relationship between religion and state in India to justify the plan. In Leitner's view an error had been committed when British administrators determined to exclude religious teaching from government institutions on account of the religious neutrality of the colonial state. Citing the example of the state of Prussia, Leitner proposed that the principle of 'religious neutrality' be reinterpreted to denote 'the impartial distribution of State funds to the religious teaching of all denominations alike'.[38] This he contrasted with the existing denial of state funding for religious instruction – a policy that, he observed, was closer to the French 'secular' model of a formal and absolute separation between state and religion, known today as 'laïcité'.[39] As in the aftermath of Mayo's resolution, concerns for the provision of religious education had provoked a critique and rethinking of Indian secularism.

During the 1870s, however, it was increasingly the alternative plan expounded by Arthur Howell for the reunion of religious and secular instruction – state withdrawal – that Leitner came to adopt. In February 1872 Leitner engineered a temporary exchange of appointments with Charles Pearson, inspector of schools in the Punjab's Rawalpindi circle: Pearson would officiate as registrar of the Punjab University College while Leitner proceeded to the frontier to devote his attention to village schooling.[40] It was during this trip, perhaps inspired by the recommendation in Mayo's recent resolution that grants-in-aid be generously dispensed to Muslim schools, that Leitner began the task of encouraging indigenous parties to establish institutions combining religious teaching and basic secular lessons, and to apply for government funding. Between February and October of 1872 Leitner toured the five frontier districts of the Rawalpindi circle – Hazara, Peshawar, Kohat, Bannu and Dera Ismail Khan – raising public subscriptions for the foundation of schools under local, Indian management to which, it was hoped, the Punjab government would contribute aid. Later he claimed to have raised subscriptions for the foundation of twenty-two Muslim and Hindu schools during his tour.[41] Though the Punjab government did not at this stage adopt the change in policy direction suggested by his efforts, it is significant that as early as 1872 the possibility of state withdrawal from the provision of education in favour of private enterprise had been raised. A desire to see secular and religious instruction conjoined, and for the advance of elementary education on the frontier, informed proposals towards that end.

Shaped by his experiences in the Rawalpindi circle, Leitner developed his misgivings over colonial education into a comprehensive critique. In his view the difficulties of indigenous schools obtaining grants-in-aid amounted to their practical exclusion from the colonial educational system; the stringency of grant-in-aid rules, Leitner argued, had effectively caused the ruin of indigenous education.[42] The solution was to be found in Indian 'self-government' in educational matters.[43] In January 1875 Leitner, who had returned to Europe on furlough, spoke before the East India Association in London and outlined in detail what educational 'self-government' would mean: not only would state funding be generously awarded to schools under the management of Indian parties; in each town and village a local committee would be established with responsibility for the administration of public instruction.[44] Leitner later added to his scheme by proposing that the Punjab education department be abolished and its responsibilities, including the allocation of public funding, the inspection of schools and the determination of courses of study, transferred to local management committees dominated by Indian members.[45]

When Sayyid Ahmad Khan had appealed to the government of the NWP in 1866 for the institution of local committees to advise on educational matters, his request had been made independently of a concern for the exclusion of religion from state education.[46] Only later, as we have noted, did Sayyid Ahmad begin to act for the reconciliation of religious and secular instruction. For Leitner, however, educational decentralization and the promotion of religious instruction were interrelated components of a radical programme of reform. After his return to India in 1875 Leitner undertook an extensive survey of Punjab education beyond the colonial system of public instruction – the findings of which were published in his *History of Indigenous Education* in 1882. A result of this enquiry was the claim that almost 120,000 pupils attended Punjab schools unsupported by the colonial state, 'the protest of the people against our system of education'.[47] To explain the unpopularity of government-sponsored schooling Leitner developed the ideas that he had first articulated ten years earlier on the prescriptive nature of instruction in the colonial system. In his opinion, however, the predominant reason why government schools had failed the

Punjab population remained the absence of religious teaching. Leitner noted in his *History* that Punjabi Muslims in particular avoided government institutions because religious subjects were not taught within them. The answer was to bestow government aid on Muslim schools in which Islamic education and secular western lessons would be combined.[48] For the state to withdraw from the direct provision of education and devote public funding to schools maintained by representatives of the Punjab's religious groups was necessary for the creation of a popular and effective educational system.[49]

As Leitner's campaign against secular colonial education gathered momentum, Muslim members of the Anjuman-i-Punjab turned their attention to the subject. They included Sayyid Muhammad Latif, editor of the Anjuman's weekly journal, the *Akhbar-i-Anjuman-i-Punjab*; Mahomed Hayat Khan, a long-serving government employee; and Rahim Khan, the first Muslim doctor of British medicine in the Punjab. The subject of Muslim education was first discussed at an Anjuman meeting in 1872. Participants voiced their support for the foundation of the MAO College and the following year they welcomed Sayyid Ahmad and his followers to Lahore. Sayyid Ahmad's son, Sayyid Mahmud, delivered a lecture on the advantages of a Muslim college at Aligarh.[50] That Punjabi Muslim elites held a concern for the conjoint imparting of secular government instruction and Islamic religious education comparable to that inspiring Muslim efforts at Aligarh is clear. In early 1872 Mayo's resolution was put before the senate of the Punjab University College – a governing body composed of some forty European and Indian gentlemen, many of whom were also members of the Anjuman-i-Punjab. The senate responded by rejecting Mayo's recommendations for the special encouragement of Muslim participation in government education, noting that in the Punjab – unlike in Bengal – the proportion of Muslims participating in the colonial educational system was not dramatically lower than in other communities.[51] However, the Muslim members of the senate led by Mahomed Hayat Khan recorded a separate minute in which, echoing Sayyid Ahmad's essay committee, they reiterated that a large proportion of Muslims feared sending their sons to government schools, lest they be led to abandon Islam. Government education, they added, would remain unpopular with Punjabi Muslims for as long as it continued to ignore their religious teaching.[52] To facilitate the conjoint imparting of religious instruction and secular lessons, the senate's Muslim members proposed that teachers of each religion be appointed to government institutions to impart religious instruction. Agreement was also expressed with Mayo's recommendation that grants-in-aid be more generously dispensed to schools founded and managed by Muslims, in which secular and religious instruction might be combined.

After 1872 the Anjuman-i-Punjab passed a series of resolutions condemning the restrictions on religious instruction in the colonial educational system.

Both the appointment of religious teachers to government institutions and the encouragement of indigenous educational agency were endorsed at Anjuman meetings as measures for the conjoining of religious and secular education.[53] One Anjuman resolution noted explicitly that the award of grants-in-aid to schools managed by Indian parties would ensure that a greater number of pupils received an education combining intellectual stimulation and religious teaching conducive to the improvement of morality.[54] While the influence of Gottlieb Leitner on this particular resolution is clear, there should be no doubt that Indian members of the Anjuman – particularly Muslim parties – also opposed the exclusion of religion from government institutions. In the view of Sayyid Muhammad Latif the omission of religious instruction from government schools was the primary cause of Muslim reluctance to participate in the colonial system of public instruction. Latif proposed that religious education, structured around extracts from books on fiqh and Hadith, be introduced into government schools, and that state financial support be more extensively given to Muslim institutions.[55] The latter proposal was supported by Rahim Khan, for whom the wider award of grants-in-aid was necessary to facilitate Muslim educational enterprise.[56] Leitner placed the views of the Muslim members of the university senate before the Punjab government to add weight to his campaign for educational reform. Submitting his plans for state withdrawal from the management of schools and colleges to the viceroy of India, Lord Lytton, in December 1876, he could convincingly claim the backing of Punjabi Muslim elites.[57]

The Indian Education Commission and After

The greatest opportunity for Punjabi parties to put before government their views on the subject of religious instruction and the wider failings of state education was provided in February 1882, when a commission was appointed by the Government of India to enquire into the workings of the colonial system of public instruction. The commission's brief was to ascertain how far governments in each province of British India had been successful in providing for the dissemination of 'useful and practical knowledge', in accordance with Wood's dispatch.[58] Presided over by William Wilson Hunter, it toured India over an eight-month period in 1882, collecting the opinions of individuals and associations – Indian and European. Scholars studying the commission have rightly noted its significance to vernacular language debates in the Punjab.[59] The commission's Punjab sittings were occasions for Indian parties to make the case for Urdu, Hindi or Punjabi as the province's vernacular medium, a debate increasingly polarized on religious lines. In total, ninety-six memorials were submitted to the commission from the Punjab's territories, a number exceeded only in the NWP; a majority of these contributed to vernacular language discussions.[60] Additionally, however, many respondents to the commission offered ideas on the exclusion of religious teaching from colonial colleges and schools. Indian and European parties expounded state withdrawal as a necessary revision of government educational provisions, with ultimately influential results.

In the years preceding the commission's appointment, amid intensifying appeals for the provision of religious education in the colonial system, a separate association had begun promoting the interests of Muslim elites in the Punjab: the Anjuman-i-Islam of Lahore. The Anjuman-i-Islam had been established in 1869. For eight years, however, its major concern was the supervision of Muslim endowments and restoration of mosques in Lahore; only in 1877 was the scope of its activities extended to include social and educational matters and the representation of Muslim views to government[61] The individual responsible for this development was Muhammad Barkat Ali Khan, a government assistant commissioner at Lahore. Formerly a member of both the senate of the Punjab University College and the Anjuman-i-Punjab, Barkat Ali was an influential supporter of the MAO College, responsible for popularizing its objectives among Punjabi Muslims. In 1873, as a member of the Anjuman-i-Punjab, he had been instrumental in organizing Sayyid Ahmad's Lahore visit; soon after he determined the organization of a separate Muslim association necessary for the advance of Muslim education in the province. Barkat Ali shared with Sayyid Ahmad concerns for both the reconciliation of Muslims to government education and the preservation of Islam under colonial rule, encouraging Punjabi Muslims to accept English language education alongside Islamic instruction.[62] By 1880 several hundred Muslim gentlemen at Lahore had been attracted to the Anjuman – many of whom had earlier participated in the activities of the Anjuman-i-Punjab.[63] Barkat Ali's Anjuman played a pivotal role in encouraging Punjabi Muslim elites to send their sons to the MAO College – an institution which, he believed, admirably combined secular and religious instruction.[64] Approximately one-quarter of Aligarh students derived from the Punjab – a success for which he and the Anjuman were chiefly responsible.[65]

When the Education Commission arrived in the Punjab, Gottlieb Leitner seized the opportunity to lead discussions about the shortcomings of colonial public instruction. Leitner submitted very extensive evidence to the commission repeating his ideas on the necessary reconciliation of religious and secular instruction in Punjab schools, via the short-term addition of religious teachers to government institutions and the longer-term withdrawal of the colonial state from the management of schools and colleges in favour of private parties. 'A moral training is an essential element of mass education', he argued, 'and it will be a long time before it can be dissociated in India from a religious sanction'.[66] In July 1882 members of the Anjuman-i-Punjab offered their support for Leitner's proposals, passing a resolution that grants-in-aid should be more extensively awarded to locally-managed schools in which religious and secular subjects would be combined.[67] Other Indian parties agreed. Before the commission, organizations representing Hindu and Sikh constituencies lamented the absence of religious teaching in colonial colleges and schools. The Lahore Arya Samaj – established in 1877 – proposed the comprehensive award of government grants to Hindu and Muslim schools, placing them on an equal footing with Christian missionary institutions.[68]

The most extensive Indian calls for state withdrawal came from Punjabi Muslim parties. From Ludhiana, Amritsar and Lahore Muslim individuals and associations submitted evidence to the commission and dwelt upon problems deriving from the exclusion of religious instruction from government institutions. Both the addition of religious classes to state schools and colleges and the more extensive award of grants-in-aid to Muslim schools were proposed as measures for the reconciliation of religious and secular instruction; wider reservations about education in government institutions meant that the latter was more consistently advocated. The evidence of the Anjuman Hamdardi Islamia – an organization composed of Muslims employed in the Punjab education department and in teaching roles in government schools – may be considered typical. The colonial separation of religion from education, it argued, was 'very wrong' and in direct contrast to pedagogical provisions in Europe, where religious instruction was offered in schools to all those who desired it.[69] For members of the Anjuman the extension of the grant-in-aid system to a wider range of indigenous schools would permit the inclusion of religious instruction into elementary curricula, while creating a decentralized system more attuned to the localized demands of Punjabi peoples. Repeatedly Muslim parties observed that primary schools under local, private management, supported by grants-in-aid, would be capable of offering courses of instruction better suited to local requirements and imparting religious instruction. With regard to higher level education, some respondents to the commission expressed a concern that the withdrawal of the state would leave Muslims no choice but to attend Christian missionary colleges.[70] However, a greater number advocated state withdrawal, accompanied by the more extensive award of grants-in-aid, as an opportunity for Muslims to found schools and colleges combining religious and secular education. The MAO College was referenced as an exemplar institution doing just that.[71]

In the final report of the Education Commission, submitted to government in the summer of 1883, a set of proposals was made for the withdrawal of the colonial state from the direct provision and management of education. Henceforth, the report stated, the principal concern of provincial education departments would be the encouragement of private educational enterprise; colleges and higher level schools would be established only on a grant-in-aid basis, and greater latitude would be given to the managers of aided schools to determine courses and media of instruction. Though the state would continue to concern itself with the provision of elementary education, the management of primary institutions would be entrusted to local or municipal boards with the power to determine courses of study. Grants-in-aid would be more generously awarded to indigenous schools in return for the secular instruction that they imparted.[72] To account for these recommendations, growing British frustration at the failure of colonial education to extend beyond a small, predominantly urban minority should be noted. The encouragement of private educational enterprise was considered a means of extending western education while reducing the administrative and financial burden on the colonial state.[73] More so, however, British parties favoured the award of grants-in-aid as a measure for the reconciliation of religious and secular instruction.

Putting aside those individuals – predominantly missionaries – who argued for state withdrawal so that western education would more often include a Christian component, two major rationalizations may be identified behind British favour for the reconciliation of religious and secular education in Indian institutions supported by government. For some British parties the teaching of religious subjects in privately-managed schools was a necessary counter to the absence of moral guidance offered by secular courses of instruction; the teaching of Hindu, Sikh or Muslim religious precepts was preferable to secular government education.[74] This of course had been the primary motivation for Arthur Howell and Gottlieb Leitner to propose state withdrawal. For other British figures, meanwhile, the conjoint imparting of religious instruction and secular lessons in grant-maintained Indian institutions was a pragmatic means of rendering secular government curricula popular. Confronted by extensive Punjabi opposition to exclusively secular instruction, many British officials had by 1882 determined that the award of grants-in-aid to indigenous institutions was the only effective way of extending instruction in western subjects to a greater portion of the Punjab's population. Several noted the imperative of reuniting religious and secular lessons if Punjabi Muslims were to be reconciled to government-prescribed courses of instruction.[75] Only the award of grants-in-aid to Muslim schools could achieve this end if the colonial secular education commitment was to be preserved.

To explain definitively the commission's proposals, the views of its president, William Wilson Hunter, must be considered. That Hunter was sympathetic to the idea of state withdrawal is suggested by the list of seventy questions that he drew up for answer by commission witnesses: more than a third aimed at interrogating the legitimate boundaries of state participation in education, and raised possibilities for encouraging indigenous educational agency.[76] Hunter was well disposed towards the case made by Leitner for the inclusion of indigenous schools in the state educational system, requesting that he be granted leave by the Punjab administration to complete his survey of indigenous education, and later writing a note, which he appended to the Education Commission's report, in support of his research.[77] When the veracity of Leitner's evidence on the exclusion of indigenous schools from the colonial system was challenged by the Punjab director of public instruction, William Holroyd, Hunter subjected Holroyd to an extensive interrogation before the commission.[78]

By December 1882, after the evidence of witnesses across India had been collected by the commission, Hunter was acutely aware of growing British concerns over the difficulties of inculcating moral improvement in government schools and colleges that were committed to delivering secular instruction alone. The commission responded by recommending a series of proposals for the extension of moral training in government institutions, including the opening of playgrounds and gymnasia, the encouragement of teachers to exercise a moral influence on students and the compilation of a moral textbook independent of religious precepts to be taught in government colleges.[79] No doubt, however, the president was also conscious that in the view of many officials, only the teaching of religious principles – whether Christian, Hindu, Muslim or Sikh – could effect moral improvement. One such official was the viceroy of India from 1880, Lord Ripon, with whom Hunter was in regular contact while the commission was at work. A convert to Catholicism, Ripon was convinced that education should include a religious component. Visiting the MAO College he explained:

> I hold the belief ... that the division between those two branches of education which go by the name of religious and secular is altogether an artificial division, and that a complete education can only be secured by their close and intimate union.[80]

As lord president in Gladstone's Liberal cabinet between 1869 and 1873, Ripon had been instrumental in the composition of the English Elementary Education Act (1870), which confirmed the importance of religion to education in the metropolis by permitting religious instruction in schools under local board management and awarding government aid to institutions controlled by religious bodies.[81] While on tour in the Punjab, Ripon affirmed his conviction that one 'cannot have a true education unless religious and secular training are combined'.[82] The viceroy was a firm supporter of the Education Commission's proposals for state withdrawal and the encouragement of indigenous educational agency.[83]

When Hunter and the commission proposed greater government support for private educational institutions, however, his concern was less for the conjoint imparting of religious and secular instruction on principle, than for the encouragement of Indian participation in the colonial system of public instruction. Hunter's correspondence reveals that the recommendations of the commission were greatly influenced by the evidence submitted to it by Punjabi parties; the president took from the Punjab a conviction that the conjoining of religious and secular instruction via state withdrawal was indispensable for the creation of a popular system of state-sponsored education. Reporting to Ripon on the progress of the commission's enquiries, Hunter noted that the evidence received from Punjabi parties had convinced him that 'any system of education, to be a truly national system in India, must avail itself of the desire of the great religious sections of the people to provide each for its own wants, on the basis of its own beliefs'.[84] He continued:

> I was ... impressed by the amount of work which might be done at a small cost to the state, by aiding the sectarian efforts of the great religions, Hindu & Muhammadan as well as Christian, on an impartial system of payments for purely secular results.[85]

In 1871, as we noted in chapter two, Hunter had gained notoriety after the publishing of *Indian Musalmans* – a text in which the advance of western education among Muslim subjects was proposed as a remedy for religious fanaticism and the disposition of Muslims to rebel against British rule. A decade on, there is a compelling evidence that it was particularly Muslim parties that the commission president had in mind when proposing state withdrawal and the extension of the grant-in-aid system for the popularization of secular government instruction. In the commission's report, some twenty-five pages were devoted to Muslim education: the commission reviewed the success of measures adopted by provincial governments after Mayo's resolution and made seventeen fresh recommendations for reconciling Muslims to the study of a secular, government curriculum.[86] A number of the recommendations concerned the attendance of Muslims at government-managed schools and colleges: special scholarships might be awarded to Muslim pupils, for example, and vernacular media chosen with Muslim interests in mind. The extension of government aid to schools under Muslim management was also recommended: the educational agency of Muslim individuals and associations was to be encouraged. By early 1883 Hunter had arrived at the conclusion, shaped by the evidence of Muslim parties in the Punjab, that it was chiefly through this means that the reconciliation of Muslims to western education would be achieved. The model that he desired to see emulated was the MAO College. In April 1882 Hunter visited Aligarh before offering praise for the college's role in encouraging western education among Muslim subjects; to Sayyid Ahmad he admitted that 'the true solution of that [Muslim education] problem will be arrived at by private efforts such as yours'.[87] The recommendations of the Education Commission for state withdrawal were critically shaped by Muslim appeals for the conjoining of religious and secular instruction in privately-managed institutions – to which Hunter, on account of his determination to see the progress of secular, western education among Muslims, was especially sensitive. Summarizing to Ripon the proposals of the commission, he explained: '[t]he essentially religious basis of Muhammadan education is allowed for by the recognition [and financial support] of their maktabs, or indigenous schools, if they impart any secular instruction whatever'.[88] Through state withdrawal and the support of institutions managed by Muslim parties, the reconciliation of Muslims to secular, western education would be achieved.

The response of the Punjab government to the recommendations of the commission was to introduce a collection of measures that tended towards the decentralization of control over education and the promotion of indigenous educational agency. In 1884 a reorganization of the Punjab education department was effected with the appointment of additional Indian school inspectors. The management of schools was transferred to municipal committees and the first public educational conference was held in the province, to which Indian and European elites were invited.[89] Crucially, grant-in-aid rules were revised: the Punjab administration accepted the proposal that in future institutions of secondary education would be established only on the grant-in-aid principle and government aid given more generously to lower level indigenous schools.[90] The lieutenant governor of the Punjab, Charles Aitchison, was aware that the fundamental issue at stake in state withdrawal was the provision of religious instruction. Determined to uphold the colonial secular education commitment, he recorded that the Punjab government 'cannot establish religious schools ... but we can rightly help the people if they choose to establish schools for themselves'.[91] Like Hunter, the lieutenant governor considered that the award of grants-in-aid to schools managed by Muslim parties was the most likely method of encouraging the Muslim study of a secular, western curriculum. A system of payment-by-results was introduced, rendering the award of state funding in the Punjab partially contingent on the externally assessed achievements of pupils in the prescribed subjects of a government curriculum. In this way, Aitchison held, the continued teaching of 'useful' western subjects in institutions under Indian management would be ensured.[92]

Punjabi parties responded enthusiastically to the government's invitation that they establish institutions within the colonial system. In 1886 a college was opened at Lahore under the direction of the Arya Samaj; the Majlis-i-Islami, an association composed of Muslim elites at Amritsar, allied itself with the Lahore-based Anjuman-i-Islam and brought under its control the management of an Anglo-Vernacular school.[93] The most significant educational development for Punjabi Muslims was the establishment in September 1884 of the Anjuman-i-Himayat-i-Islam – an organization reaching beyond the restricted membership of the Anjuman-i-Islam to attract 900 Muslims at Lahore.[94] Existing scholarship suggests that the foundation of the Anjuman-i-Himayat-i-Islam was provoked by a Muslim desire to refute the attacks of Christian missionaries on Islam. To this end, the Anjuman published a journal – the *Risala-i-Anjuman-i-Himayat-i-Islam* – and sponsored itinerant preachers.[95] The provision of religious education to Muslim children was an additional major motivation for the Anjuman's organization. Encouraged by the withdrawal of the colonial state and the promise of grants-in-aid, the Anjuman moved quickly to organize Muslim education in Lahore. In 1886 its first primary school was established, with government support. Three years later it attained the status of a high school, attracting 400 students with its combination of Islamic religious instruction and the secular curriculum of a government institution.[96] By 1890 the Anjuman had under its control five primary schools for the education of Muslim boys. It also undertook the publication of a series of textbooks in English, Urdu, Persian and Arabic for the learning of each language alongside basic Islamic precepts – a revealing example of innovation in Islamic learning inspired by colonial educational forms.[97] The Anjuman assumed widespread responsibility for the instruction of Lahori Muslims, taking over a task formerly claimed by officials to be the preserve of the colonial state.

Hunter's commission had disclaimed any intention of wishing to encourage the denominalization of Indian education with its recommendations for the encouragement of indigenous educational agency. Its proposals included the stipulation that the award of a grant-in-aid remain conditional on an institution accepting pupils without regard for their religious affiliation.[98] Nevertheless, the inevitable result of state withdrawal and the wider award of grants-in-aid was the establishment of institutions under the management of religious constituencies that offered instruction in a particular religion and attracted members of that religious group. Punjabi Muslim appeals for the reconciliation of religious and secular instruction had brought about a major revision of colonial educational policy, provoking the Anjuman-i-Himayat-i-Islam and other Muslim associations to embark on the provision of education. With the transfer of responsibility for the management of schools and colleges from government to civil society, the colonial secular education commitment was preserved, but schooling in the Punjab was rapidly denominalized.

5 THE CAMPAIGN FOR A MUSLIM UNIVERSITY

In March 1898 the campaign for a Muslim university in India was begun. The idea of founding a university for Indian Muslims had been raised by Sayyid Ahmad and others as early as 1872, during discussions culminating in the establishment of the Muhammadan Anglo-Oriental College (hereafter MAO college) at Aligarh. Only after the death of the college's founder, however, was a movement for the realization of the university proposals launched. This chapter considers the university campaign in its early stages, leading up to the establishment of the All-India Muslim League in December 1906. The university demand in this period has been primarily studied by scholars for its political significance. In the most influential of existing studies, Gail Minault and David Lelyveld argue that the campaign for a university constituted 'an effort to create an all-India Muslim constituency and to carve out for it a decisive piece of political power'.[1] For Minault and Lelyveld, the university demand was politicised in that it attempted to define and consolidate a Muslim interest to represent before government, to influence government policy and to challenge British control of the 'educational access to power'.[2] In a detailed account of the university campaign, S. Y. Shah agrees: the demand for a university provided an opportunity for Muslim elites to mobilize large numbers of their co-religionists across geographically disparate areas and enter into the political arena.[3] The educational details in Muslim university proposals have been primarily studied for their political significance: that, for example, the establishment of a separate university would promote English education among Muslims, strengthening their position in the competition for public employment and political power.[4]

That the campaign for a Muslim university played a major role in the development of an all-India Muslim constituency is affirmed in the course of this chapter. The call for a university was voiced by Muslims located in northern India – in Bengal, the North-Western Provinces (hereafter NWP) and the Punjab, and further afield in the Bombay and Madras provinces; Muslim parties across the subcontinent shared similar aspirations and met together in pursuance of the university goal. Alongside an intensification of competition for government employment and the revival of vernacular language debates, the campaign for a university contributed to the idea of a distinct Muslim political interest to be protected and promoted in India. The first attempt to form a northern Indian Muslim political association was made in 1898, setting in motion events culminating in the inaugural session of the All-India Muslim League at Dacca. However, it is necessary to caution against a historiographical tradition in which the campaign for a Muslim university is subsumed into endeavours to explain the developments contributing to Muslim political organization or 'separatism'. Such an approach conflates motivation and consequence. While the campaign for a university would have important consequences for Muslim political consciousness and organization, the motivations informing university demands cannot be explained simply in these terms. Muslim leaders were of course aware that the campaign for a university would bring together their co-religionists across India, furthering understandings of Muslim community and lending credibility before government to the idea of an all-India Muslim political interest. The university demand was not advanced without a consciousness of the political and socioeconomic benefits to be obtained by its realization. To account for the desire to found a Muslim university in this way is nevertheless insufficient. It is because of the privileging of an approach centred on the political that scholars have failed to situate the university campaign within prevailing contemporary debates over the shortcomings of colonial education in India, and in particular the deficit of moral or religious education in the government system of public instruction. The campaign for a Muslim university involved a coalition of interests and frequent disagreements between participants: almost all agreed, however, that at a Muslim university an education in secular western subjects would be combined with Islamic religious instruction. The university campaign was the climax of a series of Muslim movements against the exclusion of religion from colonial education in the later nineteenth century.

The first section of this chapter reveals how, from 1888, Muslims in Bengal, the NWP and the Punjab seeking permission to introduce religious instruction in government schools and colleges capitalized on growing British concerns over the deficit of moral training and religious teaching in the colonial system of public instruction. Adopting and employing the prevailing colonial language of ethics and morality, they negotiated state educational provisions and engineered small but significant revisions of the colonial secular education commitment – most notably when an experiment was commenced with the teaching of Islam in a government school at Amroha in the NWP. The confluence of British and Muslim concerns over moral and religious instruction provided great encouragement to supporters of the plan for a Muslim university. As section two documents, Muslim leaders advanced the university scheme from 1898 within the context of critical British introspection over the failings of government education to effect moral improvement. Repeated, persuasive arguments were made that a Muslim university would succeed where the existing Indian universities had failed, to provide for the moral supervision and religious education of students. In 1902, however, the Indian Universities Commission pronounced itself in opposition to the formation of a Muslim university – a setback forcing Indian Muslims to interrogate their position as a minority religious community and devise possibilities for survival in a modern Indian state and nation. Muslim leaders advancing the university cause not only contested the exclusion of religion from colonial education, but also rethought the relationship between religion and state on the subcontinent, developing alternative models of Indian secularism.

The MEC and the Amroha Experiment

The institution at the forefront of the Muslim university campaign in the period 1898–1906 was the Muslim Educational Conference (hereafter MEC).[5] Founded at Aligarh in 1886, the MEC was intended to be an organization for the discussion of educational questions affecting Muslims in India. Its headquarters was at Aligarh, but its aim to bring together Muslims from across the NWP, the Central Provinces, Bihar and the Punjab.[6] In this respect the MEC constituted a bid by the hierarchy at Aligarh – in particular Sayyid Ahmad – for leadership of a wider Muslim community in upper India. Opinion differs over the extent to which Sayyid Ahmad's founding of the MEC was provoked by the first meeting, one year earlier, of the Indian National Congress. It is well known that Sayyid Ahmad urged Muslims not to participate in the Congress.[7] The MEC, which, he argued, differed by virtue of being an educational rather than a political body, provided an alternative focus for Muslim public activity.[8] What is important for our purposes is that the MEC was an organization of particular vicissitude. Initially little more than an annual gathering, in 1889 it established a permanent organizational structure with a standing committee at Aligarh that oversaw the work of committees in each locality. Local committees were expected to collect regular information on the progress of Muslim education and submit reports to Aligarh in advance of annual meetings.[9] During the lifetime of Sayyid Ahmad, MEC participants derived predominantly from the NWP and the Punjab. Five of the first nine meetings of the conference were held at Aligarh with the others at Lucknow, Lahore, Allahabad and Delhi. Until 1898 management of the conference rested firmly in Sayyid Ahmad's hands. The most enthusiastic MEC participants were his supporters in the Punjab – among them members of the Anjuman-i-Islam and the Anjuman-i-Himayat-i-Islam. Membership of the conference grew steadily, from forty-six in the first year, to 247 in 1888, when it first visited the Punjab.[10] By the time that the MEC was hosted in Delhi in 1892 it had 595 paid-up members.[11] After Sayyid Ahmad's death the MEC spread from its upper India base to visit Calcutta (1899), Madras (1901), Bombay (1903) and Dacca (1906). The work of popularizing it was undertaken by Mohsin-ul-Mulk who, after a brief interregnum, had succeeded Sayyid Ahmad as secretary of the MAO College and the conference.[12] Under Mohsin-ul-Mulk's direction the MEC developed into the most high-profile Muslim association in India, leading elite Muslim negotiations with the colonial state.

One of the principal aims of the MEC was the popularization of western learning among Indian Muslims, spreading the message that Muslims must become acquainted with western science and the English language. The first meeting of the conference was held at Aligarh in December 1886. Sayyid Ahmad proposed a resolution – passed unanimously – that Muslims 'stand in great need of high education in European Science and Literature'.[13] Two years later, at Lahore, a resolution was passed calling on Muslims to raise subscriptions to support their young co-religionists through a government collegiate education.[14] Sayyid Ahmad used the MEC to argue that efforts for the encouragement of western education among Muslims must be concentrated on the college at Aligarh. However, members of the MEC were equally concerned for the religious education of members of their community. At each of the conference's first two meetings a resolution was passed expressing concern that the number of Muslims with knowledge of the Qur'an was decreasing on a daily basis.[15] Mirza Irfan Ali Beg argued at Lucknow in 1887 that while it was incumbent on Muslims to learn the English language, the importance of studying the Qur'an could not be overlooked.[16] The following year, Mahomed Hayat Khan, president of the conference at Lahore, argued that the decline of religious learning among Muslims was an evil to be remedied as a matter of priority.[17] His particular concern was the absence of arrangements for the religious education of Muslim boys attending government schools and colleges.

In 1895 the MEC achieved a remarkable and little noticed success when one of its members was granted permission to arrange for the religious education of Muslim boys in a government Anglo-Vernacular school at Amroha – a small town 140 kilometres east of Delhi. The Amroha experiment is significant for its interrogation of the colonial commitment to the exclusion of religious teaching from state education, and reveals the extent to which in the final decade of the nineteenth century European and Muslim parties shared a concern over the pernicious effects of western education divorced of religious or moral content. Both European and Muslim parties contended that the exclusive imparting of secular western lessons in government institutions should be revised. In the previous chapter we saw that major concerns about the deficit of religious or moral training in the government system of public instruction were brought by European and Muslim parties before the Indian Education Commission of 1882. The commission had responded by recommending state withdrawal from the management of higher level educational institutions in favour of private bodies which, sponsored by government grants-in-aid, might establish institutions combining secular and religious instruction. Unwilling to recommend a departure from the colonial secular education commitment, the commission also made a series of proposals for those schools and colleges remaining under government management – including the compilation of a moral textbook independent of religious precepts to be taught in government colleges. These proposals were widely condemned by British observers for having failed to resolve satisfactorily the problem of the absence of moral training in government schools and colleges. In December 1887 the Government of India under Lord Dufferin responded by proposing new measures to improve the discipline and moral conduct of students in government institutions: boarding houses would be attached to schools and colleges, in which students would reside under the supervision of teachers selected on the basis of their moral probity; conduct registers would be introduced to monitor student behaviour; and breaches of discipline would be more severely punished. The plan for a moral textbook – shelved by Dufferin's predecessor, Lord Ripon – was revived.[18]

The growth of British concerns over the moral deficiency of students and graduates of the government system of public instruction through the 1880s might be explained as a response to increasing instances of opposition to government on the part of the western-educated Indian. In such a view, widespread in existing scholarship, condemnation of the character of the Indian student or graduate is considered a manifestation of colonial anxiety grounded in the realization that the western-educated Indian subject posed the most significant threat to the perpetuation of the British government of India. To censure that subject for his moral deficiency was to affirm the continued indispensability of colonial rule, and defer the possibility of Indian self-government.[19] There is no doubt a great deal of truth in such accounts. In December 1887 the Government of India stated for the first time that the advance of western education was encouraging such unfavourable traits as ill discipline and irreverence in Indian students.[20] That contention was made within two years of the foundation of the Indian National Congress, amid widespread British complaints – particularly in Bengal – about the increasingly oppositional nature of the Indian press. When European parties were requested by Dufferin's government to submit opinions on the question of morality and discipline in state education, responses very often included references to increasing political unrest.[21] H. E. M. James represented a portion of British opinion when in an article published in the *National Review* in November 1893 he equated the spread of western knowledge in India with the destruction of indigenous religion, and the concomitant creation of a moral void productive of bad manners, disrespect of authority and disloyalty towards government.[22]

To explain the growth of British concerns over the lack of moral education in the government system of public instruction simply in terms of the increasing threat of the western-educated subject to British rule is, however, a simplification.

In December 1893 Theodore Beck, principal of the MAO College, responded to James's article by denying a causal link between higher western education and disloyalty towards government.[23] As we shall see, few Europeans in the 1890s were more concerned than Beck about moral instruction in Indian education, or voiced more consistent objections to the colonial system of public instruction with regard to moral training. Beck, however, refused to condemn the moral deficiency of the Indian graduate in explanation of opposition to government. His opinions – in addition to his actions at Aligarh – serve as a reminder that British concerns over moral education were not solely a response to an anxiety generated by the perceived threat posed by the western-educated Indian. The efforts of Beck and many of his contemporaries to extend moral training derived from a conviction independent of growing signs of opposition to British rule that colonial attempts to effect the moral regeneration of India through education had erred in their course.

Dufferin's administration initiated India-wide discussions on the most effective means for improving moral instruction in Indian schools and colleges. During the course of 1888, interested European and Indian parties submitted opinions to provincial governments on the subject. Extensive agreement was expressed with the contention that more should be done for the moral education of Indian youth. On the question of means, however, opinions differed. While general support was offered for many of the Government of India's December 1887 proposals tending towards the greater regulation of student conduct, the government was widely observed to have left one crucial question untouched: how far could the morality of students in state schools and colleges realistically be improved in the absence of religious education? The enquiries of provincial governments into means for the extension of moral training engendered widespread debate on the relationship between morality and religion.

The education of Indian students in government schools and colleges was premised on the assumption that moral improvement might be inculcated without recourse to religious instruction. Teaching of the tenets of Christianity and of all Indian religions would be avoided in state-managed institutions, yet the morality of students would be improved. Moral lessons were to be imparted indirectly through the teaching of western subjects – particularly English literature. In 1888 this set of arguments was defended by a number of influential British administrators. In Bengal the director of public instruction, Alfred Croft, argued that while western education had undermined the traditional religious and moral foundations of Indian, and particularly Hindu, society, a new morality would be gradually introduced by the teaching of western subjects.[24] The ideological foundation upon which this contention rested was explicitly stated by some: that moral improvement was not dependent on religious direction.[25] However, others vehemently disagreed, questioning the colonial claim to effect moral improvement through secular western lessons. The break up of morality, argued the Lord Bishop of Bombay, was the inevitable result of a secular system of education: the indispensable foundation of morality was religion.[26] This opinion was not confined to religious authorities. As we previously observed, Arthur Howell was among the first in the 1870s to argue that if the colonial state would not renege on its commitment to the imparting of secular instruction alone, it must withdraw from the foundation and management of schools and colleges in favour of private agencies. The belief underpinning this argument was stated candidly by Howell in 1888: 'religion is to morality what the soil is to the plant – the source of its vitality, strength, and beauty ...; toiling, struggling, ordinary humanity must find its morality, its aspirations and its consolations in religion alone'.[27] He continued:

> Holding these views, I look upon our Indian educational system as one of the most appalling experiments on the largest scale that the world has ever seen. ... [O]ur public educational institutions ... are dealing annually with over two and a half millions of children. We catch them young; we keep them during the school-going age; the longer we keep them the more we destroy their religion; and then we turn them loose upon society without any religion at all.[28]

The extent of divisions of opinion within the British community on the relation of morality to religion becomes clear when proposals for the compilation of a moral textbook are considered. To recall, the introduction of a moral textbook to Indian college classes had been proposed by the Education Commission in 1882, but rejected by Ripon's Indian administration soon after. During Dufferin's viceroyalty, the Conservative politician and secretary of state for India, R. A. Cross, revived the textbook plan. The idea of a moral textbook free of religious doctrine gained favour with members of the British Indian Association and was endorsed by the governing body of the Calcutta University, which suggested the compilation of a textbook consisting of prose and poetry extracts to shape student morality by way of precept and example.[29] Others proposed the compilation of a moral textbook based on Aristotle's *Ethics* to be taught in higher level school and college classes.[30] Two responses were available to those convinced of the indissoluble union of morality and religion when confronted with these proposals. The first was outright rejection. The Church Missionary Society in Madras argued to government that morality could not be separated from religion: an effective moral education would be guaranteed only by the introduction of Bible lessons to government institutions.[31] A second and more original response was the suggestion that a moral anthology be compiled, not excluding religious precepts but containing lessons extracted from each of the religions of India. British officials in Madras, Assam and Coorg made similar proposals that a textbook be composed consisting of Christian, Muslim, Hindu and Buddhist moral teachings.[32]

The significance of British debates over moral education in the late 1880s for Muslim attempts to see religious instruction admitted into government institutions may be summarized as twofold. It is clear first and foremost that widespread European dissatisfaction existed over the deficit of moral instruction in government schools and colleges. It is further evident that a large number of European administrators and educationalists viewed religious education – whether in Christianity or other faiths – as necessary for effective moral training. These two factors offered encouragement to Muslim parties seeking the teaching of Islam in government colleges and schools. In December 1887 the Government of India had sought to pre-empt suggestions that permission be granted for members of each religious community to organize religious instruction in state institutions, when it reiterated that only in schools and colleges under private management might religious lessons be offered. The government concurred with the earlier recommendations of the Education Commission that through an increase in the number of privately-managed institutions imparting religious education, the best solution to the question of extending moral training would be found.[33] However, this declaration came with a significant new adjunct: that the religious instruction of pupils in state schools and colleges might be arranged by external parties to take place outside of regular school hours. Dufferin's administration attached a series of conditions to this notice: not only would instruction be given before or after the ordinary school day, but teachers would also be selected independently of government, and lessons attended by students only with the permission of parents or guardians. Crucially, the government would not interfere with the content of religious instruction and no charge would be made on public revenues to meet the cost of religious teaching. Through these stipulations it was envisaged that the colonial secular education commitment would be preserved. Advertising the possibility of religious instruction for pupils of state institutions nevertheless marked a change of emphasis in colonial practice: Indian subjects were tacitly invited to provide for the religious instruction of boys attending state colleges and schools.

Muslim leaders responded quickly to the government's invitation, circulated in the *Aligarh Institute Gazette*.[34] In April 1888 the third annual meeting of the Punjab general educational conference – introduced by government as a means for interesting Indian elites in colonial education – was held at Lahore. Top of its agenda was the subject of moral education in government schools and colleges. Following discussions on the encouragement of physical exertion, the construction of boarding houses and the compilation of a moral textbook, two Muslim attendees brought forward a resolution on religious education: Muharram Ali Chishti and Maulvi Yusuf Ali Khan requested that religious instruction be permitted in Punjab government schools outside of school hours in accordance with the principles outlined by the Government of India in December 1887.

The debate provoked by this resolution extended into the conference's second day: Muharram Ali Chishti's arguments in its favour were supported by, among others, Reverend J. P. McKee of the United Presbyterian Church – a revealing example of Muslim and Christian parties together contesting the exclusion of religion from state education.[35] Ultimately a revision of the Punjab Educational Code was won: religious instruction would be permitted outside of school hours on a voluntary basis, provided it be independently arranged and funded.[36] At the Lahore meeting of the MEC in December 1888 resolutions were unanimously passed thanking the Punjab government for this concession and determining that all other provincial governments be petitioned to grant the same.[37]

This provided the context for the successful attempt of Viqar-ul-Mulk to introduce Muslim religious instruction at the government Anglo-Vernacular school in his hometown of Amroha. Born in 1841, Viqar-ul-Mulk entered public life when in 1861 he was appointed by Sayyid Ahmad Khan to oversee arrangements for famine relief at Amroha. Soon after he followed Sayyid Ahmad to Aligarh and acted as his deputy when the latter was employed as a subordinate judge in the town. In 1872 Viqar-ul-Mulk won second prize in the essay competition organized by Sayyid Ahmad on the causes of Muslim educational backwardness, with the first prize taken by Mohsin-ul-Mulk. Thereafter the careers of Mohsin-ul-Mulk and Viqar-ul-Mulk were closely interwoven. After playing a part in the foundation of the MAO College, Viqar-ul-Mulk followed Mohsin-ul-Mulk to Hyderabad where both served in the Nizam of Hyderabad's government between 1875 and 1892. Viqar-ul-Mulk retired from service and returned to Amroha shortly before Mohsin-ul-Mulk's settling at Aligarh in 1893.[38] In December 1892 Viqar-ul-Mulk attended the MEC's meeting at Delhi. Here he proposed a resolution that religious education be encouraged in government schools and colleges. This of course was nothing new. During the speech accompanying his resolution, however, Viqar-ul-Mulk made a radical suggestion: that Islam be taught in government institutions not merely out of school hours, but as an integral part of the school curriculum; half of the class time devoted each week to the learning of a second language should be reallocated for the imparting of religious instruction, on a twice weekly basis.[39] This plan carried the support of Nawab Abdul Latif and other members of the Mahomedan Literary Society (hereafter MLS) in Calcutta. In the summer of 1888 Latif had reminded the Bengal government of his conviction that religious education was indispensable for a rising generation of Muslim youth. In one of his boldest submissions to government he stated that morality was inseparable from the revealed religion of Islam. Proposals for the compilation of a moral textbook independent of religion, or incorporating extracts from different religions, he described as 'unacceptable' to Muslims.[40] Noting that constraints of time made it very difficult for Muslim pupils attending government institutions to receive religious instruction outside of school hours,

Latif anticipated Viqar-ul-Mulk by proposing that boys in government schools be permitted to withdraw from vernacular language lessons and attend religious classes organized by the Muslim community. Only then might the twin imperatives of religious and secular education be reconciled.

After the meeting of the MEC at Delhi, Viqar-ul-Mulk personally set about seeing the plan for religious instruction during government school hours realized. In September 1894 a 'Scheme for the Introduction of Religious Instruction in Government Schools and Colleges' was submitted to the Government of the NWP. In this pamphlet Viqar-ul-Mulk emphasized the impossibility of religious instruction being kept up alongside secular education if the former was confined to periods before or after regular school hours. To be effective, religious education would have to be imparted in the course of the regular school day.[41] Viqar-ul-Mulk stressed that attendance at religious lessons would be dependent on the sanction of each pupil's parents and that the cost of religious instruction would be met by members of the Muslim community. The 'Scheme', he insisted, was consistent with the conditions suggested in the Government of India's December 1887 letter with the sole exception that religious lessons be imparted during rather than outside of regular school hours.[42] In his correspondence with government, Viqar-ul-Mulk capitalized on growing British concerns by elaborating on the problems caused by the absence of religious education from state institutions, adopting and employing ideas prevalent in colonial discourse on the shortcomings of exclusively secular instruction. Education without religious content, he suggested, might produce candidates for government employment, but could achieve no higher goals. In the absence of effective moral training, meanwhile, the resistance of educated Indians to British authority was likely to grow.[43]

When Sayyid Ahmad had forwarded to the NWP administration a copy of the MEC's 1888 resolution, appealing for permission to arrange religious instruction in government institutions outside of school hours, the response had not been encouraging for supporters of the religious education cause. Edmund White, director of public instruction, had offered his firm opposition to the plan, founded on a belief that the imparting of religious instruction in government schools would accentuate Hindu-Muslim antagonism.[44] When district boards in the NWP were consulted on the question, a consensus of opinion was returned that religious teaching in government schools would be likely to increase discord between different communities.[45] The lieutenant governor of the NWP, Auckland Colvin, therefore refused to follow the course set upon by the neighbouring Punjab administration and sanction the MEC's proposal. Colvin, who in 1888 had ventured his government's support for measures including the construction of boarding houses and maintenance of conduct registers, was convinced that permitting religious instruction in state institutions would create an impression that the government was deliberately fostering antagonism between religious parties.[46] The response of Thomas Crompton Lewis – Edmund White's successor as director of public instruction – was very similar when Viqar-ul-Mulk's 'Scheme' came under consideration. Lewis cited increasing rancour between Hindu and Muslim as reason enough for preserving the colonial secular education commitment: neither school premises nor school hours should be used for religious instruction.[47] For the director of public instruction, Viqar-ul-Mulk's 'Scheme' was a futile reaction to the declining influence of Islam over Muslims educated in government schools and colleges. Implicit in his response was that this decline ought to be welcomed.

How then are we to explain the decision of the government of the NWP to sanction Viqar-ul-Mulk's proposals? In September 1895 a six-month trial was begun in which boys attending the government Anglo-Vernacular High School at Amroha were given the choice of opting out of the second half of twice-weekly second language lessons, to attend Muslim religious classes organized in a mosque adjacent to the school premises. At the end of this trial period external parties were granted permission to arrange religious instruction during second language hours for the pupils of Anglo-Vernacular schools throughout the NWP.[48] The officiating lieutenant governor whose word sanctioned the Amroha experiment was Alan Caddell. A former district magistrate at Aligarh, Caddell was sympathetic towards the MAO College and convinced of its merits as an educational institution. During a visit to the college in August 1895 he offered praise for its emphasis on the development of character and moral conduct among students.[49] From this we might infer that Caddell favoured the union of secular and religious education at Aligarh, and sought its extension into state-managed institutions.

A clearer picture emerges when we consider Caddell's permanent successor, Antony MacDonnell, lieutenant governor from November 1895. In existing scholarship MacDonnell's administration in the NWP is remembered for its unfavourable impact on Muslim subjects.[50] MacDonnell deliberately sought to increase the number of Hindus relative to Muslims in government service in the territories under his command, and in April 1900 he determined that the Nagri script might be used instead of the Persian in government courts – employment in the courts would be dependent on a candidate's knowledge of both.[51] This decision provoked the opposition of Muslims in the NWP. Mohsin-ul-Mulk organized an Urdu Defence Association which met in the summer of 1900 at Lucknow with 350 Muslim delegates.[52] MacDonnell was mistrustful of Mohsin-ul-Mulk, believing him intent on reversing Sayyid Ahmad's policy of Muslim loyalty towards government.[53] More widely the lieutenant governor was suspicious of what he perceived as an ongoing Islamic revival in the NWP, and was convinced of the possibility of anti-government insurrection on the part of a Muslim population directing its political allegiance to the sultan of Turkey.[54]

On the subject of religious education, however, MacDonnell's views were closely in accord with those of his Muslim subjects. MacDonnell arrived in the

NWP with extensive knowledge of colonial debates on morality and religion in government education. In 1888 he had served as secretary to the Government of India in the Home Department, and in this capacity exercised a critical influence during attempts at the extension of moral training under Lord Dufferin. MacDonnell it was who had composed the Government of India's December 1887 letter, in which it was first officially stated that western education was productive of moral deficiency and irreverence in Indian students. As lieutenant governor, MacDonnell was publicly critical of government education in India for its tendency to cultivate the intellectual capacity of students at the expense of their moral character.[55] Measures including the tightening of school and college discipline, the improved training of teachers and the construction of hostels and boarding houses were introduced under his direction for the extension of moral supervision and training.[56] MacDonnell placed particular faith in the removal of students from their home environment into residences attached to schools and colleges where they might live under European supervision. Laying the foundation stone of a Hindu residence at the Muir College, Allahabad, he declared his aspiration that boarding houses become an integral part of the state educational system for the moral uplift of students.[57]

The lieutenant governor was convinced, however, that the greatest moral improvement would be brought about by religious education. One concern was the Christian instruction of the European population in his province. Within weeks of assuming office, MacDonnell visited the Allahabad high schools, founded by public subscription to provide for the education of European boys and girls in the city. Here he applauded the combination of Christian and secular instruction imparted to pupils, and stated openly that secular education should not be separate from religious instruction.[58] Visiting La Martiniere College at Lucknow the following year, MacDonnell would be dismayed to discover that religious instruction was not systematically imparted to students, and that attendance at church services each Sunday was irregular. The lieutenant governor took the unusually interventionist approach towards a private institution of consulting with the Anglican and Roman Catholic Bishops of Lucknow to ensure that religious lessons were offered for members of each denomination.[59] MacDonnell's views on the centrality of religion to education were most fully developed in a speech delivered at the Convocation of the Allahabad University in 1899. In this speech the Lieutenant Governor contended that the spread of western knowledge in India had encouraged students to question religious ideas: the decline of morality, he explained, was as an inevitable consequence of the loosening of the ties of religion in the minds of those schooled in western thought.[60]

What then could be done for raising the moral standard? MacDonnell was convinced that the great principles of morality belonged not only to Christianity, but were shared by other religions including Hinduism and Islam.[61] While religious ideas incompatible with modern scientific enquiry would be discarded by western-educated Indians, Hindus and Muslims might extract moral lessons from their respective creeds while studying western ideas. Through the award of grants-in-aid, therefore, it was incumbent on government to encourage the foundation of private institutions in which advanced secular lessons would be combined with Hindu, Muslim or Christian religious teaching.[62] MacDonnell welcomed the religious education not only of Protestant and Catholic, but also of Hindu and Muslim – each in his respective creed – as a means for the improvement of morality. In January 1896 he paid his first visit to the MAO College where he was addressed by Sayyid Ahmad and the other college trustees. The trustees emphasized to MacDonnell that a particular strength of the college was its combining of modern secular lessons with religious instruction for both Sunni and Shia students.[63] MacDonnell responded that he was a greater admirer of the combination of western learning and Muslim religious teaching at the institution. Extracting from the trustees' address, he added: 'it is a great satisfaction to me to know that the Directors of this College accept, and act upon, the rule, that ... secular education without religious training is "comparatively futile and ineffectual work"'.[64] With an awareness of MacDonnell's views on the importance of religion to education it is clear why he endorsed an experiment involving the teaching of Islam at the Amroha government school, and later issued a circular order sanctioning similar arrangements at schools throughout the NWP.

During the course of administrative discussions over the possible arrangement of religious teaching for pupils of state institutions, British officials had attempted to maintain the commitment of the colonial state to the provision of secular education alone. With the drafting of the Government of India's December letter (1887), the revision of the Punjab Educational Code (1888), the determining of rules governing the Amroha experiment (1895) and the composition of a draft circular by the Government of the NWP (1896) conditions were worked out by which, it was envisaged, that commitment would be preserved. At Amroha, the granting of permission to students to attend religious classes during school hours was conditional on the arrangement and funding of religious instruction by an external party. No teacher employed at the school would be permitted to act as religious instructor and, most importantly of all, no state funding was to be spent on religious instruction.[65] This, however, was not as simple as it might appear. Consider the debate at Amroha over where religious instruction would take place. Sanctioning Viqar-ul-Mulk's 'Scheme' the Government of the NWP had determined that religious classes must be offered outside of school premises: the imperative of committing public funds only to secular education meant that no existing school building, constructed at the expense of the state, could be used. If boys were to attend religious lessons during second language hours, however, the classes would have to be held in close proximity to the school site. Administrative discussions over the distancing of the colonial state from religious instruction took on a literal form in response to Viqar-ul-Mulk's suggestion that the Muslim community of Amroha be permitted to construct a building for religious lessons at a distance of 18 feet from the school classrooms.[66] In the event, a nearby mosque was used. When it came to drafting the government circular extending the Amroha scheme, however, the question of location was again raised. What if – in other towns – a suitable building close to school premises could not be found? MacDonnell's decision that where this problem arose, buildings on school premises might be used for religious instruction after all, involved a deliberate adjustment of the parameters of the secular education commitment.[67]

In several other ways the nature of that commitment was interrogated during the Amroha trial. From the outset the government had determined that it would play no part in the arrangement of religious lessons. However, the question of attendance was problematic. If students were to opt out of second language lessons, ought not their attendance at religious classes be regulated and enforced? What would prevent boys from declining language lessons and then playing truant? The government resolved that it was incumbent on the headmaster of the Amroha school to monitor attendance at religious classes and punish boys for their absence.[68] The rules governing the Amroha experiment stated that if examinations were to be held in religious subjects these would be conducted not by the school but by the Muslim community. The headmaster at Amroha was, however, permitted to distribute awards for religious learning at the school's annual prize-giving ceremony, which he duly did in 1896. Through the regulation of attendance and distribution of prizes, religious instruction was incorporated into the regular life of the Amroha school, and the distancing of the state from religious education was compromised. The government's circular of August 1896 endorsed the role of headmasters in regulating attendance and distributing prizes; the parameters of the secular education commitment were revised.[69]

The question of the content of religious lessons and their impact on students also had important ramifications. Prior to the commencement of the Amroha experiment, the Government of the NWP had declared that it would in no way attempt to interfere with what was taught in religious classes.[70] The Amroha scheme, however, was a six-month trial sanctioned because of British concerns over the deficit of moral training in government institutions. Clearly the impact of religious instruction on the moral conduct and character of students would have to be assessed. After the close of the trial in March 1896 the headmaster of the Amroha school submitted a series of reports to government on the effects of religious teaching. In these it was suggested that religious lessons had had no detrimental impact on student conduct and may indeed have elevated the moral standard.[71] MacDonnell requested the headmaster's personal views on the experiment, and may have been gratified to read that Amroha students were more regularly attending prayers as a result of the classes. Fears that religious instruction would provoke conflict between Hindus and Muslims, or Sunnis and Shias, were allayed. Though the content of religious lessons at Amroha was not interfered with by government, the processes of observing and evaluating the effects of religious instruction was a further compromise of the colonial separation of religion and pedagogy. British administrators were well aware of the difficulties involved in monitoring the impact of religious instruction, while maintaining an official concern for secular education alone – a sufficient reason for some to decry the Amroha trial from the start.[72] This, however, did not prevent the case being made when the Amroha scheme was extended to schools throughout the NWP that the government would need to ensure that religious instruction 'was not contrary to morality or calculated to provoke a breach of peace'.[73] The introduction of Muslim religious instruction to government Anglo-Vernacular schools at Almora (1898) and Shahjahanpur (1899) was accompanied by attempts to monitor the effect of religious teaching on students, in spite of arguments founded on the government's secular commitment to the contrary.[74]

Between September 1894 and August 1896 Viqar-ul-Mulk made repeated and ultimately successful appeals to the concern of members of the NWP's administration for the deficit of moral or religious training in government institutions. In the course of his exchanges with government he displayed a detailed awareness of the colonial secular education commitment and negotiated important revisions of its terms. Viqar-ul-Mulk deserved the vote of thanks offered by the MEC when it met at Meerut in December 1896.[75] Not only had he obtained permission for the religious instruction of Muslim boys at government schools in the NWP. His successful appeal to British concerns over the deficiency of moral and religious education in the colonial system of public instruction had charted a path to be followed when, within two years, the campaign for a Muslim university was begun.

The Muslim University Movement

The immediate stimulus for the commencement of the Muslim university campaign was the death of Sayyid Ahmad in March 1898. Four days after the founder's parting an assembly of the students of the MAO College was convened and the goal of expanding the college into a university was announced. Theodore Beck spoke before the students on the desirability of a Muslim university at Aligarh and was seconded by one of the college's professors, Theodore Morison, who was later to succeed Beck as principal.[76] On the same day, the college's board of management met and resolved to establish a Sir Syed Memorial Fund to collect subscriptions for the proposed university. Members of the fund committee charged with furthering the university cause included Beck, Mohsin-ul-Mulk, Viqar-ul-Mulk and, in the Punjab, Muhammad Barkat Ali Khan.[77]

Through the 1880s and 1890s the MAO College had developed in such a way as to avoid the criticisms of a deficit of moral training and supervision directed at institutions under government management. Not only did the college combine secular and religious instruction in its daily course, but a large majority of students resided in boarding houses under the close supervision of European and Muslim superiors. Physical exertion was encouraged as part of a vibrant corporate life that also included clubs and debating societies.[78] The college was praised by British officials for its 'esprit de corps' and development of student 'character'. Some noted approvingly that with its emphasis on the moral upbringing of students in addition to their acquisition of knowledge it more closely resembled an English public school or Oxbridge college than it did a government institution in India.[79] This resemblance was not accidental. In the previous chapter we noted that Sayyid Ahmad's decision to found the college was inspired by his visit to England in 1869–70. David Lelyveld has convincingly shown that in the course of this trip Sayyid Ahmad selected the model of an English public school for the institution.[80] Theodore Beck was later recruited from Cambridge – from where he had recently graduated – to serve as principal. Under Beck's direction the college was consciously developed upon Cambridge lines – most noticeably with the foundation of a Union club that, staging weekly debates on social and political topics, became central to the experience of Aligarh students and the definition of a corporate ethos shared by students and staff. Beck's vision for the MAO College was additionally shaped by perceived failings of state education in India. Like many of his British contemporaries he condemned the tendency of government schools and colleges to encourage 'superficial' learning centred solely on the passing of examinations.[81] Beck argued that the Indian universities stifled intellectual development by rigidly prescribing what could be taught in government colleges; the colleges for their part were 'shamefully' deficient in all features tending towards the cultivation of student character, including organized sports and games, and the personal contact of students with teachers.[82] For Beck the MAO College would be different. Where government institutions trained only the intellect – and this solely in preparation for examinations – Aligarh would offer a holistic education cultivating both intellect and character. Students would live and receive instruction in an environment fostering the highest moral standards.

An important component of the environment that Beck sought to create at Aligarh was Islam. We have seen that a principal motivation for the foundation of the MAO College was the desire for an institution in which Muslims would receive advanced western education in conjunction with religious instruction. With the establishment of the college, committees had been appointed to determine courses of religious education for Sunni and Shia students. Students sat annual examinations on religious subjects, though attendance was not strictly enforced; in 1885 145 of 187 Muslim students were examined on their religious lessons.[83] As principal, Theodore Beck attempted to extend the influence of religion in the daily life of students at Aligarh. In November 1885 attendance at morning prayers was made compulsory for all those boarding at the college; observance of the five daily prayers was later enforced for pupils in lower level classes.[84] Beck borrowed directly from Cambridge when he introduced a system by which pupils attended prayers immediately after regular lessons.[85] In an earlier period complaints had often been made about the difficulties of arranging for students to read regularly the Qur'an. Beck saw this problem overcome by insisting that the Qur'an be studied for half an hour each morning before the regular school day began. The hours set aside each week for religious instruction on top of this commitment were increased from one to two.[86] The principal's enthusiasm for the extension of religious instruction derived in part from a fundamental conviction that education must include a religious component.[87] Additionally, Beck valued the enforcing of religious observances as a means for improving college discipline: a section assessing student attendance at prayers and religious lessons was included in his annual college reports either side of notes on boarding house discipline and student hygiene.[88] Beck's endeavours to extend religious education and encourage religious observances were assisted by members of staff including Shibli Numani, professor of Arabic, and, after his arrival in 1893, Mohsin-ul-Mulk. What Theodore Beck had begun was then continued by his successor, Theodore Morison. The principal of the college between 1899 and 1905, Morison was even more enthusiastic than Beck for the religious instruction of pupils. Soon after assuming office he introduced daily, compulsory religious education for all school- and college-level pupils; Sunni and Shia committees were reconstituted to determine courses and conduct annual examinations in religious subjects.[89] Morison had earlier convinced Beck and Sayyid Ahmad to appoint Abdullah Ansari, a maulvi from Deoband, to lead prayers and see to the religious supervision of Sunni students.[90]

In the composition of plans for a Muslim university in 1898 it was Morison rather than Beck who played the crucial role. Morison followed Beck in condemning government colleges in India for their imparting of a 'purely intellectual' education and failure to mould the character of students: state institutions, he argued, lacked the corporate life and close association of student and teacher that were so vital to an effective education.[91] In government colleges, Morison believed, a remedy for this problem would be the construction of boarding houses in which scholars would reside under the supervision of college staff.[92] As principal at Aligarh he oversaw the construction of new boarding houses and extension of arrangements for the supervision of boarders by members of staff.[93] For Morison, however, the greatest failing of government colleges was the absence of religious teaching and a religious milieu in which students might live and learn – a conviction founded on the belief that the immovable foundation of morality in India was religion.[94] In the summer of 1898 Morison unveiled plans for a Muslim university in which religion was at the fore. Three faculties would exist at Morison's envisaged institution for the study of European Arts, European Science and Oriental Learning; students would be permitted to choose subjects from across these faculties. Two subjects, however, would be compulsory: the English language and Islam.[95] In Morison's scheme students would attend a course of lectures on Islamic subjects immediately after matriculation and pass an examination on religious teaching before progressing to the rest of their course. All pupils would reside at the university and live according to the moral code of Islam: prayers would be offered daily and actions that contravened Islamic precepts would be prohibited. Morison composed an article for the London-based *National Review* in which he sought to convince English observers of the merits of a residential Muslim university at Aligarh.[96] The most important audience to win over, however, was an Indian Muslim one. Morison's university proposals were widely circulated in India in the months preceding the December 1898 meeting of the MEC at Lahore.

The Lahore conference must be regarded as a defining moment in the history of the MEC. The first meeting of the conference after the death of Sayyid Ahmad, it witnessed the unanimous passing of a resolution in favour of the establishment of a Muslim university. For six years thereafter the campaign for a university dominated the agenda of the MEC and brought into its fold Muslim parties from across the subcontinent. Theodore Morison moved the resolution that a Muslim university be established. Before the MEC he argued that two major defects existed in the Indian university system: that no religious education was offered and that no provisions were made for the moral training of students. While the latter problem might be overcome through the conversion by government of the universities or attached colleges into residential and teaching institutions, the Muslim community alone could found a university in which Islam was taught.[97] What would be the difference between a Muslim university and a Muslim college – such as the MAO College – affiliated to one of the existing Indian universities? Morison noted the potential of a Muslim university to foster 'national' feeling among Indian Muslims.[98] Most importantly, however, a Muslim university would be able to design its own degrees and thereby insist on the religious education of pupils. Morison followed his first resolution with a second that religious instruction be compulsory for the university's pupils.

To suggest that any one reason accounted for the MEC's unanimous resolve to establish a Muslim university at this juncture would be misleading. Members of the conference, including Theodore Beck and Mian Shah Din, viewed the foundation of a university as the surest means of fostering intellectual and material progress among Indian Muslims: promoting the temporal interests of the Muslim community was a powerful incentive to back the university plan.[99]

There is no doubt, however, that the possibility of conjoining religious education and instruction in modern subjects – on a scale larger than that permitted at the MAO College – was a principal motivation for supporting the university cause. Though opinions differed over whether or not religious education ought to be compulsory at the university, the importance of Islamic teaching for Muslim students was made clear.[100] Mohsin-ul-Mulk spoke at the conference on the necessity of religious instruction constituting part of any Muslim university course. The importance of religious education was also noted by Badruddin Tyabji – a pre-eminent member of the Anjuman-i-Islam in Bombay – who submitted a letter to the MEC in support of Morison's plans.[101]

To illuminate further the extent to which the demand for a Muslim university was motivated by concerns for the provision of religious education, it is instructive to consider the views of two individuals from outside of the hierarchy at Aligarh who came to play influential roles in the university campaign. Sayyid Husain Bilgrami was born at Gaya in 1842 where his father, Sayyid Zainuddin Husain, had been appointed a deputy collector after studying at the Calcutta Madrasa.[102] Bilgrami received an Arabic education until the age of 14, when he began studying English. In 1859 he arrived in Calcutta and entered La Martiniere College in the city, before graduating with a BA from the Calcutta University with a first class degree. After several years teaching Arabic at Canning College, Lucknow, where he also acted as editor of the *Lucknow Times*, Bilgrami met Salar Jung I, prime minister under Asaf Jah VI in Hyderabad, and was invited to serve in the dominions of the Nizam. Bilgrami acted as private secretary to Salar Jung and travelled to Europe with the prime minister in 1876. Bilgrami's lifelong concern was education. In 1877 he played a leading role in the foundation of Hyderabad College – modelled on a government institution in British Indian territories – and the Madrasa-i-Aliya, for the education of Hyderabadi nobles in Arabic, Persian, Urdu and English.[103] Following the succession of Salar Jung II the Hyderabad administration was reorganized and Bilgrami was appointed as director of public instruction. In this role he directed the development of a modern educational system in the territories of the Nizam: as in British India, institutions under the management of government would exist alongside those supported by grants-in-aid and monitored by a state inspectorate.[104] Bilgrami ensured that the Hyderabad state continued to support oriental learning. Under his direction the Dar-ul-Ulum – a college founded in 1854 for the study of Arabic and Persian subjects – was revived and affiliated to the Punjab University for the award of oriental degrees. The Dairatul Maarif – a society for the preservation and republication of rare Arabic texts – was established and a public library was opened in which Arabic, Persian, Urdu and English titles were collected.[105]

Bilgrami was convinced of the indispensability of religion to education and made that conviction known. In early 1888 he composed a response to the Government of India's enquiries into moral training, positing that education in government schools and colleges encouraged not only ill discipline and irreverence but, most seriously, the revolt against religion. As a result of 'godless' government instruction, not only were certain precepts of religion ignored, but religion as a moral or ethical foundation for the imposing on self of discipline and restraint had been undermined.[106] As director of public instruction, Bilgrami set about ensuring that the introduction of western learning in the Nizam's dominions did not produce similar results. In 1885 religious instruction and enforced observances were introduced at the Madrasa-i-Aliya to ensure that a rising generation of Hyderabadi elites would know and practice Islam.[107] Soon after, Bilgrami made religious instruction compulsory for all Muslim boys attending government institutions in the Hyderabad state – a measure for which he was congratulated by Gottlieb Leitner.[108]

A firm supporter of the MAO College, Bilgrami played a pivotal role ensuring its continued financial support by the Nizam of Hyderabad through the 1880s and 1890s.[109] In 1886 he was made a college trustee and became a close acquaintance of Theodore Beck's. Bilgrami and Beck shared with Sayyid Ahmad in condemning the activities of the Indian National Congress and urging Muslims to abstain from participation.[110] Moreover, the pair held very similar views on the importance of Muslims studying both western subjects and their religion. It would appear that Beck's decision to extend religious education at Aligarh in the late-1880s was in part inspired by the example set by Bilgrami in Hyderabad.[111] In 1896 Bilgrami was invited to preside over the meeting of the MEC at Meerut. Here he used his presidential address to advance the thesis that Indian Muslims constituted a national group transcending racial difference and united by religious belief. Education without religion was 'denationalizing': to accept the purely secular education offered in colonial institutions was positively injurious to Muslim interests.[112] At the Meerut conference Bilgrami supported a resolution calling for the introduction of arithmetic and other elementary subjects into private madrasas as a means by which religious and basic secular instruction might be conjoined.[113]

In 1898 Bilgrami prepared a paper outlining his plan for a Muslim university which, in his absence, was read out at the Lahore meeting of the MEC by Mohsin-ul-Mulk. It began with a rallying call in which he suggested that Indian subjects were perhaps the only population in the world to submit without protest to a system of education devoid of religious content.[114] Similarly to Beck and Morison, Bilgrami noted the failings of government institutions affiliated to the Indian universities to provide a holistic education: most colleges, he argued, had no corporate life and made no attempt to cultivate morality in students. University courses encouraged teachers to prepare students only for examinations: students studied degrees for no reason but their market value. Most serious of all for Bilgrami was the absence of religious teaching from almost all university colleges, as a result of which Muslims studying for degrees grew up ignorant of their religion and sacred history.[115] Bilgrami's vision for a Muslim university was an expanded MAO College in which the defects of government institutions would be remedied. Students and professors would reside on university premises – living and learning in close association; the best European professors would be recruited so that Muslims might benefit from direct contact with advanced western ideas. European subjects including biological science, mathematics, history, philosophy, economics and political science would be studied, and religious teaching – avoiding dogmatic minutiae and centred on the moral guidance of students – would be imparted.[116] Returning as president of the MEC at Rampur in 1900, Bilgrami urged delegates to concentrate the conference's efforts on expanding the MAO College into a Muslim university.[117] Bilgrami particularly valued the efforts made by Theodore Morison to extend religious instruction at Aligarh.[118] Morison was at this point urging Bilgrami to retire from Hyderabad service and settle at Aligarh as secretary of the college. The principal suggested that only Bilgrami was capable of filling the void left by the death of Sayyid Ahmad and of inspiring Aligarh's staff and students to work towards the university goal.[119]

In March 1899 Muslim elites in Calcutta declared themselves in support of the plan for a university at Aligarh and established a local branch of the Sir Syed Memorial Fund.[120] Soon after, Mohsin-ul-Mulk determined that the next meeting of the MEC would be held in Calcutta. The first meeting of the conference beyond its upper India base, this would provide the opportunity for Sayyid Amir Ali to assume a prominent position in the university campaign. As the founder of the National Muhammadan Association, an organization which had come to rival Nawab Abdul Latif's MLS as the main body representative of the interests of Bengali Muslim elites, Amir Ali had gained a national profile when in 1882 he submitted to the Government of India a memorial detailing the social and economic plight of Indian Muslims under British rule. In 1887 he had attempted to organize a political conference for Muslim leaders across India in response to the foundation of the Indian National Congress.[121] Now, more than a decade on, he played a leading role convincing Bengali Muslims to support the MEC and its university demand. The MEC and its objects were discussed at public meetings across the Bengal province – at Calcutta, Patna, Dacca, Ranchi, Birbhum and Kidderpore – in the months leading up to December 1899.[122]

Amir Ali held simultaneous anxieties over the failure of Indian Muslims to obtain English education and compete for public employment, and for the fate of Islam under colonial rule. In December 1898 he submitted a letter to be read at the Lahore meeting of the MEC, in which he argued that at a Muslim university modern western subjects would have to be studied so that Muslims might acquire knowledge on par with the people of Europe.[123] Indeed a Muslim university would need to follow a very similar curriculum to that of the existing

Indian universities so as not to disadvantage Muslims in the competition for temporal advancement. The one major difference in the course of instruction at a Muslim university would be the teaching of Islam. Over the course of the preceding decade, Amir Ali had attempted to stress the ethical teachings of Islam, urging European and Muslim parties to recognize the moral guidance contained within the Qur'an and life of Muhammad.[124] In the campaign for a Muslim university, this ethical interpretation of Islamic teachings was deployed. In plans put before the MEC Amir Ali argued that the existing Indian universities had failed to provide students with a sound moral education: the teaching of Islamic ethics at a Muslim university would achieve this end. When the MEC met at Calcutta Amir Ali was selected as president. In his presidential address – delivered before British observers including the lieutenant governor of Bengal, John Woodburn – he argued that the Muslim community might succeed where the colonial state had failed: in establishing a university combining intellectual and ethical instruction.[125] Amir Ali went further than most of his Muslim contemporaries with his suggestion that prescribed Islamic rituals, such as praying five times each day, might be abandoned with the ethical interpretation of Islam. Nevertheless, delegates of the MEC at Calcutta welcomed his proposals for the teaching of Islamic ethics at a Muslim university, passing a resolution in their support.[126] At a Calcutta meeting of the Sir Syed Memorial Fund, held several days after the close of the MEC, Amir Ali and Theodore Morison shared the stage. The pair were in agreement that at a Muslim university English education would proceed alongside the teaching and enforcing of an Islamic ethical code.[127]

The arrival of Lord Curzon as viceroy of India in January 1899 engendered great hopes of a successful ending to the Muslim university campaign. Curzon was convinced of the necessary reform of colonial educational provisions and it is to his administration that the attention must now turn. As viceroy, Curzon attempted the introduction of significant administrative and military changes. His government extended provisions for famine relief and undertook major public works projects concentrated on irrigation and railway building. Curzon attempted to centralize authority in the Government of India and personally oversaw many of the projects in which his administration was engaged. Other measures that he instigated included his cultivation of the support of the rulers of India's princely states and successful defensive policy on the north-west frontier.[128] Curzon's most extensive reforms, however, and those to which he devoted greatest personal attention, were of government education. In September 1901 the viceroy convened an educational conference at Simla, attended by European officials and educationalists. The agenda was comprehensive: delegates discussed the extension of primary instruction, agricultural and commercial education; the course of studies in secondary institutions; female education; university reform and the vexed question of moral training.[129] The first sitting of the conference was set aside for a speech by the viceroy. Curzon critiqued the narrow focus of former Indian governments on the literary education of an elite minority through the English medium. State efforts, he argued, must in the future be concentrated on the extension of popular instruction in the vernacular languages: mass education would be more practical in character, concentrating on agricultural and commercial training.[130] Curzon personally composed resolutions on these subjects which were unanimously passed at Simla and became state policy with the Government of India's educational resolution of March 1904.[131]

The more complex and – it would prove – controversial area of reform announced by Curzon at Simla was university education. Curzon was an outspoken critic of the existing Indian universities. As mere examining bodies, he argued, the universities played very little role in the education and upbringing of students. Responsibility for instruction lay solely with affiliated colleges which, spread across geographically diffuse areas, could not be relied upon to provide sound teaching. Failing to accommodate students, and without a residential teaching staff, most colleges did not provide effective intellectual or moral training.[132] Curzon expounded the view that the failure of the Indian universities had accentuated certain characteristic defects of the Indian intellect.[133] Indian students, he held, committed facts to memory but did not think independently – a tendency encouraged by the examination-centred nature of university education. The Indian graduate preferred words to action and was often guilty of excessive hyperbole. While he would follow rules and precepts, he was incapable of using his initiative and of acting autonomously. Speaking at the Calcutta University, Curzon urged an audience of students to avoid the characteristically Indian defects of exaggeration, invention and imputation and stated with typical brazenness that the 'tyranny of words' among educated Indians required substitution for independence of thought and action.[134] The responsibility of government, he held, was to reform the university system in such a way that the distinctive vices of the Indian graduate would be overcome.

Curzon's attention had been directed to university reform during his first year in office. In February 1901 the viceroy composed a confidential minute summarizing ongoing administrative discussions and raising a series of points for further consideration. The main question raised was one of the upmost importance for our study: how far was it expedient to convert the Indian universities into teaching and residential institutions?[135] A precedent for the addition of teaching faculties to the Indian universities had been set in 1898 when the University of London was granted power to appoint professors and offer instruction additional to that provided by affiliated colleges. No longer would the London university simply examine students and award degrees.[136] Members of Curzon's administration stated their favour for a similar course in India. To permit the Indian universities to teach as well as examine, they suggested, would raise the standard of instruction in higher education. Moreover, a moral benefit would be reaped by the extended influence of professors on university students.[137] This benefit, it was added, would be augmented by the foundation of hostels attached to universities and affiliated colleges. With the support of directors of public instruction in Bengal and the NWP, delegates at the Simla conference resolved that efforts be extended to attach hostels and boarding houses to university colleges for the moral benefit of students.[138] The Government of India under Curzon was edging towards a conception of teaching and residential institutions as a means for the improvement of university education in its intellectual and – particularly – moral aspects.

Supporters of the plan for a Muslim university derived particular encouragement from Curzon's personal views on moral training in Indian education. The viceroy concurred with members of his administration that university colleges must provide residences for students in which they might live under close moral supervision. The conversion of the universities into teaching institutions was a proposal he was willing to entertain.[139] As far as government institutions were concerned, Curzon advocated the careful selection of teachers and use of textbooks that would indirectly imbue moral lessons as means for elevating the moral standard.[140] For the viceroy, however, these measures were secondary to religious education for effecting moral improvement. In the first month of his viceroyalty, Curzon recorded privately that it was imperative for education to have a moral as well as an intellectual impact: an effective means of moral improvement would be the education of Indian pupils in their respective faiths.[141] The viceroy later publicized his conviction that religious instruction in institutions under private management was the best way of providing moral training: 'We must look for religious instruction, Christian, Mohammedan, or Hindu, to the private institutions, where the tenets of those faiths are taught by their own votaries, and to which we can lend the assistance of Government grants-in-aid'.[142] In April 1901 Curzon visited Aligarh, where he offered praise for the MAO College's residential system and close moral supervision of students. On the subject of religious education, he added:

> Adhere to your own religion, which has in it the ingredients of great nobility and of profound truth, and make it the basis of your instruction, for education without a religious basis is, though boys at school and at the University are often too young to see it, like building a house without foundations.[143]

Curzon refused to commit a definite answer to the Aligarh trustees' request that permission be granted to convert the college into a Muslim university. He did, however, hint at his favour for such a course when paying compliment to the ethos and corporate life of the college. With its provisions for student residence and religious education, Curzon observed, the MAO College was set apart from most institutions attached to the Indian universities, and closer in spirit to the historic universities of England.[144]

Before determining on a definite course of university reform, Curzon appointed a commission to enquire further into the subject. Sayyid Husain Bilgrami was selected as one of two Indian members of the seven man commission and in this capacity composed questions on moral training and supervision in university colleges to be put before witnesses.[145] The Indian Universities Commission collected the evidence of more than 150 individuals between February and April of 1902, and inspected sixty colleges affiliated to the universities.[146] An opportunity was presented for proponents to put directly before government the case for a Muslim university. The final meeting of the MEC before the appointment of the commission was at Madras. Mohsin-ul-Mulk and Theodore Morison travelled to the conference with the intention of gathering further support for the conversion of the MAO College into a Muslim university. In this goal, they succeeded: Morison spoke before the Madras audience on the necessity of a university for Indian Muslims, and introduced a resolution – passed unanimously – on the subject.[147] The Aligarh leadership could now plausibly claim that the university campaign was supported by Muslims in each of India's major urban centres. It is notable how far local delegates at the Madras conference shared with their northern Indian co-religionists a concern for the reconciliation of religious and secular education. The conference passed a set of resolutions by which religious teaching and instruction in the subjects of a government curriculum might be imparted conjointly in the Madras province – including, most conspicuously, that the Government of Madras be petitioned to grant permission for the arrangement of religious education in government schools during second language hours. It also resolved that the Madras administration be requested to convert the Madrasa-i-Azam – a government college for the education of Muslims in the Triplicane area of Madras – into a grant-in-aid institution under the management of a local Muslim committee. The Madrasa would be remodelled along the lines of the MAO College, and offer Muslim students an Islamic education and upbringing alongside instruction in western subjects.[148]

The Universities Commission visited Aligarh in April 1902. One month earlier the MAO College trustees had made a representation to James La Touche, Antony MacDonnell's successor as lieutenant governor of the NWP, stating their desire to expand the college into a Muslim university. A familiar strategy had been employed: the trustees had emphasized to La Touche the arrangements for religious and moral training at Aligarh, and suggested that an Aligarh Muslim university would constitute a great improvement on existing higher education provisions.[149] Before the Universities Commission a similar course was followed. Aftab Ahmad Khan, one of the most senior college trustees, extolled to the visiting commissioners the virtues of the MAO College's residential system for the development of student character. A student, Zarif Mahomed, was brought before the commissioners as proof.[150] The main task of stating the case for a Muslim university was left to Mohsin-ul-Mulk. Displaying a detailed knowledge of colonial educational debates, Mohsin-ul-Mulk engaged in an extensive critique of existing university provisions. The Indian universities, he argued, compelled students to study too many subjects and sit examinations too regularly, encouraging the acquirement of superficial learning. Instruction in the Arabic and Persian languages was very deficient; religious education and moral training were entirely ignored. Each of these criticisms paved the way for the case for a Muslim university to be made. A Muslim university would set an independent curriculum and stage its own examinations: true rather than superficial learning would be ensured. A Muslim university would offer advanced instruction in the Arabic and Persian languages for those desiring it. Above all, a Muslim university would guarantee the religious education and moral upbringing of students. Mohsin-ul-Mulk explained to the commissioners the arrangements for boarding at the MAO College and made the case that effective moral supervision in a student boarding house was dependent on religious teaching and the enforcing of religious observances. The government, he argued, would be unable to undertake this task, on account of its commitment to impart secular education alone.[151]

The report of the Indian Universities Commission was submitted to the Government of India in June 1902 and made public two months later. Among its recommendations was that the existing Indian universities appoint professors, and organize higher level teaching through the foundation of schools of advanced study to complement the undergraduate courses taught in affiliated colleges.[152] British witnesses before the commission had overwhelmingly stated their favour for the development of the universities as teaching institutions. A proposal was soon after brought forward for the foundation of science and law faculties at the Allahabad University.[153] Considerable support was offered by European witnesses for the extension in colleges and universities of the residential system. The Universities Commission responded by praising the residential arrangements in place at the MAO College, with their attention to the moral supervision of students, and recommending that similar arrangements be made elsewhere. University students, it suggested, should be compelled to reside in hostels or boarding houses at universities or affiliated colleges, where authority would be exercised by morally upright members of staff.[154] The commission also encouraged universities and colleges to cultivate a corporate spirit, through the establishment of libraries, debating clubs, sports teams and other societies.[155]

Why then did the Universities Commission announce itself in opposition to the establishment of a Muslim university? Part of the answer to this question must be found in the general direction of the commission's proposals. Consistent with the course outlined by Curzon's administration prior to 1902, the commission recommended a strengthening of government control over the Indian universities. A number of proposals were made for ensuring the representation and influence of government officials on university senates, while the introduction of a government veto on textbooks and staff appointments was considered.[156] Of more significance was the tendency of the commission's recommendations to limit the provision of university education. Justified as measures for improving the quality of higher education, the commission recommended tougher rules for the affiliation of colleges to universities and the disaffiliation of those colleges not teaching up to the BA standard.[157] When Curzon's government considered the introduction of legislation enacting these proposals and raising the minimum fee for university education, it was widely accused of deliberately restricting Indian access to higher education – an accusation which, the proceedings of Curzon's council reveal, was not without foundation.[158] To endorse the plan for a Muslim university would have been counter to the general direction of Curzon's policies. The government also threw out proposals for the foundation of new universities in the Central Provinces and Burma.[159]

The Universities Commission's rejection of the Muslim university proposition cannot, however, be explained by these factors alone. Noting briefly the demand for a Muslim university at Aligarh, the report of the commission declared its members' opposition not only to the foundation of new universities but also to the idea of a denominational university in India. '[W]hile no obstacle should be placed in the way of denominational colleges', the report read, 'it is important to maintain the undenominational character of the Universities'.[160] The president of the Universities Commission was Thomas Raleigh, a member of Curzon's executive council and a close adviser to the viceroy. Raleigh held sympathies for the MAO College and recorded his belief in its merits as an educational institution. In December 1899 he had attended the meeting of the MEC at Calcutta and become acquainted with plans for a Muslim university. Raleigh stated his agreement with Sayyid Husain Bilgrami's views on the necessary extension of moral training in the Indian universities.[161] However, the president held a conception of what a university should be that was unfavourable to the Muslim university scheme. In an April 1900 letter Raleigh recorded that his ideal university would include contact and co-operation between men of different religions.[162] For Raleigh a university ought to consist of students and teachers of diverse religious opinions and beliefs. In 1871 religious testing had been abolished at the universities of Oxford and Cambridge. The opening up of fellowships to non-Anglican parties was a landmark step away from denominationalism in higher education in the metropolis. We can assume that Raleigh was not alone among members of the Indian Universities Commission and British community in India, in considering the foundation of a Muslim university a regressive plan counter to trends in Europe, particularly in England, where, despite the continued centrality of religion to education, the idea of universities for the exclusive benefit of one religious constituency was being departed from. Notwithstanding a dispensation towards religious instruction and the development of denominational colleges, Raleigh and others looked unfavourably on the proposal for a university exclusively for members of one religious group. Curzon was content to follow Raleigh in leaving the demand for a Muslim university unanswered.[163]

In her recent study of the historical development of the concept of secularism in India, Shabnum Tejani has shown how in the course of discussions over constitutional reform in the period 1906-9 the term 'communalism' was first used to denote the political mobilization of a minority religious community.[164] The designation 'communal' was applied to Muslim demands for the establishment of separate electorates in representative institutions. Significantly, the words 'communal' and 'communalism' were not neutral but pejorative, suggesting the pursuance of a religious group's interests to the detriment of an Indian whole. To be communal was to act for the gain of a religious community at the expense of the progress of the nation. The campaign for a Muslim university reveals a striking antecedent for this development. Declaring the plan for a Muslim university 'denominational', the Universities Commission implied its sanctioning and establishment to be contrary to the interests of India – a suggestion adopted and disseminated by some within Indian society and the press. In response, Muslim parties would subject to scrutiny the desirability of founding a university for their co-religionists. During a crucial period after the decision of the Universities Commission the position of a Muslim constituency in India was interrogated. Possibilities were devised and projected for the coexistence of heterogeneous religious communities within the Indian nation and a modern Indian state.

The most high-profile of Muslims arguing against the foundation of a Muslim university after the publication of the commission's report was Akbar Hydari. In December 1903 the MEC travelled to Bombay, where it was presided over by Badruddin Tyabji. Tyabji used his presidential address to restate the need for a Muslim university to inculcate moral principles and impart religious education to Muslim students.[165] However, Tyabji's nephew Hydari disagreed. In the final months of 1903 he composed an extensive paper arguing against the foundation of a Muslim university. In deference to the wishes of MEC organizers he abstained from presenting it at the December meeting and instead had it published in the Bombay journal *East and West*.[166] Hydari's oppositional article has been noted in other research on the campaign for a Muslim university. Scholars have recorded Hydari's conviction that a Muslim university would be unable to offer secular instruction on par with that in the other Indian universities and that advanced religious education would be better confined to private madrasas.[167] What has been overlooked, however, is that Hydari was above all arguing against the concept of a university in India exclusively for members of one religion. Indian interests, he posited, would be best served by the development of a common national consciousness, which could not be achieved in a 'denominational' university; denominationalism was a bane to be avoided in favour of the conjoint higher education of members of all religious groups.[168] Support for this contention was offered by a small but tangible number of Muslims in other provinces.[169]

The prevailing Muslim response to the report of the commission, however, was to restate the case for a Muslim university: Indian Muslims required religious education to be imparted alongside instruction in an advanced course of western study; the best means for providing that education was the foundation of a Muslim university where students would live and learn under the guidance of Islam.[170] The commission was criticized for having made a decision counter to prevailing Muslim public opinion. Sayyid Husain Bilgrami was rebuked for his failure to represent Muslim interests and oppose its verdict.[171] In December 1902 the MEC met at Delhi. Aftab Ahmad Khan made a speech notable for its outright rejection of the idea that the movement for a Muslim university might be stalled 'by any passage or remarks in any Commission report' while the Aga Khan offered his substantial support for the Muslim university plan.[172] One significant feature of demands for a Muslim university in this period was the more frequent reference to Indian Muslims as a distinct national constituency. For Mohamed Hayat, the Universities Commission had failed to recognize Muslim 'national' as well as religious requirements, by rejecting the university scheme.[173] Aftab Ahmad Khan projected the idea of a Muslim nation unified by religion with a national university at its heart.[174]

The idea of a Muslim university as 'denominational' was engaged with in several ways as the university campaign advanced. An initial response to the Universities Commission's report was to ask how the idea of a denominational university could be rejected, when the desirability of conjoining religious and secular education was so widely conceived of by European and Muslim parties. The establishment of colleges for members of one religious group had been recognized by British administrators as an effective way of extending moral training and the residential university system: in what way would the chartering of a denominational university be different?[175] The *Aligarh Institute Gazette* came closest to explaining the commission's opposition to a Muslim university when it suggested that the trend in Europe was against the foundation of universities exclusive in matters of religion.[176] This it followed with a cogent critique of the importing into India of the term 'denominational', and its use to describe the Muslim university plan. The Universities Commission, it argued, had done a disservice to Muslims by using a term loaded with negative connotations in European higher education to explain a scheme perfectly suited to present circumstances and public opinion in India. To reject the idea of universities for specific religious constituencies was to ignore the needs and wants of a population comprised of multiple religious groups. If the term 'denominational' was to be used in reference to a Muslim university, the article's anonymous writer added, it ought to be stripped of its pejorative European associations. Muslim parties advanced the thesis that only a denominational university could ensure the religious education and moral supervision of degree level Muslim students.[177] The case was repeatedly made that a denominational university would not endanger friendly relations between diverse religious communities – the MAO College encouraged respect and enquiry towards other religions and a Muslim university would follow suit.[178]

A growing number of Muslims turned at this juncture to the idea that a system of denominational universities might be established in India – a proposal expounded most influentially by Theodore Morison. Earlier we saw that in 1898 Morison put before the MEC detailed plans for a Muslim university providing for the religious and secular education of students. Soon after, he published an extensive text, *Imperial Rule in India*, to which he appended a 'Note on Education'. The note began with the contention that religious education was indispensable for elevating the moral standard in India. Working from this premise Morison proposed the handing over of government colleges to local committees composed of members of one religious group. Committees would be responsible for converting government institutions into denominational, residential colleges that imparted religious lessons alongside a regular university course. Hindu colleges might in this way be established throughout India; a Sikh college would be developed at Amritsar; and a Parsi institution at Bombay. The MAO College would be expanded and become a Muslim university.[179] In 1903, after the publication of the Universities Commission report, Morison developed this plan into a scheme for fully fledged denominational universities. Ostensibly writing a history of the MAO College, he proposed that the existing system of Indian universities – with jurisdiction defined on a territorial basis – be replaced by a structure based on religious community. Rather than universities of Calcutta, Madras, Bombay, Punjab and Allahabad, there would Muslim, Sikh, Parsi and Hindu universities in India. The existing arrangement of affiliated colleges spread across large geographical areas would be abandoned: denominational universities would have responsibility for teaching, and would insist on the residence of students. Thriving university towns would be created in which students and teachers would be brought together among their co-religionists. Religion would be a pervasive influence at each university and religious education would be imparted to all.[180]

It is evident that Morison's plan for a denominational university system involved a repositioning of the colonial state in relation to the religions of its subjects. Morison argued that it was necessary for the Government of India to recognize and respond to the requirements of the diverse religious constituencies under its rule; no longer could the colonial state seek to ignore or dissolve religious difference. For Morison the major requirement of each religious community was a university in which religious and secular education would be conjoined. In his writings on the subject Morison left ambiguous the question of whether or not the colonial state would directly support religious education in the projected new universities. If religious teaching at each institution was funded through public subscription, British administrators might have been able to maintain that the colonial commitment to sponsor only secular education had been preserved. However, a more likely result of the state-sanctioned foundation of a denominational higher education system – which surely Morison had in mind – was the abandonment of the colonial secular education commitment in favour of the government support of both religious and secular instruction, entailing a redefinition of the relationship between religion and state in the educational domain. As early as 1888 Nawab Abdul Latif had determined that such a redefinition was necessary. Arguing for the provision of religious instruction in government schools and colleges, Latif followed Gottlieb Leitner and other

European figures in proposing that the colonial commitment to 'religious neutrality' be reinterpreted as the impartial support of all religions, rather than the forced separation of religion from state.[181] His suggestion constituted a critique and revision of the nature of Indian secularism in all but name.

It is surely more than a coincidence that among those Muslims most vociferously contesting the exclusion of religion from government education during the 1880s and 1890s were three who had served for considerable periods in the Nizam's dominions in Hyderabad: Viqar-ul-Mulk, Mohsin-ul-Mulk and Sayyid Husain Bilgrami. Under the reforms effected by Salar Jung II from 1884, a modern bureaucratic state apparatus had been developed in Hyderabad with the support and direction of British officials. The Hyderabad state differed from its British Indian counterpart in one crucial respect, however: religion was not excluded, but patronized and encouraged through a variety of state institutions and practices. We have noted that Sayyid Husain Bilgrami introduced compulsory religious education for Muslim pupils in schools and colleges under the jurisdiction of the Nizam. This was just one part of the Nizam's support of religious learning. The Hyderabad state maintained a large number of madrasas within its territories; substantial annual grants were awarded to the Muslim religious seminary at Deoband and the MAO College.[182] The support of the Hyderabad state for religious institutions was not confined to Islam. In the mid-1890s the Nizam's government was endowing in excess of 15,000 Hindu temples, in addition to approximately 6,000 mosques and Muslim shrines in its territories. Churches and Christian schools were also maintained and salaries were paid to clergymen of the Anglican and Roman Catholic churches in Hyderabad city. The support of religion in the Nizam's dominions was managed by a separate government department that counted among its regular tasks the allocation of money to be spent on religious festivals and pilgrimages, including but not confined to, the Haj.[183] Hyderabad, then, provided an alternative model for the relationship of state to religion: the government support of all faiths. Sayyid Husain Bilgrami, Mohsin-ul-Mulk and Viqar-ul-Mulk did not articulate to colonial authorities possible alternative conceptions of the relationship of religion to state in British India as part of their respective efforts for the extension of religious instruction. However, the possibility of an alternative – derived from their knowledge and experience of the Nizam's dominions – cannot have escaped their attention.

Ultimately it was after the report of the Indian Universities Commission that a redefinition of the relationship between religion and state in India was most fully articulated by Muslim parties. In June 1903 Amir Ali spoke in London on the need to develop a denominational Indian university system. Repeating the contention that the existing Indian universities failed to impart a sound religious and ethical education, he proposed the establishment of Muslim, Hindu and Christian universities on the subcontinent.[184] For the development of this idea we must turn to Mohamed Ali, who was later to become one of the outstanding Muslim leaders in India.[185] Born in 1878, Mohamed Ali studied at the MAO College between 1890 and 1898 before departing for England to sit a degree in modern history at Oxford. Following his return to India he held official positions in the states of Rampur and Baroda and was among the founding members of the All-India Muslim League in 1906. Soon after moving to Calcutta and founding the newspaper *The Comrade*, he gained prominence. In his journalistic writings he critiqued what he perceived to be the attempt of Indian nationalist leaders to force a surrender of Muslim identity into an idea of the Indian nation that was increasingly Hindu in its aspirations and symbolism.[186] Within the context of increasing Congress activity, and a revival of the campaign for a Muslim university after 1910, Mohamed Ali argued that the identity of religious communities required preservation rather than dissolution in conceptions of the Indian nation. For Ali, affiliation to religious community was compatible with an Indian national identity. India, he argued, should be considered a 'federation of faiths' in which Hindu and Muslim organizations and institutions might coexist and thrive.[187]

The final contention of this chapter is that Mohamed Ali's conception of the Indian nation – which he would later widely expound – was formulated during the crucial period of inquisition and rationalization provoked by the announcement of the Universities Commission against a Muslim university. Ali was convinced of the importance of religion to education. In 1902, while employed as Chief Educational Officer in the Muslim-ruled state of Rampur, he followed Sayyid Husain Bilgrami's Hyderabad example in ensuring that pupils in the Rampur government college received religious instruction alongside a western course of studies.[188] That Ali backed the plan for a Muslim university in spite of the opposition of the Universities Commission should therefore come as no surprise. In October 1904 Ali's entry into public life was marked with a speech at Ahmadabad re-stressing the indispensability of a Muslim university in India. Ali argued that a Muslim university was necessary for the moral training of young men according to the prescripts of Islam: religious instruction and the residential system would define the university to be created through the expansion of the MAO College.[189] This recommendation was coupled with a proposal for the foundation of a Hindu University at Benares. In explanation Ali argued that India must be understood as a 'Federation of Religions': the institutions of the country, he advanced, must reflect the heterogeneity of a population composed of multiple religious groups.[190] A conclusion was therefore articulated that had been moved towards by Muslim parties contesting the exclusion of religion from government education over the preceding four decades: that the colonial state support, rather than detach itself from, the religions of India. In response to the decision of the Universities Commission, Mohamed Ali devised and advanced a conception of how multiple religious communities might coexist in modern India. Far from something to condemn and eschew, 'denominationalism' would be the essence of India – for preservation and strengthening in an Indian state and nation.[191]

CONCLUSION: SECULARISM CONTESTED

In October 1915, when the Government of India legislated for the foundation of Benares Hindu University, the colonial secular education commitment was finally compromised. Under the terms of Act XVI of 1915, a university was established at Benares for the teaching of religious subjects alongside an extensive secular course. With the sanction and endowment of the colonial state, the university would impart compulsory religious instruction; examinations would be sat in religious subjects, prayers would be offered between classes and Hindu festivals would be celebrated.[1] Though no retreat was made from the policy of exclusively imparting secular education in schools and colleges under state management following this decision, the British government had committed itself to the preservation of an institution in which the study of religious subjects would be enforced. No longer could it be claimed that the colonial state provided and patronized secular education alone.

From its inception in 1904 the demand for a Hindu university at Benares shared a great deal in common with the campaign for a Muslim university at Aligarh. Like its Muslim counterpart, the proposed Hindu university was a residential and teaching institution; the study of western scientific and technical subjects would be combined with thorough instruction in Hindu faith, history and literature. The prime mover behind the university plans was Pandit Madan Mohan Malaviya – a prominent educationalist and member of the Indian National Congress at Allahabad, for whom the reconciliation of religious and secular instruction in a distinctly Hindu institution of higher education was necessary for the worldly and spiritual revival of the Hindu community.[2] Urging the establishment of a Hindu university, Malaviya elaborated at length on the relationship between faith and temporal welfare: the advancement of Hindu society, he proposed, was dependent on the restoration of faith to a central position in the life of the social body.[3] In a similar vein to exponents of the demand for a Muslim university, Malaviya critiqued the colonial separation of religion from education, arguing that comprehensive religious training was required for the inculcation of morality and development of character. His promise that the graduates of a Hindu university would be men of high principle, rectitude and integrity, public-spirited, enterprising and physically and mentally robust reads like a direct response to British anxieties over the failings of secular western instruction – inspired no doubt by the precedent set by those seeking a Muslim university at Aligarh.[4]

When the Indian National Congress met at Allahabad in December 1905, the opportunity was taken by Malaviya to convene a meeting of Hindu leaders from across the subcontinent and introduce his university scheme; a resolution in its support was unanimously passed. Thereafter, the Hindu campaign gathered momentum. In 1911 the Central Hindu College – founded at Benares by the theosophist Annie Beasant to combine moral teachings centred on the Hindu religion with a scientific and literary course – was brought under the direction of Malaviya's Hindu University Society and, analogous to the role played by the MAO College in the campaign for a Muslim university, became the foundation of Hindu university plans. A residential Hindu university teaching religious and secular subjects was projected as the development of Beasant's college, with the support of Muslim leaders including the Aga Khan and Mohamed Ali.[5] The plan for a Hindu university resonated – of course – with the latter's conception of a 'Federation of Religions' within the Indian nation.

Explanations of the Government of India's decision to retreat from the exclusive patronage of secular education and permit the establishment of a Hindu university in which religious subjects would be taught have traditionally focused on the growth of Indian nationalism during the first two decades of the twentieth century. In her recent study of the establishment and early years of Benares Hindu University, Leah Renold argues that the government's decision to sanction the university derived from a perception of the role played by secular western education in encouraging such unfavourable traits as irreverence and disrespect for authority – productive in turn of anti-government critique and nationalist sedition. In Renold's view, the foundation of a university teaching Hindu religious precepts and encouraging faith observances was the result of a British realization of the failings of secular western instruction to produce Indian subjects loyal and submissive to colonial rule. Through the teaching of religion alongside a secular course of study, British administrators aspired to cultivate university graduates of stronger moral fibre, who would be better disciplined and more likely to comprehend the virtues of colonial government: the university's creation was 'an attempt to use religion to prop up the British throne'.[6] Renold adds that British officials sought via the establishment of the university to consolidate the support of a loyalist class of Hindu elites championing the scheme, and in doing so to counter the growing influence of a younger generation of Hindu leaders less well disposed towards British rule. Through the university's foundation the growing forces of Indian nationalism would be opposed.[7]

This book has taken a longer-term view. It has been shown that after the Indian Rebellion the commitment of the colonial state to patronize only secular education was confirmed. However, that commitment was far from universally popular among European parties, and in the final three decades of the nineteenth century it was increasingly maligned. Supporters of the exclusive colonial provision of secular instruction advanced a number of arguments in its favour. Through the dissemination of western scientific and literary knowledge, it was held, the moral and intellectual improvement of Indian subjects would be ensured; to introduce religious education to state institutions – whether Hindu, Muslim, Christian or other – would be practically very difficult, would encourage inter-religious discord and would place the success of colonial pedagogy in jeopardy. Some critics of the colonial secular education commitment, among them William Gifford Palgrave and Alfred Lyall, argued for the teaching of Indian religions in government institutions as a strategic measure to consolidate the support of indigenous elites as early as 1871. The arguments of other European parties, including Gottlieb Leitner and Arthur Howell, for the admittance of Hindu and Muslim religious lessons into government schools and colleges derived from a more fundamental conviction that education should not be divorced from religion.

After its establishment in 1835 the colonial secular education commitment passed through a series of mutations. Refused by the administration of William Bentinck, state support was in 1854 awarded to institutions under private management teaching religious subjects in return for the secular instruction that they imparted. Initially the operation of the grant-in-aid system principally meant the government endowment of Christian missionary institutions, but following Mayo's resolution of 1871 and the recommendations of the Education Commission, the award of grants-in-aid became a crucial institutional mechanism by which secular instruction was conjoined with Muslim religious teaching in the government system. By the early 1880s British concerns over the shortcomings of secular education had converged into a dominant discourse on the moral deficiencies of the Indian student educated in a western scientific and literary course; the impudence, insolence and irreverence of the western-educated Indian was widely explained as a result of the absence of religious training in colonial schools. Though the growth of this discourse broadly coincided with the inauguration and escalation of nationalist opposition to colonial rule, it is a mistake to view British concerns over the failings of secular western instruction solely through the lens of anti-government opposition. Debates over the absence of moral training in government institutions revealed deep-rooted colonial anxieties concerning the possibilities for effecting moral improvement without religious instruction.

The reforms that were introduced to higher education provision under Lord Curzon – among them the construction of hostels and boarding houses, the encouragement of physical exercise and the revival of moral textbook plans – should be considered a final attempt to extend moral training in the Indian universities while preserving the colonial secular education commitment. In spite of his personal favour for the conjoint imparting of religious and secular instruction, Curzon was unwilling to countenance the establishment of a Muslim university considered by members of his council to be a retrograde, 'denominational' scheme. No sooner had Curzon's reforms been announced, however, than they were denounced by European observers for failing to address satisfactorily the deficiency of moral training in higher education.[8] In light of widespread British scepticism over the possibility of cultivating morality without religious instruction it should come as no surprise that plans for the foundation of Hindu and Muslim universities were finally endorsed. With the reallocation of the Mohsin endowment in 1875, state withdrawal and the Amroha experiment, solutions had been found for the reconciliation of Islamic and secular instruction in the colonial system of public instruction consistent with the commitment of government to sponsor secular education alone. Ultimately, however, that commitment was compromised in order that the separation of religion from higher education might be overcome.

This study has argued that conceiving of public instruction as part of the exercise of colonial governmentality in nineteenth-century India permits us to understand its potential as a set of practices for the regulation of conduct and fashioning of subjectivities. Colonial education was considered by British figures to be a means of transforming the moral and intellectual condition of the people of India, and of generating a population composed of enlightened subjects who in future would be capable of regulating and ultimately governing themselves. With each negotiation of government educational provisions, however, European and Muslim parties contested an aspect of colonial governmentality; with each revision of colonial public instruction, the nature of governmentality in the domain of education was revised. The colonial secular education commitment dictated that in state-managed institutions the fashioning of subjectivities would be achieved through instruction in scientific and literary subjects devoid of religious content. As European and Muslim parties negotiating with British authorities secured revisions of the colonial secular education commitment, the exercise of governmentality through colonial education was modified.

The history of the colonial secular education commitment compels scholars of colonial governmentality to incorporate instances of negotiation and resistance into understandings of the operation of the British government of India as a modern regime of power. To this end they should return to Foucault's understanding of civil society as a domain in which both the exercise of governmentality and the negotiation of governmental practices takes place. In later nineteenth-century India, emergent civil institutions such as public associations and newspapers contributed to the dissemination of new knowledge and ideas, shaping subjectivities in ways that reflected the pedagogical imperatives of colonial authorities; in civil society the British project for the western education of India – part of the exercise of colonial governmentality – was aggrandized. Simultaneously, however, colonial educational provisions were also opposed and negotiated in civil society. In civil institutions the exclusion of religious instruction from state schools and colleges was contested and small revisions of the exercise of governmentality through education were engineered. Processes of negotiation and exchange between British and Indian parties shaped the development of state practices and the nature of colonial government to an extent that is rarely recognized in research.

The motivations informing the development of Muslim public activity and the negotiation of Muslim parties with colonial authorities on the subject of education were multifarious. A number of studies point to the concern of elite Muslims to safeguard the temporal interests of their religious group, widely perceived as 'backward' in the competition for education and employment under colonial rule.[9] In view of a governmentalized colonial state acting through public instruction to create a new type of Indian subject, however, there can be little doubt that the survival and strengthening of Islam was an additional major motivation for Muslim public organization and engagement with government. In Bengal, the North-Western Provinces and the Punjab, the desire to see provisions for religious education in the colonial system of public instruction extended contributed towards the development of Muslim civil institutions, bodied by actors carrying and expressing faith-based concerns. The idea of a distinct Muslim community to be represented before government at local, provincial and – with the campaign for a Muslim university – all-India level, gained ground.

The end point of this study is the moment when the model of negotiation between British officials and Muslim elites that was central to the operation of colonial administration and the development of governmental practices in the post-Rebellion period, was superseded by the advent of modern politics. After the death of Sayyid Ahmad Khan, Muslim leaders connected to the MAO College had departed from his policy of political quietism by seeking to found a popular organization for the representation of Muslim interests. In 1901 Mohsin-ul-Mulk had been reprimanded by the Government of the NWP for rallying Muslim opposition to the use of the Nagri script in colonial courts; Viqar-ul-Mulk attempted the foundation of a political association for Muslims in upper India soon after.[10] The refusal of the Indian Universities Commission to accede to Muslim university plans in 1902 should be considered a watershed after which even those leaders of the Aligarh movement, such as Theodore Morison and Sayyid Husain Bilgrami, who were capable of exercising considerable influence on British administrators began to doubt the efficacy of rejecting political action in favour of acquiescence to government.[11] The events had been set in motion that would culminate in the inauguration of the All-India Muslim League in December 1906.

That the establishment of an independent political body to represent Indian Muslims was an event of seismic importance in the history of modern India is today recognized. It is well known that the Muslim League ultimately played the pivotal role in the demand for Pakistan. In explanation of the League's foundation, scholars have successfully charted the realization among Muslim elites of the need for a political body to represent Muslim interests, within the context of the increasingly agitational politics of the Indian National Congress.[12] The significance to an Urdu-speaking, sharif Muslim class of securing separate Muslim representation on district and municipal boards, university senates and legislate councils has been demonstrated – alongside the importance of Muslim demands for a reserved proportion of positions in the civil, judicial and military branches of government. Much has been made of the fact that the Muslim individuals appealing to the Government of India for the granting of these concessions at Simla in October 1906 sought the securing of Muslim interests in proportion not only to the numerical strength, but also to the historical significance and social status of their community.[13]

It is not the intention here to deny the relevance to Muslim political organization of concerns over government employment and representation on public bodies, clearly outlined in the memorial submitted by Aligarh's Muslim leaders to Lord Minto – Curzon's successor as viceroy of India – at Simla.[14] What must be added, however, is that an interest in the provision of religious education also contributed to Muslim political formation. Among the leading players in the establishment of the Muslim League were Mohsin-ul-Mulk, Viqar-ul-Mulk and Sayyid Husain Bilgrami, each of whom, as we have seen, played a dynamic role in contesting the colonial separation of religion from education. Mohsin-ul-Mulk and Viqar-ul-Mulk were named the League's joint secretaries, while Bilgrami was responsible for drafting the Simla memorial.[15] Other founding members of the League included Aftab Ahmad Khan, Mohamed Ali and the Aga Khan – all influential in the Muslim university campaign. The final draft of the Simla memorial included a paragraph repeating the necessity of founding a Muslim university to act as a religious and intellectual centre for Indian Muslims.[16] Following Partha Chatterjee, it might be argued that in colonial India civil society, with its modern, western-style associational institutions participated in by an elite minority, was superseded in the twentieth century by 'political society' – a domain centred on mass public formations with the political party as its characteristic institution.[17] Muslim negotiations of the colonial secular education commitment remind us, however, that Islam did not simply enter into Indian public spheres in this later period: faith-based concerns were important to Muslim public activity prior to the development of mass political organizations and popular politics. Scholars researching particular regions of colonial India must consider more closely the contribution of concerns for the provision of religious education in the colonial system to the localized emergence of Muslim organizations and the evolution of conceptualizations of Muslim community.

The demand for a Muslim university was finally satisfied in September 1920. Aligarh Muslim University would be a residential and teaching institution raising students in an Islamic atmosphere and imparting religious instruction alongside a regular secular course. Its establishment marked the culmination of Muslim negotiations of the colonial secular education commitment over the preceding decades. The Muslim parties who negotiated with colonial authorities were not of one type. After 1875 members of a Persian- and Urdu-speaking sharif class, typified by Nawab Abdul Latif and the Mahomedan Literary Society, were joined by professional, urban Muslims represented in organizations like the Anjuman-i-Himayat-i-Islam. No one set of theological prescripts united Muslims contesting the exclusion of religion from government education; associations such as the Muslim Educational Conference brought together individuals with very different religious ideas and beliefs. The campaign for a Muslim university exposed disagreements about what Muslim children should be taught. While Amir Ali and others suggested that religious instruction might be imparted through vernacular media, for example, many such as Sayyid Husain Bilgrami and Mahomed Hayat Khan countered that the Qur'an must be read in its original, sacred language, insisting that the revival of Islamic education be accompanied by the teaching of Arabic.[18] Nevertheless, supporters of the campaign for a Muslim university all shared the same incentive that had informed Muslim negotiations of colonial educational provisions over the preceding decades: a desire to see the provision of religious instruction in the state educational system.

This study should be read alongside recent scholarship that has returned to the nineteenth century to reconsider the origins and development of Indian secularism in the colonial supervision of endowments, administration of law and management of inter-religious relations. In the course of their negotiations of the colonial secular education commitment, Muslim and British parties scrutinized and rethought the relationship between state and religion in India. The possibility was raised that Indian secularism might mean not the formal and absolute separation of state from religion, but the impartial government support of a plurality of faiths. Advanced by British critics of restrictions on religious instruction in the colonial educational system from the early 1870s, the idea of the state patronage of all Indian religions was strikingly captured and developed in Mohamed Ali's vision of India as a 'federation of faiths'. To draw the conclusion that those seeking the admittance of religious instruction into colonial educational institutions opposed Indian secularism would be false. Rather, through negotiation of the colonial secular education commitment, meanings of secularism on the subcontinent were worked out.

In the present day a prevalent academic and intellectual assumption remains that politics and other public activities should be secular. Despite recent scholarly efforts, faith is widely equated with the irrational or premodern – a normative approach contributing to the emergence of peculiarly modern forms of exclusivist religious politics in South Asia and beyond. Public manifestations of religion are considered unhelpful or pernicious to the effective practice of government and the processes ensuring that governmental practices are scrutinized and checked. Muslim negotiations of the colonial secular education commitment oblige us to challenge this set of views. For Muslim subjects under colonial rule, faith could be a source of empowerment. Actors seeking the reconciliation of religious and secular instruction entered into the public domain and founded vibrant civil institutions capable of negotiating with the colonial state. If the development of understandings of religious community in colonial India is to be more fully comprehended, the complex, dynamic role of faith in the lives of individuals and collectivities that responded to governmental practices should be enquired into and understood.

In February 1903, an anonymous editorial in *Aligarh Monthly* – the MAO College's magazine – correctly identified what scholars in the past three decades have increasingly realized: that the predicted decline of religion with the advance of scientific rationality has failed to materialize. Restating the case for a Muslim university to combine religious and secular instruction, the author noted that both in India and the West faith had not 'as many might have prophesised, and did prophesy, declined, with the spread of science and learning', before adding: 'Religion can no longer afford to be associated in the minds of men with ignorance, bigotry and fanaticism'.[19] We would do well to take this advice to heart and follow the example of those Muslim leaders who in the first decade of the twentieth century rethought the concept of secularism for the accommodation of multiple religious identities and beliefs in modern India.

WORKS CITED

Primary Material

Proceedings, Consultations and Reports

Bengal Education Consultations, India Office, British Library, London. (BEC)

Bengal Education Proceedings, India Office, British Library, London. (BEP)

Bengal Education Reports, India Office, British Library, London. (BER)

Bengal General Proceedings, State Archives of West Bengal, Kolkata.

Bengal Public Consultations, India Office, British Library, London.

Bengal Revenue Consultations, India Office, British Library, London. (BRC)

Board of Control Records, India Office, British Library, London. (Board Records)

Correspondence and Proceedings of the General Committee of Public Instruction, State Archives of West Bengal, Kolkata. (GCPICP)

India Education Proceedings, National Archives of India, New Delhi. (IEP)

India Public Consultations, India Office, British Library, London. (IPC)

North-Western Provinces Education Proceedings, India Office, British Library, London. (NWPEP)

North-Western Provinces Education Reports, India Office, British Library, London. (NWPER)

Punjab Education Proceedings, India Office, British Library, London. (PEP)

Punjab Education Reports, India Office, British Library, London. (PER)

Punjab Home Proceedings, India Office, British Library, London. (PHP)

Private Papers

Antony Patrick MacDonnell Papers, MS. Eng. hist. c. 352–64, Bodleian Library, University of Oxford. (MacDonnell Papers)

Badruddin Tyabji Papers, National Archives of India, New Delhi. (Tyabji Papers)

Benjamin Disraeli Papers, Dep. Hughenden, 1–382, Bodleian Library, University of Oxford. (Disraeli Papers)

Charles Edward Trevelyan Manuscripts, Microfilm Acc. No. 1242, National Archives of India, New Delhi. (Trevelyan Manuscripts)

Charles Edward Trevelyan Papers, GB 186 CET, Robinson Library, Newcastle University. (Trevelyan Papers)

Charles Wood Papers, Mss. Eur. F78, Borthwick Institute, University of York. (Wood Papers)

First Earl of Lytton Papers as Viceroy of India, 1876–80, Mss. Eur. E218, India Office, British Library, London.

George Nathaniel Curzon Papers, Mss. Eur. F111–2, India Office, British Library, London. (Curzon Papers)

H. H. Wilson Papers, Mss. Eur. E301, India Office, British Library, London.

Lord Mayo Papers, Add. MS 7490, Manuscripts Department, Cambridge University Library. (Mayo Papers (India))

Lord Mayo Papers, Collection List No. 126, National Library of Ireland, Dublin. (Mayo Papers (Ireland))

Lord William H. Cavendish Bentinck Papers, Portland (Welbeck) Collection, GB 159 Pw Ja-Jg, Department of Manuscripts and Special Collections, University of Nottingham. (Bentinck Papers)

Ripon Papers, Ms. Add. 43,617, Western Manuscripts, British Library, London. (Ripon Papers)

Sayyid Husain Bilgrami Papers, Nehru Memorial Library, New Delhi. (Bilgrami Papers)

Spencer Harcourt Butler Papers, Mss. Eur. F116, India Office, British Library, London. (Harcourt Butler Papers)

Parliamentary Papers

Copy of a Despatch to the Government of India on the Subject of General Education in India, House of Commons Parliamentary Papers, 1854, 393, xlvii.155. (HCPP)

Fourth Report from the Select Committee on Indian Territories; Together with the Minutes of Evidence and Appendix, House of Commons Parliamentary Papers, 1852–3, 692, xxviii.149. (HCPP)

House of Commons Hansard, Third Series, vols 101–92 (1848–68). (HC Hansard)

Second Report from the Select Committee of the House of Lords, Appointed to Enquire into the Operation of the Act 3 & 4 Will. 4, c. 85, for the Better Government of Her Majesty's Indian Territories; And to Report their Observations thereon to the House; And to whom Leave was Given to Report from Time to Time to the House; Together with the Minutes of Evidence, and Appendix, House of Commons Parliamentary Papers, 1852–3, 627–I, xxxii.1. (HCPP)

Sixth Report from the Select Committee on Indian territories; Together with the Proceedings of the Committee, Minutes of Evidence and Appendix, House of Commons Parliamentary Papers, 1852–3, 897, xxix.1. (HCPP)

Reports and Correspondence on Progress of Education in India, 1866–70, House of Commons Parliamentary Papers, 1870, 397, lii.1. (HCPP)

Newspapers and Periodicals

Aligarh Institute Gazette (Aligarh).

Aligarh Monthly (Aligarh).

Asiatic Journal and Monthly Register for British and Foreign India, China, and Australasia (London).

Civil and Military Gazette (Lahore).

The Comrade (Calcutta).

East and West (Bombay).

The Englishman (Calcutta).

Friend of India (Calcutta).

Indian Magazine (London)

Journal of the East India Association (London).

Lahore Chronicle (Lahore).

Mahomedan Anglo-Oriental College Magazine (Aligarh).

Moslem Chronicle (Calcutta).

National Review (London).

Nineteenth Century (London).

The Pioneer (Allahabad).

Punjab Observer (Lahore).

The Spectator (London).

Published Works

Act No. XVI of 1915: An Act to Establish and Incorporate a Teaching and Residential University at Benares (Delhi: Superintendent of Government Printing, 1915).

Addresses, Poems and Other Writings of Nawwab Imadul-Mulk Bahadur (Sayyid Husayn Bilgrami, C. S. I.) (Hyderabad: Government Central Press, 1925).

Administration Report of His Highness the Nizam's Dominion for 1294 Fasli (1884–85) (Bombay: 'Times of India' Steam Press, 1886).

Ahmad, R., 'The Proposed Muslim University in India', *Nineteenth Century*, 44 (1898), pp. 915–21.

Ali, A., *The Life and Teachings of Mohammed, or the Spirit of Islam* (London: W. H. Allen & Co., 1891).

—, *The Spirit of Islam, or the Life and Teachings of Mohammed* (Calcutta: S. K. Lahiri & Co., 1902).

Ali, M., *Short Essays by Moulvee Mohommed Ulli, An English Teacher of the Calcutta Government Madrassa College* (Calcutta: I.C. Bose & Co., 1858).

Ali, M., *The Proposed Mohamedan University: Being an Address Delivered at the Bombay Presidency Mohamedan Educational Conference, at Ahmadabad, on 16th October, 1904* (Bombay: Caxton Printing Works, 1904).

—, *My Life, A Fragment: An Autobiographical Sketch of Maulana Mohamed Ali*, ed. A. Iqbal (Lahore: Sh. Muhammad Ashraf, 1946).

Anon., *What Shall We Do with the Musulmans?* (Calcutta: Sanders, Cones and Co., 1858).

Arnold, E., *Education in India: A Letter from the Ex-Principal of an Indian Government College to his Appointed Successor* (London: Bell and Daldy, 1860).

Bilgrami, S. H., 'Moral and Religious Education', in *Addresses, Poems and Other Writings of Nawwab Imadul-Mulk Bahadur (Sayyid Husayn Bilgrami, C. S. I.)* (Hyderabad: Government Central Press, 1925), pp. 21–4.

Bowen, H. C., *Muhammadanism: Its Present Condition and Influence in India* (London: Macmillan and Co., 1873).

Burne, O. T., *Memories* (London: Edward Arnold, 1907).

[Church Missionary Society], *A Memorial to the Queen from the Church Missionary Society, on the Religious Policy of the Government of India. With an Explanatory Statement on the Past and Present Policy of the Indian Government in Respect to Religion, and the Education of the Natives* (London: Church Missionary House, 1858).

—, *Religious Neutrality in India: Delusive and Impracticable* (London: Church Missionary House, 1858).

Correspondence Connected with the Removal of Mr. W. Tayler from the Commissionership of Patna (Calcutta: John Gray, 1858).

Croft, A., *Review of Education in India in 1886, with Special Reference to the Report of the Education Commission* (Calcutta: Superintendent of Government Printing, 1888).

Din, M. S., 'Mohamedan Societies in the Punjab', *Indian Magazine*, 208 (1888), pp. 186–92.

Duff, A., *New Era of the English Language and English Literature in India; Or, an Exposition of the late Governor-General of India's Last Act, Relative to the Promotion of European Literature and Science, through the Medium of the English language, amongst the Natives of that Populous and Extensive Province of the British Empire* (Edinburgh: John Johnstone, 1837).

—, *The Rev. Dr. Duff's Letters, Addressed to Lord Auckland, on the Subject of Native Education: With his Lordship's Minute (for the Sake of Reference) Prefixed* (Calcutta: Baptist Mission Press, 1841).

—, *Lord Ellenborough's Blunder Respecting the Cause of the Mutiny* (Calcutta: Baptist Mission Press, 1857).

Grant, C., *Observations on the State of Society among the Asiatic Subjects of Great Britain, Particularly with Respect to Morals. Written Chiefly in the Year 1792* (n. p., 1797).

Gupta, K. P. S. (ed.), *Speeches of the Marquis of Ripon, Viceroy and Governor General of India* (Calcutta: Star Press, 1883).

Halliday, F., *Minute by F. J. Halliday on Necessary Reforms at the Madrusseh, or Mahommedan College, Calcutta* (Calcutta: 1858).

[Hay, G.], *Minute of the Marquis of Tweeddale, Late-Governor of Madras, on the Introduction of the Bible as a Class-Book into Government Schools in India* (London: Church Missionary House, 1859).

Hayat, M., 'The Proposed Mohammadan University in India', *East and West*, 1:13 (1902), pp. 1379–84.

Hodgson, B. H., *Miscellaneous Essays relating to Indian Subjects* (London: Trubner & Co., 1880).

Howell, A., *Education in British India, prior to 1854, and in 1870–71* (Calcutta: Superintendent of Government Printing, 1872).

Hunter, W. W., *The Indian Musalmans* (1871) (Lahore: Sang-e-Meel Publications, 1999).

—, *A Life of the Earl of Mayo, Fourth Viceroy of India* (London: Smith, Elder, & Co., 1875).

Husain, Y. (ed.), *Selected Documents from the Aligarh Archives* (London: Asia Publishing House, 1967).

Hydari, A., 'A Mahomedan University in India', *East and West*, 3:34 (1904), pp. 765–73.

Hyland, A. and K. Milne (eds), *Irish Educational Documents. A Selection of Extracts from Documents Relating to the History of Irish Education from the Earliest Times to 1922* (Dublin: C.I.C.E., 1987).

Indian Education Policy: Being a Resolution Issued by the Governor-General in Council, on the 11th March 1904 (Calcutta: Office of the Superintendent, Government Printing, 1904).

James, H. E. M., 'Reflections on the Way Home', *National Review*, 22 (1893–4), pp. 335–51.

Johnston, J., *Abstract and Analysis of the Report of the "Indian Education Commission", with Notes, and "the Recommendations" in Full* (London: Hamilton, Adams & Co., 1884).

Kerr, J., *A Review of Public Instruction in the Bengal Presidency from 1835 to 1851* (London: WM. H. Allen & Co., 1853).

Khan, S. A., *Review on Dr. Hunter's Indian Musalmans: Are they Bound in Conscience to Rebel against the Queen?* (Benares: 1872).

—, *Translation of the Report of the Members of the Select Committee for the Better Diffusion and Advancement of Learning among Muhammadans in India* (Benares: Medical Hall Press, 1872).

La Touche, J., *Selections from Speeches of Sir J. J. D. La Touche, K. C. S. I., Lieutenant-Governor of the United Provinces from 1901 to 1906* (Naini Tal: United Provinces Government Camp Press, 1906).

Latif, A., *A Paper on Mahomedan Education in Bengal Read by Mouvlie Abdool Luteef Khan Bahadoor at the Second Session of the Bengal Social Science Association, Held at the Town Hall of Calcutta, on the 30th January 1868* (Calcutta: 1868).

—, 'A Short Account of My Public Life', *Nawab Bahadur Abdul Latif, C.I.E* (Calcutta: Thacker Spink & Co., n.d. [1915]), pp. 165–206.

—, 'A Minute on the Hooghly Mudrussah Written at the Request of the Hon'ble Sir J. P. Grant, K. C. B., Lieutenant Governor of Bengal', in E. Haque (ed.), *Nawab Bahadur Abdul Latif: His Writings & Related Documents* (Dacca: Samudra Prokashani, 1968), pp. 19–42.

—, 'A Short Account of My Humble Efforts to Promote Education, Specially among the Mahomedans', in E. Haque (ed.), *Nawab Bahadur Abdul Latif: His Writings & Related Documents* (Dacca: Samudra Prokashani, 1968), pp. 187–242.

Latif, S. M., 'A Brief Account of the History and Operations of the Anjuman-i-Punjab from its Foundation in 1865 to the End of the Year 1877', Supplement to the *Civil and Military Gazette*, Lahore, 12 January 1878.

Lawrence, J., *Despatches by Sir John Lawrence, G.C.B., Chief Commissioner of the Punjab, on Christianity in India (Reprinted from the 'Times' of Oct. 23rd, 1858.)* (London: Church Missionary House, 1858).

Lees, W. N., *A Biographical Sketch of the Mystic Philosopher and Poet Jami being the Preface to his 'Lives of the Mystics'* (Calcutta: W. N. Lees's Press, 1859).

—, *Indian Musalmans: Being Three Letters Reprinted from the 'Times', with an Article on the Late Prince Consort and Four Articles on Education, Reprinted from the 'Calcutta Englishman'* (London: William and Norgate, 1871).

Leitner, G. W., *The Theory and Practice of Education with Special Reference to Education in India* (Lahore: Indian Public Opinion Press, n. d. [1870]).

—, *A Lecture on the Races of Turkey (Both of Europe and Asia,) and the State of their Education: Being, Principally, a Contribution to Muhammadan Education* (Lahore: Indian Public Opinion Press, 1871).

—, 'Native Self-Government in Matters of Education', *Journal of the East India Association*, 9 (1876), pp. 1–46.

—, *History of Indigenous Education in the Panjab Since Annexation and in 1882* (Calcutta: Superintendent of Government Printing, 1882).

Lushington, C., *The History, Design and Present State of the Religious, Benevolent and Charitable Institutions, Founded by the British in Calcutta and its Vicinity* (Calcutta: Hindostanee Press, 1824).

Lyall, A. C., *Asiatic Studies: Religious and Social* (London: John Murray, 1882).

MacDonnell, A. P., *Selections from Speeches of Sir A.P. MacDonnell, G.C.S.I., Lieutenant-Governor, N.W.P., and Chief Commissioner of Oudh, from 1895 to 1901* (Naini Tal: N.W. Provinces and Oudh Government Camp Branch Press, 1901).

[Mahomedan Literary Society], *A Quarter Century of the Mahomedan Literary Society of Calcutta. A Resumé of its Work from 1863 to 1869, etc.* (Calcutta: 1889).

Majumdar, J. K. (ed.), *Indian Speeches and Documents on British Rule, 1821–1918* (Calcutta: Longmans, Green & Co., 1937).

[Malaviya, M. M.], 'Prospectus of a Proposed Hindu University', in S. L. Dar and S. Somaskandan (eds), *History of the Banaras Hindu University* (Varanasi: Banaras Hindu University Press, 1966), pp. 49–74.

—, 'The Hindu University of Benares: Why it is Wanted and What it Aims at', in S. L. Dar and S. Somaskandan (eds), *History of the Banaras Hindu University* (Varanasi: Banaras Hindu University Press, 1966), pp. 114–49.

Monteath, A. M., 'Note on the State of Education in India (Compiled in 1862)', in P. Kirpal (ed.), *Selections from Educational Records of the Government of India. Volume I. Educational Reports, 1859–71* (Delhi: Government of India, 1960), pp. 1–119.

—, 'Note on the State of Education in India, 1865–66' in P. Kirpal (ed.), *Selections from Educational Records of the Government of India. Volume I. Educational Reports, 1859–71* (Delhi: Government of India, 1960), pp. 121–298.

Morison, T., 'A Muhamadan University', *National Review*, 32 (1898–9), pp. 243–9.

—, *Imperial Rule in India: Being an Examination of the Principles Proper to the Government of Dependencies* (Westminster: Archibald Constable & Co., 1899).

—, *The History of the M.A.O. College, Aligarh: From its Foundation to the Year 1903; Together with the Annual Report for the Year 1902–1903 and Appendices* (Allahabad: Pioneer Press, 1903).

Muhammad, S. (ed.), *The Aligarh Movement. Basic Documents: 1864–1898* (Meerut: Meenakshi Prakashan, 1978).

— (ed.), *The All-India Muslim Educational Conference (Select Presidential Addresses) 1886–1947* (New Delhi: A.P.H. Publishing Corporation, 2003).

[Muhammadan Anglo-Oriental College Management Committee], *Scheme for the Proposed Mahomedan Anglo-Oriental College* (n. p., n. d. [1872]).

—, *Scheme of Studies for the Mahomedan Anglo-Oriental College, Aligarh* (Benares: Medical Hall Press, 1875).

Naik, J. P. (ed.), *Selections from Educational Records of the Government of India Vol. II. Development of University Education, 1860–87* (Delhi: Government of India, 1963).

Obaidulla, M., *The Madrasah Scheme* (Calcutta: Urdoo Guide Press, 1873).

Palgrave, W. G., *Narrative of a Year's Journey Through Central and Eastern Arabia (1862–63)* (London: Macmillan and Co., 1865).

—, *Essays on Eastern Questions* (London: Macmillan and Co., 1872).

Philips, C. H. (ed.), *The Evolution of India and Pakistan 1858 to 1947: Selected Documents* (London: Oxford University Press, 1962).

Pirzada, S. S. (ed.), *Foundations of Pakistan: All-India Muslim League Documents: 1906–1947* (Karachi: National Publishing House, 1969).

Raleigh, T. (ed.), *Lord Curzon in India: Being a Selection from his Speeches as Viceroy and Governor-General of India, 1898–1905* (London: Macmillan and Co., 1906).

Report by the Bengal Provincial Committee; With Evidence taken Before the Committee, and Memorials Addressed to the Education Commission (Calcutta: Supt. of Govt. Printing, 1884).

Report by the Panjab Provincial Committee; With Evidence taken Before the Committee, and Memorials Addressed to the Education Commission (Calcutta: Supt. of Govt. Printing, 1884).

Report of the Administration of His Highness the Nizam's Dominion for 1303 Fasli (8th October 1893 to 7th October 1894) (Bombay: 'Times of India' Steam Press, 1895).

Report of the General Committee of Public Instruction of the Presidency of Fort William in Bengal, for the Year 1836 (Calcutta: Baptist Mission Press, 1837).

Report of the Indian Education Commission Appointed by the Resolution of the Government of India Dated 3rd February 1882 (Calcutta: Superintendent of Government Printing, 1883).

Report of the Indian Universities Commission (Simla: Government Central Printing Office, 1902).

Report on the Administration of His Highness the Nizam's Dominions for the Four Years 1304 to 1307 Fasli (8th October 1894 to 7th October 1898.) (Madras: Lawrence Asylum Press, 1899).

Richey, J. A. (ed.), *Selections from Educational Records. Part II: 1840–1859* (Calcutta, Superintendent Government Printing, 1922).

Selections from the Records of the Government of Bengal, No. 14: Papers relating to the Establishment of the Presidency College of Bengal (Calcutta: Military Orphan Press, 1854).

Selections from the Records of the Government of India, Home Department No. CCLXV: Papers relating to Discipline and Moral Training in Schools and Colleges in India (Calcutta: Superintendent of Government Printing, 1890).

Selections from the Records of the Government of India, Home Department No. CCV: Correspondence on the Subject of the Education of the Muhammadan Community in British India and their Employment in the Public Service Generally (Calcutta: Superintendent of Government Printing, 1886).

Skrine, F. H., *Life of Sir William Wilson Hunter, K.C.S.I., M.A., LL.D., a Vice-President of the Royal Asiatic Society, etc.* (London: Longmans, Green and Co., 1901).

Sprenger, A., *The Life of Mohammad, from Original Sources* (Allahabad: Presbyterian Mission Press, 1851).

—, *A Catalogue of the Arabic, Persian and Hindu'sta'ny Manuscripts, of the Libraries of the King of Oudh, compiled by Order of the Government of India* (1854) (Osnabruck: Biblio Verlag, 1979).

Stocqueler, J. H., *A Review of the Life and Labours of Dr G. W. Leitner* (Brighton: Tower Press, 1875).

Trevelyan, C. E., *A Treatise on the Means of Communicating the Learning and Civilization of Europe to India* (Calcutta: Bengal Hurkaru, 1834).

[—], *The Letters of Indophilus to 'The Times'* (London: Longman, Brown, Green, Longmans, and Roberts, 1858).

Trevelyan, C. E. et al., *The Application of the Roman Alphabet to all the Oriental Languages; Contained in a Series of Papers Written by Messrs. Trevelyan, J. Prinsep, and Tytler, Rev. A. Duff, and Mr. H.T. Prinsep and Published in Various Calcutta Periodicals in the Year 1834* (Serampore: Serampore Press, 1834).

Zastoupil, L. and M. Moir (eds), *The Great Indian Education Debate: Documents Relating to the Orientalist-Anglicist Controversy, 1781–1843* (Richmond: Curzon, 1999).

Secondary Material

Abbasi, M. Y., *Muslim Politics and Leadership in South Asia, 1876–92* (Islamabad: Institute of Islamic History, Culture and Civilization, 1981).

Ahmad, A., *Islamic Modernism in India and Pakistan, 1857–1964* (London: Oxford University Press, 1967).

Ahmed, A. F. S., *Social Ideas and Social Change in Bengal, 1818–1835* (Calcutta: Raddhi, 1976).

Ahmed, R., *The Bengal Muslims 1871–1906: A Quest for Identity* (New Delhi: Oxford University Press, 1988).

Akenson, D. H., *The Irish Education Experiment: The National System of Education in the Nineteenth Century* (London: Routledge & Kegan Paul, 1970).

Akkad, B. J., *Malaviyaji (A Brief Life Sketch of Pandit Madan Mohan Malaviya)* (Bombay: Vora, 1948).

Allan, M., *Palgrave of Arabia: The Life of William Gifford Palgrave, 1826–88* (London: Macmillan, 1972).

Allender, T., *Ruling through Education: The Politics of Schooling in the Colonial Punjab* (New Delhi: New Dawn Press, Inc., 2006).

—, 'Bad Language in the Raj: The "Frightful Encumbrance" of Gottlieb Leitner, 1865–1888', *Paedagogica Historica*, 43:3 (2007), pp. 383–403.

Anderson, M. R., 'Islamic Law and the Colonial Encounter in British India', in D. Arnold and P. Robb (eds), *Institutions and Ideologies: A SOAS South Asian Reader* (Richmond: Curzon Press, 1993), pp. 165–85.

[Anon.], *Anjuman-i-Himayat-i-Islam Lahore: A Short History and Account of its Constructive Activities* (Lahore: Anjuman-i-Himayat-i-Islam, n. d.).

Arnold, D., *Police Power and Colonial Rule: Madras 1859–1947* (Delhi: Oxford University Press, 1986).

—, *Colonizing the Body: State Medicine and Epidemic Disease in Nineteenth-Century India* (Berkeley, CA: University of California Press, 1993).

—, *Science, Technology and Medicine in Colonial India* (Cambridge: Cambridge University Press, 2000).

Asad, T., *Genealogies of Religion: Discipline and Reasons of Power in Christianity and Islam* (Baltimore, MD: The John Hopkins University Press, 1993).

—, *Formations of the Secular: Christianity, Islam, Modernity* (Stanford, CA: Stanford University Press, 2003).

Bakshi, S. R., *Madan Mohan Malaviya: The Man and his Ideology* (New Delhi: Anmol Publications, 1990).

Ballantyne, T., 'Race and the Webs of Empire: Aryanism from India to the Pacific', *Journal of Colonialism and Colonial History*, 2:3 (2001), pp. 1–25.

Ballhatchet, K. A., 'The Home Government and Bentinck's Educational Policy', *Cambridge Historical Journal*, 10:2 (1951), pp. 224–9.

Banchoff, T. (ed.), *Religious Pluralism, Globalisation and World Politics* (New York, NY: Oxford University Press, 2008).

Barnard, H. C., *A History of English Education from 1760* (London: University of London Press, 1960).

Barrier, N. G., 'Muslim Politics in the Punjab, 1870–1890', *Panjab Past and Present*, 5:1 (1971), pp. 84–127.

Barry, A., 'Ethical Capitalism', in W. Larner and W. Walters (eds), *Global Governmentality: Governing International Spaces* (London: Routledge, 2004), pp. 195–211.

Bayly, C. A., *Empire and Information: Intelligence Gathering and Social Communication in India, 1780–1870* (Cambridge: Cambridge University Press, 1996).

—, 'Ireland, India and Empire: 1780–1914', *Transactions of the Royal Historical Society, Sixth Series*, 10 (2000), pp. 377–97.

—, *Recovering Liberties: Indian Thought in the Age of Liberalism and Empire* (Cambridge: Cambridge University Press, 2012).

Bearce, G. D., 'Lord William Bentinck: The Application of Liberalism to India', *Journal of Modern History*, 28:3 (1956), pp. 234–46.

Bellot, H. H., *The University of London: A History* (Bristol: Western Printing Services, 1969).

Bhargava, R., 'What is Secularism For?', in R. Bhargava (ed.), *Secularism and its Critics* (New Delhi: Oxford University Press, 2004), pp. 486–542.

Birla, R., *Stages of Capital: Law, Culture, and Market Governance in Late Colonial India* (Durham, NC: Duke University Press, 2009).

Boylan, C., 'Victorian Ideologies of Improvement: Sir Charles Trevelyan in India and Ireland', in T. Foley and M. O'Connor (eds), *Ireland and India: Colonies, Culture and Empire* (Dublin: Irish Academic Press, 2006), pp. 167–78.

Bruce, S. (ed.), *Religion and Modernization: Sociologists and Historians Debate the Secularization Thesis* (Oxford: Clarendon Press, 1992).

Casanova, J., *Public Religions in the Modern World* (Chicago, IL: University of Chicago, 1994).

Chadwick, O., *The Secularization of the European Mind in the Nineteenth Century* (Cambridge: Cambridge University Press, 1975).

Chaghatai, M. I., 'Dr Aloys Sprenger and the Delhi College', in M. Pernau (ed.), *The Delhi College: Traditional Elites, the Colonial State, and Education before 1857* (New Delhi: Oxford University Press, 2006), pp. 105–24.

Chakrabarti, P., *Western Science in Modern India: Metropolitan Methods, Colonial Practices* (Delhi: Permanent Black, 2004).

Chakraborty, A. K., *Bengali Muslim Literati and the Development of Muslim Community in Bengal* (Shimla: Indian Institute of Advanced Study, 2002).

Chakravarty, D., *Muslim Separatism and the Partition of India* (New Delhi: Atlantic, 2003).

Chandhoke, N., *Beyond Secularism: The Rights of Religious Minorities* (New Delhi: Oxford University Press, 1999).

Chatterjee, N., *The Making of Indian Secularism: Empire, Law and Christianity, 1830–1960* (Basingstoke: Palgrave Macmillan, 2011).

Chatterjee, P., *The Nation and its Fragments: Colonial and Postcolonial Histories* (Princeton, NJ: Princeton University Press, 1993).

—, 'On Civil and Political Society in Post-Colonial Democracies', in S. Kaviraj and S. Khilnani (eds), *Civil Society: History and Possibilities* (Cambridge: Cambridge University Press, 2001), pp. 165–78.

—, 'Secularism and Tolerance', in R. Bhargava (ed.), *Secularism and its Critics* (New Delhi: Oxford University Press, 2004), pp. 345–79.

Churchill, E. D., 'Muslim Societies of the Punjab, 1860–1890', *Panjab Past and Present*, 8:1 (1974), pp. 69–91.

—, 'The Muhammadan Educational Conference and the Aligarh Movement 1886–1900', *Panjab Past and Present*, 8:2 (1974), pp. 366–81.

Clive, J., *Macaulay: The Shaping of the Historian* (Cambridge, MA: Belknap Press, 1973).

Cohn, B. S., *An Anthropologist among the Historians and Other Essays* (Delhi: Oxford University Press, 1987).

—, *Colonialism and Its Forms of Knowledge: The British in India* (Princeton, NJ: Princeton University Press, 1996).

Collingham, E. M., *Imperial Bodies: The Physical Experience of the Raj, c. 1800–1947* (Cambridge: Polity Press, 2001).

Cook, S. B., *Imperial Affinities: Nineteenth Century Analogies and Exchanges between India and Ireland* (New Delhi: Sage Publications, 1993).

Cox, J., *Imperial Fault Lines: Christianity and Colonial Power in India, 1818–1940* (Stanford, CA: Stanford University Press, 2002).

Cruickshank, M., *Church and State in English Education: 1870 to the Present Day* (London: Macmillan & Co., 1964).

Cutts, E. H., 'The Background of Macaulay's Minute', *American Historical Review*, 58:4 (1953), pp. 824–53.

Dar, B. A., *Religious Thought of Sayyid Ahmad Khan* (Lahore: Institute of Islamic Culture, 1971).

Dar, S. L. and S. Somaskandan (eds), *History of the Banaras Hindu University* (Varanasi: Banaras Hindu University Press, 1966).

Davison, R. H., *Reform in the Ottoman Empire, 1856–1876* (Princeton, NJ: Princeton University Press, 1963).

Dean, M., *Governmentality: Power and Rule in Modern Society* (London: Sage Publications, 1999).

Denholm, A., *Lord Ripon 1827–1909: A Political Biography* (London: Croom Helm, 1982).

Diamond, J. M., 'Narratives of Reform and Displacement in Colonial Lahore: The *Intikaal* of Muhammad Hussain Azad', *Journal of Punjab Studies*, 16:2 (2009), pp. 159–77.

—, 'The Orientalist-Literati Relationship in the Northwest: G. W. Leitner, Muhammad Hussain Azad and the Rhetoric of Neo-Orientalism in Colonial Lahore', *South Asia Research*, 31:1 (2011), pp. 25–43.

Dilks, D., *Curzon in India* (London: Rupert Hart-Davis, 1969–70).

Dirks, N., *Castes of Mind: Colonialism and the Making of Modern India* (Princeton, NJ: Princeton University Press, 2001).

Dodson, M. S., *Orientalism, Empire and National Culture: India, 1770–1880* (Basingstoke: Palgrave Macmillan, 2007).

Duncan, J. S., *In the Shadow of the Tropics: Climate, Race and Biopower in Nineteenth Century Ceylon* (Aldershot: Aldgate, 2007).

Edwardes, M., *High Noon of Empire: India under Curzon* (London: Eyre & Spottiswoode, 1965).

Fisher, M., 'The Office of Akhbar Nawis: The Transition from Mughal to British Forms', *Modern Asian Studies*, 27:1 (1993), pp. 45–82.

Foley, T. and M. O'Connor (eds), *Ireland and India: Colonies, Culture and Empire* (Dublin: Irish Academic Press, 2006).

Forbes, G. H., *Positivism in Bengal: A Case Study in the Transmission and Assimilation of an Ideology* (Calcutta: Minerva, 1975).

Foucault, M., *Discipline and Punish: The Birth of the Prison* (London: Allen Lane, 1977).

—, *The Will to Knowledge: The History of Sexuality, Volume 1* (London: Penguin Books, 1998).

—, 'The Subject and Power', in J. D. Faubion (ed.), *Power. The Essential Works of Foucault 1954–1984* (London: Penguin, 2002), pp. 326–48.

—, *'Society Must be Defended': Lectures at the Collège de France, 1975–76* (London: Penguin Books, 2004).

—, *Psychiatric Power: Lectures at the Collège de France, 1973–74* (Basingstoke: Palgrave Macmillan, 2006).

—, *Security, Territory, Population: Lectures at the Collège de France, 1977–78* (Basingstoke: Palgrave Macmillan, 2009).

—, *The Birth of Biopolitics: Lectures at the Collège de France, 1978–79* (Basingstoke: Palgrave Macmillan, 2010).

—, *The Government of Self and Others: Lectures at the Collège de France, 1982–83* (Basingstoke: Palgrave Macmillan, 2010).

Fraser, L., *India under Curzon and After* (London: William Heinemann, 1911).

Frykenberg, R. E., *Christianity in India: From Beginnings to the Present* (Oxford: Oxford University Press, 2008).

Ghosh, S. C., *Dalhousie in India, 1848–1856: A Study of his Social Policy as Governor-General* (Delhi: Munshiram Manoharlal, 1975).

Gilmartin, D., 'Customary Law and *Shari'at* in British Punjab', in K. P. Ewing (ed.), *Shari'at and Ambiguity in South Asian Islam* (Berkeley, CA: University of California Press, 1988), pp. 43–62.

Gopal, S., *Patna in the 19th Century (A Socio-Cultural Profile)* (Calcutta: B. Mitra, 1996).

Goswami, M., *Producing India: From Colonial Economy to National Space* (Chicago, IL: Chicago University Press, 2004).

Green, N., *Bombay Islam: The Religious Economy of the West Indian Ocean, 1840–1915* (Cambridge: Cambridge University Press, 2011).

Gupta, C., *Sexuality, Obscenity, Community: Women, Muslims, and the Hindu Public in Colonial India* (Delhi: Permanent Black, 2001).

Gupta, S. L., *Pandit Madan Mohan Malaviya: A Socio-Political Study* (Allahabad: Chugh Publications, 1978).

Habermas, J., *The Structural Transformation of the Public Sphere: An Inquiry into a Category of Bourgeois Society* (Great Britain: Polity Press, 1989).

—, *Between Naturalism and Religion* (Cambridge: Polity Press, 2008).

Hardy, P., *The Muslims of British India* (Cambridge: Cambridge University Press, 2007).

Harte, N., *The University of London 1836–1986: An Illustrated History* (London: Athlone Press, 1986).

Hasan, M., *Mohamed Ali: Ideology and Politics* (New Delhi: Manohar, 1981).

—, *A Moral Reckoning: Muslim Intellectuals in Nineteenth-Century Delhi* (New Delhi: Oxford University Press, 2007).

Hassan, R., 'Islamic Modernist and Reformist Discourse in South Asia', in S. T. Hunter (ed.), *Reformist Voices of Islam: Mediating Islam and Modernity* (New York, NY: M. E. Sharpe, 2009), pp. 159–86.

Heath, D., *Purifying Empire: Obscenity and the Politics of Moral Regulation in Britain, India and Australia* (Cambridge: Cambridge University Press, 2010).

Herbert, D., *Religion in Civil Society: Rethinking Public Religion in the Contemporary World* (Aldershot: Ashgate, 2003).

Ikram, S. M., *Indian Muslims and Partition of India* (New Delhi: Atlantic Publishers, 1992).

Imadi, S. H., *Nawab Imad-ul-Mulk (Social and Cultural Activities of Nawab Imad-ul-Mulk Syed Husain Bilgrami in Hyderabad)* (Hyderabad: Government of Andhra Pradesh, 1978).

Iqbal, A., *The Life and Times of Mohamed Ali: An Analysis of the Hopes, Fears and Aspirations of Muslim India from 1778 to 1931* (Lahore: Institute of Islamic Culture, 1974).

Ivermee, R., 'Islamic Education and Colonial Secularism: The Amroha Experiment of 1895–96', *South Asian History and Culture*, 5:1 (2014), pp. 21–36.

—, 'Shari'at and Muslim Community in Colonial Punjab, 1865–85', *Modern Asian Studies*, 48:4 (2014), pp. 1068–95.

Jain, M. S., *The Aligarh Movement* (New Delhi: Icon Publications, 2006).

Jalal, A., *Self and Sovereignty: Individual and Community in South Asian Islam Since 1850* (London: Routledge, 2000).

Joas, H. and K. Wiegandt (eds), *Secularization and the World Religions* (Liverpool: Liverpool University Press, 2009).

Jones, J., *Shi'a Islam in Colonial India: Religion, Community and Sectarianism* (Cambridge: Cambridge University Press, 2012).

Jones, K. W., 'Religious Identity and the Indian Census', in N. G. Barrier (ed.), *The Census in British India: New Perspectives* (New Delhi: Manohar, 1981), pp. 73–102.

—, *Socio-Religious Reform Movements in British India. The New Cambridge History of India III.1* (Cambridge: Cambridge University Press, 1989).

Joyce, P., *The Rule of Freedom: Liberalism and the Modern City* (London: Verso, 2003).

Kalpagam, U., 'Colonial Governmentality and the "Economy"', *Economy and Society*, 29 (2000), pp. 418–38.

—, 'Colonial Governmentality and the Public Sphere in India', *Journal of Historical Sociology*, 15 (2002), pp. 35–58.

Khan, A. R., *The All India Muslim Education Conference: Its Contribution to the Cultural Development of Indian Muslims 1886–1947* (Karachi: Oxford University Press, 2001).

Kochhar, S. K., *Pivotal Issues in Indian Education* (New Delhi: Sterling, 2005).

Kopf, D., *British Orientalism and the Bengal Renaissance: The Dynamics of Indian Modernization, 1773–1835* (Berkeley, CA: University of California Press, 1969).

Kozlowski, G. C., *Muslim Endowments and Society in British India* (Cambridge: Cambridge University Press, 1985).

Laird, M. A., *Missionaries and Education in Bengal, 1793–1837* (Oxford: Clarendon Press, 1972).

Legg, S., *Spaces of Colonialism: Delhi's Urban Governmentalities* (Oxford: Blackwell, 2007).

Lelyveld, D., *Aligarh's First Generation. Muslim Solidarity in British India* (Princeton, NJ: Princeton University Press, 1978).

Liddle, S., 'Azurda: Scholar, Poet and Judge', in M. Pernau (ed.), *The Delhi College: Traditional Elites, the Colonial State, and Education before 1857* (New Delhi: Oxford University Press, 2006), pp. 125–44.

Losonczi, P. and A. Singh (eds), *Discoursing the Post-Secular: Essays on the Habermasian Post-Secular Turn* (Berlin: Lit Verlag, 2010).

Lütt, J., *The Movement for the Foundation of the Benares Hindu University* (Heidelberg: Südasien-Institut der Universität Heidelberg, 1976).

Madan, T. N., 'Secularism in Its Place', in R. Bhargava (ed.), *Secularism and Its Critics* (New Delhi: Oxford University Press, 1998), pp. 297–320.

Majeed, J., *Ungoverned Imaginings: James Mill's The History of British India and Orientalism* (Oxford: Clarendon Press, 1992).

Malik, H., *Sir Sayyid Ahmad Khan and Muslim Modernization in India and Pakistan* (New York, NY: Columbia University Press, 1980).

Mansergh, N., *The Prelude to Partition: Concepts and Aims in Ireland and India* (Cambridge: Cambridge University Press, 1978).

Mantena, K., *Alibis of Empire: Henry Maine and the Ends of Liberal Imperialism* (Princeton, NJ: Princeton University Press, 2010).

McCully, B., *English Education and the Origins of Indian Nationalism* (Gloucester, MA: Peter Smith Publications, 1966).

Mehrotra, S. R., *The Emergence of the Indian National Congress* (Delhi: Vikas Publications, 1971).

Mehta, H. R., *A History of the Growth and Development of Western Education in the Punjab, 1846–1884* (Punjab: Govt. Record Office, 1971).

Mehta, U. S., *Liberalism and Empire: A Study in Nineteenth-Century British Liberal Thought* (Chicago, IL: Chicago University Press, 1999).

Metcalf, B. D., *Islamic Revival in British India: Deoband, 1860–1900* (Princeton, NJ: Princeton University Press, 1982).

Metcalf, T. R., *The Aftermath of Revolt: India, 1857–1870* (Princeton, NJ: Princeton University Press, 1965).

—, *Ideologies of the Raj* (Cambridge: Cambridge University Press, 1994).

Meyer, B. and A. Moors (eds), *Religion, Media and the Public Sphere* (Bloomington, IN: Indiana University Press, 2006).

Minault, G., *Secluded Scholars: Women's Education and Muslim Social Reform in Colonial India* (Delhi: Oxford University Press, 1998).

—, 'Qiran al-Sa'adain: The Dialogue between Eastern and Western Learning at Delhi College', in J. Malik (ed.), *Perspectives of Mutual Encounters in South Asian History, 1760–1860* (Leiden: Brill, 2000), pp. 260–77.

—, 'Aloys Sprenger: German Orientalism's "Gift" to Delhi College', *South Asia Research*, 31:1 (2011), pp. 7–23.

Minault, G. and D. Lelyveld, 'The Campaign for a Muslim University, 1898–1920', *Modern Asian Studies*, 8:2 (1974), pp. 145–89.

Mir, F., *The Social Space of Language: Vernacular Culture in British Colonial Punjab* (Berkeley, CA: University of California Press, 2010).

Monypenny, W. F. and G. E. Buckle, *The Life of Benjamin Disraeli, Earl of Beaconsfield* (London: John Murray, 1929).

Moody. T. W., 'The Irish University Question of the Nineteenth Century', *History*, 43 (1958), pp. 90–109.

Moore, R. J., 'The Composition of Wood's Education Dispatch', *English Historical Review*, 80:314 (1965), pp. 70–83.

—, *Sir Charles Wood's Indian Policy 1853–66* (Manchester: Manchester University Press, 1966).

Mukherjee, S. N., 'Class, Caste and Politics in Calcutta, 1815–38', in E. Leach and S. N. Mukherjee (eds), *Elites in South Asia* (London: Cambridge University Press, 1970), pp. 33–78.

Murshid, T. M., *The Sacred and the Secular: Bengal Muslim Discourses, 1871–1977* (Calcutta: Oxford University Press, 1995).

Nandy, A., 'The Politics of Secularism and the Recovery of Religious Tolerance', in V. Das (ed.), *Mirrors of Violence: Communities, Riots, and Survivors in South Asia* (Delhi: Oxford University Press, 1990), pp. 69–93.

—, *The Romance of the State: And the Fate of Dissent in the Tropics* (New Delhi: Oxford University Press, 2003).

Nash, G., *From Empire to Orient: Travellers to the Middle East, 1830–1926* (London: I. B. Tauris, 2005).

Nigam, A., *The Insurrection of Little Selves: The Crisis of Secular-Nationalism in India* (New Delhi: Oxford University Press, 2006).

O'Malley, K., *Ireland, India and Empire: Indo-Irish Radical Connections, 1919–64* (Manchester: Manchester University Press, 2009).

Padamsee, A., *Representations of Indian Muslims in British Colonial Discourse* (Basingstoke: Palgrave Macmillan, 2005).

Pandey, G., *The Construction of Communalism in Colonial North India* (New Delhi: Oxford University Press, 2006).

Pernau, M., 'From a "Private" Public to a "Public" Private Sphere: Old Delhi and the North Indian Muslims in Comparative Perspective', in G. Mahajan (ed.), *The Public and the Private: Issues of Democratic Citizenship* (New Delhi: Sage Publications, 2003), pp. 103–29.

—, 'Introduction: Entangled Translations: The History of the Delhi College', in M. Pernau (ed.), *The Delhi College: Traditional Elites, the Colonial State, and Education before 1857* (New Delhi: Oxford University Press, 2006), pp. 1–31.

Pickett, B. L., 'Foucault and the Politics of Resistance', *Polity*, 28 (1996), pp. 445–66.

Pitts, J., *A Turn to Empire: The Rise of Imperial Liberalism in Britain and France* (Princeton, NJ: Princeton University Press, 2006).

Porter, A. N., *Religion Versus Empire? British Protestant Missionaries and Overseas Expansion, 1700–1914* (Manchester: Manchester University Press, 2004).

Pottinger, G., *Mayo: Disraeli's Viceroy* (Wilton: Michael Russell, 1990).

Powell, A. A., 'Scholar Manqué or Mere Munshi? Maulawi Karimu'd-Din's Career in the Anglo-Oriental Education Service', in M. Pernau (ed.), *The Delhi College: Traditional Elites, the Colonial State, and Education before 1857* (New Delhi: Oxford University Press, 2006), pp. 203–31.

—, *Scottish Orientalists and India: The Muir Brothers, Religion, Education and Empire* (Woodbridge: The Boydell Press, 2010).

Prakash, G., *Another Reason: Science and the Imagination of Modern India* (Princeton, NJ: Princeton University Press, 1999).

—, 'Body Politic in Colonial India', in T. Mitchell (ed.), *Questions of Modernity* (Minneapolis, MN: University of Minnesota Press, 2000), pp. 189–222.

Prashad, V., 'The Technology of Sanitation in Colonial Delhi', *Modern Asian Studies*, 35:1 (2001), pp. 113–55.

Quataert, D., *The Ottoman Empire, 1700–1922* (Cambridge: Cambridge University Press, 2000).

Qureshi, M. N., *Pan-Islam in British Indian Politics: A Study of the Khilafat Movement, 1918–1924* (Leiden: Brill, 1999).

Renold, L., *A Hindu Education: Early Years of the Banaras Hindu University* (New Delhi: Oxford University Press, 2005).

Robinson, F., *Separatism Among Indian Muslims: The Politics of the United Provinces' Muslims, 1860–1923* (Cambridge: Cambridge University Press, 1974).

—, *The 'Ulama of Farangi Mahall and Islamic Culture in South Asia* (London: Hurst & Company, 2001).

Rosselli, J., *Lord William Bentinck: The Making of a Liberal Imperialist* (London: Chatto & Windus, 1974).

Roy, A., *Civility and Empire: Literature and Culture in British India, 1822–1922* (London and New York, NY: Routledge, 2006).

Said, E. W., *Culture and Imperialism* (London: Vintage Books, 1994).

Sanial, S. C., 'History of the Calcutta Madrassa', *Bengal Past and Present*, 8 (1914), pp. 83–111, 225–50.

Sanyal, U., *Devotional Islam and Politics in British India: Ahmad Riza Khan and His Movement, 1870–1920* (Delhi: Oxford University Press, 1999).

Scott, D., 'Colonial Governmentality', *Social Text*, 43 (1995), pp. 191–220.

Seal, A., *The Emergence of Indian Nationalism: Competition and Collaboration in the Later Nineteenth Century* (Cambridge: Cambridge University Press, 1968).

Seth, S., *Subject Lessons: The Western Education of Colonial India* (Durham, NC and London: Duke University Press, 2007).

Shah, S. Y., *Higher Education and Politics in Colonial India: A Study of Aligarh Muslim University (1875–1920)* (Delhi: Renaissance, 1996).

Shaikh, F., *Community and Consensus in Islam: Muslim Representation in Colonial India* (Cambridge: Cambridge University Press, 1989).

Shields, A., *The Irish Conservative Party, 1852–68: Land, Politics and Religion* (Dublin: Irish Academic Press, 2007).

Silvestri, M., *Ireland and India: Nationalism, Empire and Memory* (Basingstoke: Palgrave Macmillan, 2009).

Smith, D., *India as a Secular State* (Princeton, NJ: Princeton University Press, 1963).

Spear, P., 'Bentinck and Education', *Cambridge Historical Journal*, 6:1 (1938), pp. 78–101.

Stokes, E., *The English Utilitarians and India* (Oxford: Oxford University Press, 1959).

Studdert-Kennedy, G., *Providence and the Raj: Imperial Mission and Missionary Imperialism* (New Delhi: Sage, 1998).

Tambiah, S. J., 'The Crisis of Secularism in India', in R. Bhargava (ed.), *Secularism and its Critics* (New Delhi: Oxford University Press, 2004), pp. 418–53.

Taylor, C., *A Secular Age* (London: Harvard University Press, 2007).

—, *Dilemmas and Connections: Selected Essays* (Cambridge, MA and London: The Belknap Press of Harvard University Press, 2011).

Tejani, S., *Indian Secularism: A Social and Intellectual History, 1890–1950* (Ranikhet: Permanent Black, 2007).

Troll, C. W., *Sayyid Ahmad Khan: A Reinterpretation of Muslim Theology* (New Delhi: Vikas, 1978).

Turner, B. S., *Religion and Modern Society: Citizenship, Secularisation and the State* (Cambridge: Cambridge University Press, 2011).

Van der Veer, P., *Imperial Encounters: Religion and Modernity in India and Britain* (Delhi: Permanent Black, n. d.).

Verma, A., 'Consolidation of the Raj: Notes from a Police Station in British India, 1865–1928', *Criminal Justice History*, 17 (2002), pp. 109–32.

Viswanathan, G., *Masks of Conquest: Literary Study and British Rule in India* (London: Faber and Faber, 1990).

Walters, W., *Governmentality: Critical Encounters* (London: Routledge, 2012).

Washbrook, D. A., 'Ethnicity and Racialism in Colonial Indian Society', in R. Ross (ed.), *Racialism and Colonialism: Essays on Ideology and Social Structure* (The Hague: Nijhoff for Leiden University Press, 1982), pp. 143–81.

Wasti, S. R., *Lord Minto and the Indian Nationalist Movement* (Oxford: Clarendon Press, 1964).

—, *Muslim Struggle for Freedom in British India* (Delhi: Renaissance Publishing House, 1993).

Weber, M., *The Sociology of Religion* (Boston, MA: Beacon Press, 1963).

Whitehead, C., *Colonial Educators: The British Indian and Colonial Education Service, 1858–1983* (London: I.B. Tauris, 2003).

Wolf, L., *Life of the First Marquess of Ripon, K.G., P.C., G.C.S.I, D.C.I., etc.* (London: John Murray, 1921).

Woodward, L., *The Age of Reform 1815–70* (Oxford: Clarendon Press, 1962).

Wright, J. M., *Ireland, India and Nationalism in Nineteenth Century Literature* (Cambridge University Press, 2009).

Wurgaft, L. D., *The Imperial Imagination: Magic and Myth in Kipling's India* (Middletown, CT: Wesleyan University Press, 1983).

Zachariah, K., *History of the Hooghly College, 1836–1936* (Alipore: Bengal Government Press, 1936).

Zastoupil, L. and M. Moir, 'Introduction', in L. Zastoupil and M. Moir (eds), *The Great Indian Education Debate: Documents Relating to the Orientalist-Anglicist Controversy, 1781–1843* (Richmond: Curzon, 1999), pp. 1–72.

NOTES

Introduction: Secularism Considered

1. Minute by A. P. Howell, Officiating Resident at Hyderabad, 25 June 1888, *Selections from the Records of the Government of India, Home Department, No. CCLXV: Papers relating to Discipline and Moral Training in Schools and Colleges in India* (Calcutta: Superintendent of Government Printing, 1886), pp. 226–30, on pp. 226–7.

2. S. H. Bilgrami, 'Moral and Religious Education', *Addresses, Poems and Other Writings of Nawwab Imadul-Mulk Bahadur (Sayyid Husayn Bilgrami, C.S.I.)* (Hyderabad: Government Central Press, 1925), pp. 21–4, on p. 21.

3. S. K. Kochhar, *Pivotal Issues in Indian Education* (New Delhi: Sterling, 2005), p. 20.

4. Exceptions considered below include N. Chatterjee, *The Making of Indian Secularism: Empire, Law and Christianity, 1830–1960* (Basingstoke: Palgrave Macmillan, 2011); G. Viswanathan, *Masks of Conquest: Literary Study and British Rule in India* (London: Faber and Faber, 1990); and G. Studdert-Kennedy, *Providence and the Raj: Imperial Mission and Missionary Imperialism* (New Delhi: Sage, 1998).

5. M. Weber, *The Sociology of Religion* (Boston, MA: Beacon Press, 1963), pp. 223–45.

6. C. Taylor, *Dilemmas and Connections: Selected Essays* (Cambridge, MA and London: The Belknap Press of Harvard University Press, 2011), pp. 303–13; T. Asad, *Formations of the Secular: Christianity, Islam, Modernity* (Stanford, CA: Stanford University Press, 2003), pp. 181–201.

7. J. Casanova, *Public Religions in the Modern World* (Chicago, IL: University of Chicago, 1994); D. Herbert, *Religion in Civil Society: Rethinking Public Religion in the Contemporary World* (Aldershot: Ashgate, 2003); T. Banchoff (ed.), *Religious Pluralism, Globalisation and World Politics* (New York, NY: Oxford University Press, 2008); B. Meyer and A. Moors (eds), *Religion, Media and the Public Sphere* (Bloomington, IN: Indiana University Press, 2006).

8. S. Bruce (ed.), *Religion and Modernization: Sociologists and Historians Debate the Secularization Thesis* (Oxford: Clarendon Press, 1992); H. Joas and K. Wiegandt (eds), *Secularization and the World Religions* (Liverpool: Liverpool University Press, 2009).

9. J. Habermas, *Between Naturalism and Religion* (Cambridge: Polity Press, 2008); Taylor, *Dilemmas and Connections*, pp. 303–25; C. Taylor, *A Secular Age* (London: Harvard University Press, 2007); P. Losonczi and A. Singh (eds), *Discoursing the Post-Secular: Essays on the Habermasian Post-Secular Turn* (Berlin: Lit Verlag, 2010).

10. S. Tejani, *Indian Secularism: A Social and Intellectual History, 1890–1950* (Ranikhet: Permanent Black, 2007), pp. 234–65; D. Smith, *India as a Secular State* (Princeton, NJ:

Princeton University Press, 1963); A. Nandy, *The Romance of the State: And the Fate of Dissent in the Tropics* (New Delhi: Oxford University Press, 2003), pp. 34–60.

11. A. Nigam, *The Insurrection of Little Selves: The Crisis of Secular-Nationalism in India* (New Delhi: Oxford University Press, 2006), pp. 139–75; N. Chandhoke, *Beyond Secularism: The Rights of Religious Minorities* (New Delhi: Oxford University Press, 1999); S. J. Tambiah, 'The Crisis of Secularism in India', in R. Bhargava (ed.), *Secularism and its Critics* (New Delhi: Oxford University Press, 2004), pp. 418–53.

12. A. Nandy, 'The Politics of Secularism and the Recovery of Religious Tolerance', in V. Das (ed.), *Mirrors of Violence: Communities, Riots, and Survivors in South Asia* (Delhi: Oxford University Press, 1990), pp. 69–93; Nandy, *The Romance of the State*, pp. 34–60; T. N. Madan, 'Secularism in Its Place', in R. Bhargava (ed.), *Secularism and Its Critics* (New Delhi: Oxford University Press, 1998), pp. 297–320.

13. P. Chatterjee, 'Secularism and Tolerance', in R. Bhargava (ed.), *Secularism and Its Critics* (New Delhi: Oxford University Press, 2004), pp. 345–79; Madan, 'Secularism in Its Place'.

14. Chandhoke, *Beyond Secularism*, p. 74.

15. P. Van der Veer, *Imperial Encounters: Religion and Modernity in India and Britain* (Delhi: Permanent Black, n.d.), pp. 14–15; Tejani, *Indian Secularism*, pp. 4–5.

16. Tejani, *Indian Secularism*, p. 12; Chatterjee, *The Making of Indian Secularism*, pp. 5–8.

17. On the shift away from liberal explanations of the British role in India, see T. R. Metcalf, *Ideologies of the Raj* (Cambridge: Cambridge University Press, 1994); E. Stokes, *The English Utilitarians and India* (Oxford: Oxford University Press, 1959); and K. Mantena, *Alibis of Empire: Henry Maine and the Ends of Liberal Imperialism* (Princeton, NJ: Princeton University Press, 2010). On the state as neutral arbiter, see D. A. Washbrook, 'Ethnicity and Racialism in Colonial Indian Society', in R. Ross (ed.), *Racialism and Colonialism: Essays on Ideology and Social Structure* (The Hague: Nijhoff for Leiden University Press, 1982), pp. 143–81; and G. Pandey, *The Construction of Communalism in Colonial North India* (New Delhi: Oxford University Press, 2006), p. 16.

18. Chatterjee, 'Secularism and Tolerance', p. 351.

19. R. Bhargava, 'What is Secularism For?', in R. Bhargava (ed.), *Secularism and Its Critics* (New Delhi: Oxford University Press, 2004), pp. 486–542, on pp. 492–4.

20. Van der Veer, *Imperial Encounters*, pp. 16–24; Chatterjee, *The Making of Indian Secularism*, pp. 110–20.

21. On the state management of Muslim religious endowments, see G. C. Kozlowski, *Muslim Endowments and Society in British India* (Cambridge: Cambridge University Press, 1985). On the colonial administration of Muslim law, M. R. Anderson, 'Islamic Law and the Colonial Encounter in British India', in D. Arnold and P. Robb (eds), *Institutions and Ideologies: A SOAS South Asian Reader* (Richmond: Curzon Press, 1993), pp. 165–85; B. S. Cohn, *Colonialism and Its Forms of Knowledge: The British in India* (Princeton, NJ: Princeton University Press, 1996), pp. 57–75; D. Gilmartin, 'Customary Law and *Shari'at* in British Punjab' in K. P. Ewing (ed.), *Shari'at and Ambiguity in South Asian Islam* (Berkeley, CA: University of California Press, 1988), pp. 43–62; and R. Ivermee, 'Shari'at and Muslim Community in Colonial Punjab, 1865–85', *Modern Asian Studies*, 48:4 (2014), pp. 1068–95

22. J. Cox, *Imperial Fault Lines: Christianity and Colonial Power in India, 1818–1940* (Stanford, CA: Stanford University Press, 2002); A. N. Porter, *Religion versus Empire? British Protestant Missionaries and Rverseas Expansion, 1700–1914* (Manchester: Manchester University Press, 2004); R. E. Frykenberg, *Christianity in India: From Beginnings to the Present* (Oxford: Oxford University Press, 2008); Studdert-Kennedy,

Providence and the Raj; Chatterjee, *The Making of Indian Secularism*.

23. B. S. Turner, *Religion and Modern Society: Citizenship, Secularisation and the State* (Cambridge: Cambridge University Press, 2011), pp. 127–34.

24. Tejani, *Indian Secularism*, pp. 12–21.

25. Resolution of the Governor General of India in Council, 7 March 1835, India Public Consultations, India Office, British Library, London (hereafter IPC), no. 19 of 7 March 1835.

26. The concept of governmentality was introduced by Foucault in the fourth lecture of his 1977–8 course of lectures at the Collège de France, and developed during the following year's course. These courses have been translated and published in English as M. Foucault, *Security, Territory, Population: Lectures at the Collège de France, 1977–78* (Basingstoke: Palgrave Macmillan, 2009) and M. Foucault, *The Birth of Biopolitics: Lectures at the Collège de France, 1978–79* (Basingstoke: Palgrave Macmillan, 2010).

27. Foucault, *Security, Territory, Population*, pp. 87–367; Foucault, *The Birth of Biopolitics*, pp. 1–316.

28. On the concept of 'population', see M. Foucault, *The Will to Knowledge: The History of Sexuality, Volume 1* (London: Penguin Books, 1998), pp. 135–59; and M. Foucault, *'Society Must be Defended': Lectures at the Collège de France, 1975–76* (London: Penguin Books, 2004), pp. 239–63.

29. In his useful introduction to governmentality, Mitchell Dean offers a distinction between 'techne' – the 'means, mechanisms, procedures, instruments, tactics, techniques, technologies and vocabularies' by which government over a population is accomplished – and 'episteme' –'the forms of knowledge that arise from and inform the activity of governing' – and notes Foucault's concern for the ways in which knowledge produces and is produced by techniques, practices and institutions. See M. Dean, *Governmentality: Power and Rule in Modern Society* (London: Sage Publications, 1999), pp. 31–2.

30. G. Prakash, *Another Reason: Science and the Imagination of Modern India* (Princeton, NJ: Princeton University Press, 1999); P. Chatterjee, *The Nation and Its Fragments: Colonial and Postcolonial Histories* (Princeton, NJ: Princeton University Press, 1993); N. Dirks, *Castes of Mind: Colonialism and the Making of Modern India* (Princeton, NJ: Princeton University Press, 2001); D. Scott, 'Colonial Governmentality', *Social Text*, 43 (1995), pp. 191–220.

31. On the development of colonial government after the Indian Rebellion, see T. R. Metcalf, *The Aftermath of Revolt: India, 1857–1870* (Princeton, NJ: Princeton University Press, 1965).

32. Chatterjee, *The Nation and Its Fragments*, pp. 19–20.

33. D. Arnold, *Colonizing the Body: State Medicine and Epidemic Disease in Nineteenth-Century India* (Berkeley, CA: University of California Press, 1993).

34. G. Prakash, 'Body Politic in Colonial India', in T. Mitchell (ed.), *Questions of Modernity* (Minneapolis, MN: University of Minnesota Press, 2000), pp. 189–222. See also V. Prashad, 'The Technology of Sanitation in Colonial Delhi', *Modern Asian Studies*, 35:1 (2001), pp. 113–55; and C. Gupta, *Sexuality, Obscenity, Community: Women, Muslims, and the Hindu Public in Colonial India* (Delhi: Permanent Black, 2001).

35. S. Legg, *Spaces of Colonialism: Delhi's Urban Governmentalities* (Oxford: Blackwell, 2007); P. Joyce, *The Rule of Freedom: Liberalism and the Modern City* (London: Verso, 2003).

36. D. Arnold, *Police Power and Colonial Rule: Madras 1859–1947* (Delhi: Oxford University Press, 1986); Legg, *Spaces of Colonialism*; A. Verma, 'Consolidation of the Raj: Notes from a Police Station in British India, 1865–1928', *Criminal Justice History*, 17 (2002), pp. 109–32.

37. J. S. Duncan, *In the Shadow of the Tropics: Climate, Race and Biopower in Nineteenth Century Ceylon* (Aldershot: Aldgate, 2007).

38. R. Birla, *Stages of Capital: Law, Culture, and Market Governance in Late Colonial India* (Durham, NC: Duke University Press, 2009); M. Goswami, *Producing India: From Colonial Economy to National Space* (Chicago, IL: Chicago University Press, 2004); U. Kalpagam, 'Colonial Governmentality and the "Economy"', *Economy and Society*, 29 (2000), pp. 418–38.

39. M. Foucault, *The Government of Self and Others: Lectures at the Collège de France, 1982–83* (Basingstoke: Palgrave Macmillan, 2010).

40. A. Roy, *Civility and Empire: Literature and Culture in British India, 1822–1922* (London and New York, NY: Routledge, 2006); E. M. Collingham, *Imperial Bodies: The Physical Experience of the Raj, c. 1800–1947* (Cambridge: Polity Press, 2001); D. Heath, *Purifying Empire: Obscenity and the Politics of Moral Regulation in Britain, India and Australia* (Cambridge: Cambridge University Press, 2010).

41. In his work, Foucault wrote comparatively little on the role played by educational institutions in the disciplining of individuals, which no doubt partly explains the absence of Foucauldian enquiries into education in colonial India. However, he was in doubt about the significance of education to the regulation and conduct of behaviour, and the practices of modern governmentalized states. See M. Foucault, *Discipline and Punish: The Birth of the Prison* (London: Allen Lane, 1977); M. Foucault, *Psychiatric Power: Lectures at the Collège de France, 1973–74* (Basingstoke: Palgrave Macmillan, 2006), pp. 63–91; and Foucault, *Security, Territory, Population*, p. 88.

42. S. Seth, *Subject Lessons: The Western Education of Colonial India* (Durham, NC and London: Duke University Press, 2007), p. 2.

43. 'Consideration of the means by which the present highly advanced state of learning and civilization in Europe can be most effectually communicated to the rest of the world and to our Indian Empire in particular', 21 May 1830, Charles Edward Trevelyan Manuscripts, Microfilm Acc. No. 1242, National Archives of India, New Delhi (hereafter Trevelyan Manuscripts).

44. 'The natural process by which a conquered people in an inferior grade of civilization adopt the language and system of learning of their more civilized conquerors', 8 August 1832, Trevelyan Manuscripts.

45. 'The natural process', 8 August 1832, Trevelyan Manuscripts.

46. A. Howell, *Education in British India, prior to 1854, and in 1870–71* (Calcutta: Superintendent of Government Printing, 1872), pp. 116–75.

47. On the use of censuses and colonial science of statistics, see B. S. Cohn, *An Anthropologist among the Historians and Other Essays* (Delhi: Oxford University Press, 1987), pp. 224–54; and K. W. Jones, 'Religious Identity and the Indian Census', in N. G. Barrier (ed.), *The Census in British India: New Perspectives* (New Delhi: Manohar, 1981), pp. 73–102.

48. Studies touching upon the teaching of science in the colonial system include P. Chakrabarti, *Western Science in Modern India: Metropolitan Methods, Colonial Practices* (Delhi: Permanent Black, 2004); and Prakash, *Another Reason*. On the introduction of new pedagogical techniques to India during the period, see B. D. Metcalf, *Islamic Revival in British India: Deoband, 1860–1900* (Princeton, NJ: Princeton University Press, 1982), pp. 100–25; and T. Allender, *Ruling through Education: The Politics of Schooling in the Colonial Punjab* (New Delhi: New Dawn Press, Inc., 2006), pp. 90–122.

49. M. Foucault, 'The Subject and Power', in J. D. Faubion (ed.), *Power. The Essential Works of Foucault 1954–1984* (London: Penguin, 2002), pp. 326–48, on p. 341.

50. Studies focusing on the role of education in the production of Indian nationalism often imply the uncontested advance of western learning in colonial India. See for example, B. McCully, *English Education and the Origins of Indian Nationalism* (Gloucester, MA: Peter Smith Publications, 1966); S. R. Mehrotra, *The Emergence of the Indian National Congress* (Delhi: Vikas Publications, 1971), pp. 51–106; and A. Seal, *The Emergence of Indian Nationalism: Competition and Collaboration in the Later Nineteenth Century* (Cambridge: Cambridge University Press, 1968).

51. J. Habermas, *The Structural Transformation of the Public Sphere: An Inquiry into a Category of Bourgeois Society* (Great Britain: Polity Press, 1989).

52. Habermas, *The Structural Transformation of the Public Sphere*. On the development of 'public opinion', see especially pp. 89–102.

53. C. A. Bayly, *Empire and Information: Intelligence Gathering and Social Communication in India, 1780–1870* (Cambridge: Cambridge University Press, 1996), pp. 199–207.

54. Foucault, *Security, Territory, Population*, p. 350.

55. Foucault, *Security, Territory, Population*, pp. 296–7.

56. Some have argued the existence of implicit possibilities for resistance to disciplinary practices in Foucault's work prior to *The Will to Knowledge*. See for example B. L. Pickett, 'Foucault and the politics of resistance', *Polity*, 28 (1996), pp. 445–66.

57. The watershed moment for governmentality studies in the English-speaking academy was the publication for the first time of a complete translation of Foucault's 1977–8 lectures at the Collège de France. Foucault's eighth lecture in this series was almost exclusively devoted to exploring resistance to the conduct of conduct and the institution of what he termed 'counter-conducts'. In the following year's course the idea of civil society as a transactional domain for the interplay of relations of power between governing and governed parties was developed. No longer can studies of governmentality ignore the contestations likely to accompany attempts to conduct and control. See Foucault, *Security, Territory, Population*, pp. 191–226; and Foucault, *The Birth of Biopolitics*, pp. 291–316.

58. Scott, 'Colonial Governmentality'.

59. Prakash, 'Body Politic in Colonial India'.

60. C. A. Bayly, *Recovering Liberties: Indian Thought in the Age of Liberalism and Empire* (Cambridge: Cambridge University Press, 2012), pp. 104–31.

61. Heath, *Purifying Empire*.

62. Duncan, *In the Shadow of the Tropics*.

63. Arnold, *Colonizing the Body*.

64. U. Kalpagam, 'Colonial Governmentality and the Public Sphere in India', *Journal of Historical Sociology*, 15 (2002), pp. 35–58.

65. Recent studies of governmentality beyond the South Asian context that have emphasized this point include A. Barry, 'Ethical Capitalism', in W. Larner and W. Walters (eds), *Global Governmentality: Governing International Spaces* (London: Routledge, 2004), pp. 195–211; and W. Walters, *Governmentality: Critical Encounters* (London: Routledge, 2012).

66. Metcalf, *Islamic Revival in British India*.

67. U. Sanyal, *Devotional Islam and Politics in British India: Ahmad Riza Khan and His Movement, 1870–1920* (Delhi: Oxford University Press, 1999); Metcalf, *Islamic Revival in British India*, pp. 264–347.

68. G. Minault, *Secluded Scholars: Women's Education and Muslim Social Reform in Colonial India* (Delhi: Oxford University Press, 1998), especially pp. 158–214.

69. See for example H. Malik, *Sir Sayyid Ahmad Khan and Muslim Modernization in India and Pakistan* (New York, NY: Columbia University Press, 1980); R. Hassan, 'Islamic Modernist and Reformist Discourse in South Asia', in S. T. Hunter (ed.), *Reformist Voices of Islam: Mediating Islam and Modernity* (New York, NY: M. E. Sharpe, 2009), pp. 159–86; and A. Ahmad, *Islamic Modernism in India and Pakistan, 1857–1964* (London: Oxford University Press, 1967).

70. The numerous studies of Sayyid Ahmad's religious ideas include B. A. Dar, *Religious Thought of Sayyid Ahmad Khan* (Lahore: Institute of Islamic Culture, 1971); C. W. Troll, *Sayyid Ahmad Khan: A Reinterpretation of Muslim Theology* (New Delhi: Vikas, 1978); and Malik, *Sir Sayyid Ahmad Khan*.

71. N. Green, *Bombay Islam: The Religious Economy of the West Indian Ocean, 1840–1915* (Cambridge: Cambridge University Press, 2011); and J. Jones, *Shi'a Islam in Colonial India: Religion, Community and Sectarianism* (Cambridge: Cambridge University Press, 2012).

72. Scholarship on the causes of the development of understandings of Muslim community in the colonial period is extensive. Useful starting points include F. Robinson, *Separatism among Indian Muslims: The Politics of the United Provinces' Muslims, 1860–1923* (Cambridge: Cambridge University Press, 1974); D. Lelyveld, *Aligarh's First Generation: Muslim Solidarity in British India* (Princeton, NJ: Princeton University Press, 1978); and A. Jalal, *Self and Sovereignty: Individual and Community in South Asian Islam Since 1850* (London: Routledge, 2000). On the role of the colonial state in this process, see Washbrook, 'Ethnicity and Racialism in Colonial Indian Society'; Cohn, *An Anthropologist among the Historians and Other Essays*, pp. 224–54; Jones, 'Religious Identity and the Indian Census'; and Lelyveld, *Aligarh's First Generation*, pp. 9–16.

73. E. W. Said, *Culture and Imperialism* (London: Vintage Books, 1994), pp. 1–72.

74. T. Ballantyne, 'Race and the Webs of Empire: Aryanism from India to the Pacific', *Journal of Colonialism and Colonial History*, 2:3 (2001), pp. 1–25, on p. 4.

75. Metcalf, *Ideologies of the Raj*; U. S. Mehta, *Liberalism and Empire: A Study in Nineteenth-Century British Liberal Thought* (Chicago, IL: Chicago University Press, 1999); J. Pitts, *A Turn to Empire: The Rise of Imperial Liberalism in Britain and France* (Princeton, NJ: Princeton University Press, 2006); Mantena, *Alibis of Empire*.

76. D. Arnold, *Science, Technology and Medicine in Colonial India* (Cambridge: Cambridge University Press, 2000); Chakrabarti, *Western Science in Modern India*.

77. T. Asad, *Genealogies of Religion: Discipline and Reasons of Power in Christianity and Islam* (Baltimore, MD: The John Hopkins University Press, 1993), pp. 27–64; Asad, *Formations of the Secular*, especially pp. 1–66.

78. For example: 'Government institutions ... were founded for the benefit of the whole population of India; and, in order to effect their object, it was, and is, indispensable that the education conveyed in them should be exclusively secular'. *Copy of a Despatch to the Government of India on the Subject of General Education in India*, House of Commons Parliamentary Papers (hereafter HCPP), 1854, 393, xlvii.155, p. 16.

79. On the deployment of the category of the 'secular' in projects of ideological hegemony in colonial Egypt, see Asad, *Formations of the Secular*, pp. 205–56.

80. Foucault, 'The Subject and Power', pp. 340–2.

1 Secular Education and Religious Identity

1. M. Cruickshank, *Church and State in English Education: 1870 to the Present Day* (London: Macmillan & Co., 1964), pp. 1–11; H. C. Barnard, *A History of English Education from 1760* (London: University of London Press, 1960).

2. E. Stokes, *The English Utilitarians and India* (Oxford: Oxford University Press, 1959); T. R. Metcalf, *Ideologies of the Raj* (Cambridge: Cambridge University Press, 1994), pp. 28–30.

3. N. Chatterjee, *The Making of Indian Secularism: Empire, Law and Christianity, 1830–1960* (Basingstoke: Palgrave Macmillan, 2011), pp. 23–50; K. A. Ballhatchet, 'The Home Government and Bentinck's Educational Policy', *Cambridge Historical Journal*, 10:2 (1951), pp. 224–9; P. Spear, 'Bentinck and Education', *Cambridge Historical Journal*, 6:1 (1938), pp. 78–101.

4. G. Viswanathan, *Masks of Conquest: Literary Study and British Rule in India* (London: Faber and Faber, 1990), pp.1–44; G. Studdert-Kennedy, *Providence and the Raj: Imperial Mission and Missionary Imperialism* (New Delhi: Sage, 1998), pp. 61–124.

5. Viswanathan, *Masks of Conquest*, pp. 1–44.

6. Chatterjee, *The Making of Indian Secularism*, pp. 23–50.

7. Resolution of the Governor General of India in Council, 7 March 1835, India Public Consultations, India Office, British Library, London (hereafter IPC), no. 19 of 7 March 1835. On the anglicist-orientalist debate, see D. Kopf, *British Orientalism and the Bengal Renaissance: The Dynamics of Indian Modernization, 1773–1835* (Berkeley, CA: University of California Press, 1969), pp. 215–72; and L. Zastoupil and M. Moir, 'Introduction', in L. Zastoupil and M. Moir (eds), *The Great Indian Education Debate: Documents Relating to the Orientalist-Anglicist Controversy, 1781–1843* (Richmond: Curzon, 1999), pp. 1–72.

8. The sole exception is Donald Smith, who briefly notes in his study of Indian secularism that at stake in discussions of colonial education in the 1830s was the practical application of the government principle of religious neutrality. See D. Smith, *India as a Secular State* (Princeton, NJ: Princeton University Press, 1963), pp. 335–43.

9. Spear, 'Bentinck and Education', pp. 85–95; Zastoupil and Moir, 'Introduction', pp. 5–8; E. H. Cutts, 'The Background of Macaulay's Minute', *American Historical Review*, 58:4 (1953), pp. 824–53.

10. Court of Directors' Revenue Department dispatch to the Governor General in Council, 18 February 1824, in Zastoupil and Moir (eds), *The Great Indian Education Debate*, pp. 115–17, on p. 116.

11. Court of Directors' Revenue Department dispatch to the Governor General in Council, 18 February 1824, in Zastoupil and Moir (eds), *The Great Indian Education Debate*, p. 116. On James Mill as a utilitarian thinker and writer about British India, see J. Majeed, *Ungoverned Imaginings: James Mill's The History of British India and Orientalism* (Oxford: Clarendon Press, 1992).

12. C. Grant, *Observations on the State of Society among the Asiatic Subjects of Great Britain, particularly with Respect to Morals. Written Chiefly in the Year 1792* (n.p.: 1797), pp. 146–222.

13. For example, though Charles Grant favoured the teaching of Christianity to Indian subjects he was also convinced of the potential of English literature and the English language to undermine Indian religion and lead recipients towards Christianity. See Grant, *Observations on the State of Society among the Asiatic Subjects of Great Britain*, pp. 146–81.

14. M. A. Laird, *Missionaries and Education in Bengal, 1793–1837* (Oxford: Clarendon Press, 1972), pp. 44–132.

15. Viswanathan, *Masks of Conquest*, pp. 36–8.

16. Paper written by E. H. East on the foundation of the Hindu College, 18 May 1816, cited in the evidence of W. W. Bird, 30 June 1853, *Second Report from the Select Committee of the House of Lords, Appointed to Enquire into the Operation of the Act 3 & 4 Will. 4, c. 85, for the Better Government of Her Majesty's Indian Territories; And to*

Report their Observations thereon to the House; and to whom Leave was Given to Report from Time to Time to the House; Together with the Minutes of Evidence, and Appendix, House of Commons Parliamentary Papers (hereafter HCPP), 1852–3, 627–I, xxxii.1, pp. 235–253, on pp. 235–7.

17. On the foundation and early years of the Hindu College, see A. F. S. Ahmed, *Social Ideas and Social Change in Bengal, 1818–1835* (Calcutta: Raddhi, 1976), pp. 201–16; Kopf, *British Orientalism and the Bengal Renaissance*, pp. 178–84; and S. N. Mukherjee, 'Class, Caste and Politics in Calcutta, 1815–38', in E. Leach and S. N. Mukherjee (eds), *Elites in South Asia* (London: Cambridge University Press, 1970), pp. 33–78.

18. Preliminary rules for the Calcutta School Book Society, 6 May 1817, evidence of W. W. Bird, 30 June 1853, Appendix B, *Second Report from the Select Committee of the House of Lords*, HCPP, 1852–3, 627–I, xxxii.1, pp. 252–3.

19. Mukherjee, 'Class, Caste and Politics in Calcutta', p. 69.

20. On the growth of positivism in Bengal and the role of the Hindu College in this growth, see G. H. Forbes, *Positivism in Bengal: A Case Study in the Transmission and Assimilation of an Ideology* (Calcutta: Minerva, 1975).

21. A. Duff, *The Rev. Dr. Duff's Letters, Addressed to Lord Auckland, on the Subject of Native Education: With His Lordship's Minute (for the Sake of Reference) Prefixed* (Calcutta: Baptist Mission Press, 1841), pp. 51–75.

22. Bishop of Calcutta to Bentinck, 17 December 1832, Lord William H. Cavendish Bentinck Papers, Portland (Welbeck) Collection, GB 159 Pw Ja-Jg, Department of Manuscripts and Special Collections, University of Nottingham (hereafter Bentinck Papers), Jf 525.

23. Laird, *Missionaries and Education in Bengal*, pp. 179–222.

24. A. Duff, *New Era of the English Language and English Literature in India; Or, an Exposition of the Late Governor-General of India's Last Act, relative to the Promotion of European Literature and Science, through the Medium of the English language, amongst the Natives of that Populous and Extensive Province of the British Empire* (Edinburgh: John Johnstone, 1837); Duff to Bentinck, 18 July 1835, Bentinck Papers, Jf 909.

25. Members of the local committee at Delhi to H. H. Wilson, Secretary to the GCPI, 14 April 1829, Charles Edward Trevelyan Papers, GB 186 CET, Robinson Library, Newcastle University (hereafter Trevelyan Papers), CET 101/1–8.

26. 'The natural process by which a conquered people in an inferior grade of civilization adopt the language and system of learning of their more civilized conquerors', 8 August 1832, Trevelyan Manuscripts.

27. 'The natural process', 8 August 1832, Trevelyan Manuscripts.

28. Note on education by Trevelyan, n.d. [1834], Trevelyan Papers, CET 102.

29. Trevelyan to Bentinck, 20 November 1834, Trevelyan Papers, CET 19/2.

30. Trevelyan to Bentinck, 9 April 1834, Bentinck Papers, Jf 2104.

31. Proceedings of the meeting of the GCPI, 22 October 1834, Correspondence and Proceedings of the General Committee of Public Instruction, State Archives of West Bengal, Kolkata (hereafter GCPICP), Proceedings of the Committee, vol. 1; Minute by H. Shakespear, 27 August 1834, IPC, no. 13 of 7 March 1835.

32. Minute recorded in the General Department by Thomas Babington Macaulay, 2 February 1835, IPC, no. 15 of 7 March 1835.

33. This was more than a coincidence. Macaulay had arrived in India the previous summer with little knowledge of Indian affairs. On the question of education he was advised by Trevelyan over the following months (see for example Trevelyan to Macaulay, 20 September 1834, Trevelyan Papers, CET 19/3). Trevelyan and Macaulay were close

friends and brothers-in-law after Trevelyan married Macaulay's sister, Margaret. (On the relationship between Trevelyan and Macaulay, see J. Clive, *Macaulay: The Shaping of the Historian* (Cambridge, MA: Belknap Press, 1973), especially pp. 289–399.) The origin of Macaulay's minute in Trevelyan's educational plans was noted by contemporaries, including Brian Houghton Hodgson, who recorded that 'the Macaulayism of one cycle is but the Trevelyanism of another. ... Mr. Macaulay's Minute is but a second edition of Mr. Trevelyan's Treatise'. (B. H. Hodgson, *Miscellaneous Essays relating to Indian Subjects*, 2 vols (London: Trubner & Co., 1880), vol. 2, p. 255.) In 1834 Trevelyan's manuscripts on Indian education were published under the title *A Treatise on the Means of Communicating the Learning and Civilization of Europe to India* (Calcutta: Bengal Hurkaru, 1834).

34. Minute Recorded in the General Department by Thomas Babington Macaulay, 2 February 1835, IPC, no. 15 of 7 March 1835.

35. J. C. C. Sutherland, Secretary to the GCPI, to H. T. Prinsep, Secretary to the Government of India, 22 January 1835, IPC, no. 14 of 7 March 1835.

36. Minute by H. T. Prinsep, 15 August 1834, IPC, no. 13 of 7 March 1835.

37. Trevelyan to Bentinck, 9 April 1834, Bentinck Papers, Jf 2104. On Bentinck's career in India, see J. Rosselli, *Lord William Bentinck: The Making of a Liberal Imperialist* (London: Chatto & Windus, 1974); and G. D. Bearce, 'Lord William Bentinck: The Application of Liberalism to India', *Journal of Modern History*, 28:3 (1956), pp. 234–46.

38. Marshman to Bentinck, 9 April 1836, Bentinck Papers, Jf 245.

39. Ryan to Bentinck, 13 January 1831, Bentinck Papers, Jf 1994.

40. Trevelyan to Bentinck, 20 November 1834, Trevelyan Papers, CET 19/2; Note on education by Trevelyan, n. d. [1834], Trevelyan Papers, CET 102.

41. H. T. Prinsep, Secretary to Government, to Rev. James Bryce, 10 February 1835, IPC, no. 32 of 10 February 1835.

42. 'Address by Lord William Bentinck', *Asiatic Journal and Monthly Register for British and Foreign India, China, and Australasia*, 18 (1835), Asiatic Intelligence, pp. 8–9.

43. See chapter three for the impact of this decision on the Calcutta Madrasa and other government colleges teaching Arabic, Persian and Sanscrit subjects.

44. *Copy of a Despatch to the Government of India on the Subject of General Education in India*, HCPP, 1854, 393, xlvii.155.

45. J. Kerr, *A Review of Public Instruction in the Bengal Presidency from 1835 to 1851*, 2 vols (London: W. M. H. Allen & Co., 1853), vol. 1, pp. 57–8.

46. S. C. Ghosh, *Dalhousie in India, 1848–1856: A Study of his Social Policy as Governor-General* (Delhi: Munshiram Manoharlal, 1975), pp. 3–9.

47. Useful introductions to the dispatch include R. J. Moore, *Sir Charles Wood's Indian Policy 1853–66* (Manchester: Manchester University Press, 1966), pp. 108–23; R. J. Moore, 'The Composition of Wood's Education Dispatch', *English Historical Review*, 80:314 (1965), pp. 70–83; and Ghosh, *Dalhousie in India*, pp. 1–32.

48. *Copy of a Despatch to the Government of India on the Subject of General Education in India*, HCPP, 1854, 393, xlvii.155, p. 1.

49. *Copy of a Despatch to the Government of India on the Subject of General Education in India*, HCPP, 1854, 393, xlvii.155, pp. 15–16.

50. Duff, *New Era of the English Language and English Literature in India*, p. 38.

51. Kerr, *A Review of Public Instruction in the Bengal Presidency*, vol. 1, pp. 66–7.

52. [G. Hay], *Minute of the Marquis of Tweeddale, Late-Governor of Madras, on the Introduction of the Bible as a Class-Book into Government Schools in India* (London: Church Missionary House, 1859).

53. Letter from the Public Department, 23 March 1847, *Sixth Report from the Select Com-*

mittee on Indian Territories, together with the Proceedings of the Committee, Minutes of Evidence and Appendix, HCPP, 1852–3, 897, xxix.1, appendix 2, pp. 191–2.

54. Memorial of the Church Missionary Society in reference to the renewal of the powers of the Honourable East India Company, n.d. [May 1852], *Second Report from the Select Committee of the House of Lords*, HCPP, 1852–3, 627–I, xxxii.1, appendix P, p. 621.

55. Evidence of W. W. Bird, 30 June 1853, *Second Report from the Select Committee of the House of Lords*, HCPP, 1852–3, 627–I, xxxii.1, pp. 238–9.

56. Evidence of F. H. Robinson, 13 June 1853, *Fourth Report from the Select Committee on Indian Territories; Together with the Minutes of Evidence and Appendix*, HCPP, 1852–3, 692, xxviii.149, pp. 106–21, on pp. 118–19.

57. Evidence of Thomas Erskine Perry, 26 May 1853, *Second Report from the Select Committee of the House of Lords*, HCPP, 1852–3, 627–I, xxxii.1, pp. 12–28, on p. 25; Evidence of F. J. Halliday, 25 July 1853, *Sixth Report from the Select Committee on Indian Territories*, HCPP, 1852–3, 897, xxix.1, pp. 53–73, on p. 55.

58. On the development of the grant-in-aid system in England, see Cruickshank, *Church and State in English Education*, pp. 3–13; and L. Woodward, *The Age of Reform 1815–70* (Oxford: Clarendon Press, 1962), pp. 474–501.

59. Cruickshank, *Church and State in English Education*, p. 10.

60. Note by J. C. Marshman on Education in India, 12 November 1853, Charles Wood Papers, Mss. Eur. F78, Borthwick Institute, University of York (hereafter Wood Papers), Mss. Eur. F78/25.

61. Draft educational dispatch, n.d. [early 1854], Wood Papers, Mss. Eur. F78/12.

62. Evidence of F. J. Halliday, 25 July 1853, *Sixth Report from the Select Committee on Indian Territories*, HCPP, 1852–3, 897, xxix.1, pp. 54–5; Evidence of W. W. Bird, 30 June 1853, *Second Report from the Select Committee of the House of Lords*, HCPP, 1852–3, 627–I, xxxii.1, pp. 238–9.

63. Note by J. C. Marshman on education in India, 12 November 1853, Wood Papers, Mss. Eur. F78/25.

64. Dalhousie to Wood, 4 October 1853, Wood Papers, Mss. Eur. F78/17. Trevelyan's parliamentary evidence on the subject of Indian education was put directly before Wood as he laboured to reach a decision on the question of grants-in-aid.

65. Evidence of C. E. Trevelyan, 28 June 1853, *Second Report from the Select Committee of the House of Lords*, HCPP, 1852–3, 627–I, xxxii.1, pp. 193–220, on p. 196.

66. Evidence of C. E. Trevelyan, 23 June 1853, *Second Report from the Select Committee of the House of Lords*, HCPP, 1852–3, 627–I, xxxii.1, pp. 167–92, p. 189.

67. Evidence of C. E. Trevelyan, 28 June 1853, *Second Report from the Select Committee of the House of Lords*, HCPP, 1852–3, 627–I, xxxii.1, p. 202.

68. Evidence of C. E. Trevelyan, 23 June 1853, *Second Report from the Select Committee of the House of Lords*, HCPP, 1852–3, 627–I, xxxii.1, pp. 189–92. In a rare minute written on Indian affairs in the 1840s Trevelyan had dwelt at length on Muslim religious antagonism towards British superiority in India: 'We have succeeded, in some degree, in quieting the apprehensions of the Hindoos, but the religious animosity of the Mahomedans burns as fiercely as ever against us. It breaks out from time to time, even in times of profound peace, in the dependant native states, in our own provinces, in our own regiments; and any event which held out a prospect of success, or appeared to the natives so to do, might make it burst out in flames all over India'. Confidential minute on Afghanistan, 14 March 1842, Trevelyan Papers, CET65/1–2.

69. Evidence of C. E. Trevelyan, 28 June 1853, *Second Report from the Select Committee of*

the *House of Lords*, HCPP, 1852–3, 627–I, xxxii.1, p. 204.

70. A. Duff, Brief Memorandum on the Subject of Government Education in India, 25 January 1854, Wood Papers, Mss. Eur. F78/25.

71. Evidence of C. E. Trevelyan, 28 June 1853, *Second Report from the Select Committee of the House of Lords*, HCPP, 1852–3, 627–I, xxxii.1, p. 194. On the relationship between western knowledge and Christianity, see also p. 204: 'The country will have Christian instruction infused into it in every way by direct missionary instruction, and indirectly through books of various kinds, through the public papers, through conversations with Europeans, and in all the conceivable ways in which knowledge is communicated; and then, at last, when society is completely saturated with Christian knowledge, and public opinion has taken a decided turn that way, they will come over by thousands'.

72. Evidence of C. H. Cameron, 7 July 1853, *Second Report from the Select Committee of the House of Lords*, HCPP, 1852–3, 627–I, xxxii.1, pp. 275–90, on p. 285.

73. Wood to Dalhousie, 8 February 1854, Wood Papers, Mss. Eur. F78/LBIV.

74. Wood to Dalhousie, 19 August 1853, Wood Papers, Mss. Eur. F78/LBIII.

75. N. Harte, *The University of London 1836–1986: An Illustrated History* (London: Athlone Press, 1986), pp. 44–118; H. H. Bellot, *The University of London: A History* (Bristol: Western Printing Services, 1969).

76. Harte, *The University of London*, p. 100.

77. Wood to Elphinstone, 24 January 1854, Wood Papers, Mss. Eur. F78/LBIV.

78. Wood to Halliday, 24 July 1854, Wood Papers, Mss. Eur. F78/LBV.

79. *Copy of a Despatch to the Government of India on the Subject of General Education in India*, HCPP, 1854, 393, xlvii.155, pp. 5–16.

80. Trevelyan to Macaulay, 17 April 1854, cited in Moore, 'The Composition of Wood's Education Dispatch', p. 83.

81. T. R. Metcalf, *The Aftermath of Revolt: India 1857–1870* (Princeton, NJ: Princeton University Press, 1965); Metcalf, *Ideologies of the Raj*, pp. 43–65; K. Mantena, *Alibis of Empire: Henry Maine and the Ends of Liberal Imperialism* (Princeton, NJ: Princeton University Press, 2010), pp. 1–55; Stokes, *The English Utilitarians and India*, pp. 268–7.

82. Lord Ellenborough, President of the Board of Control, to the Chairman and Deputy Chairman of the Court of Directors, 28 April 1858, Bengal Education Reports, India Office, British Library, London (hereafter BER), 1857–8, pp. 25–34.

83. [C. E. Trevelyan], *The Letters of Indophilus to 'The Times'* (London: Longman, Brown, Green, Longmans, and Roberts, 1858), pp. 49–50.

84. Minute by F. J. Halliday on Education in India, 19 November 1858, India Education Proceedings, National Archives of India, New Delhi (hereafter IEP), no. 2 of January 1860.

85. Dispatch from the Secretary of State for India, 7 April 1859, in J. A. Richey (ed.), *Selections from Educational Records. Part II: 1840–1859* (Calcutta, Superintendent Government Printing, 1922), pp. 426–50.

86. Lord Ellenborough, President of the Board of Control, to the Chairman and Deputy Chairman of the Court of Directors, 28 April 1858, BER, 1857–8, pp. 32–4. Almost all higher level schools and colleges supported by grants-in-aid in Bengal and the NWP before 1857 were managed by Christian missionaries: for statistics, see A. M. Monteath, 'Note on the State of Education in India (Compiled in 1862)', in P. Kirpal (ed.), *Selections from Educational Records of the Government of India. Volume I. Educational Reports, 1859–71* (Delhi: Government of India, 1960), pp. 1–119, on pp. 69–85. Bengal differed from upper India in that a large number of grants-in-aid had also been awarded to lower level schools under Indian management – a point made in refutation

of Ellenborough by, among others, W. G. Young, the director of public instruction in Bengal. See the marginal notes by Young on Lord Ellenborough's letter, BER, 1857–8, pp. 30–1; and A. Duff, *Lord Ellenborough's Blunder Respecting the Cause of the Mutiny* (Calcutta: Baptist Mission Press, 1857).

87. [Church Missionary Society], *A Memorial to the Queen from the Church Missionary Society, on the Religious Policy of the Government of India. With an Explanatory Statement on the Past and Present Policy of the Indian Government in respect to Religion, and the Education of the Natives* (London: Church Missionary House, 1858), p. 4. See also [Church Missionary Society], *Religious Neutrality in India: Delusive and Impracticable* (London: Church Missionary House, 1858).

88. J. Lawrence, *Despatches by Sir John Lawrence, G.C.B., Chief Commissioner of the Punjab, on Christianity in India. (Reprinted from the 'Times' of October 23rd, 1858.)* (London: Church Missionary House, 1858), p. 3.

89. Minute by F. J. Halliday on Education in India, 19 November 1858, IEP, no. 2 of January 1860.

90. Dispatch from the Secretary of State for India, 7 April 1859, in Richey (ed.), *Selections from Educational Records*, p. 450.

91. Wood to Canning, 11 July 1859, Wood Papers, Mss. Eur. F78/LB1; Wood to Elphinstone, 2 September 1859, Wood Papers, Mss. Eur. F78/LB1; Wood to Trevelyan, 25 June 1859, Wood Papers, Mss. Eur. F78/LB1.

92. [Trevelyan], *The Letters of Indophilus to 'The Times'*, pp. 75–80.

93. Trevelyan to Wood, 28 July 1859, Wood Papers, Mss. Eur. F78/59/1; Trevelyan to Wood, 14 August 1859, Wood Papers, Mss. Eur. F78/59/1.

94. Wood to Canning, 11 July 1859, Wood Papers, Mss. Eur. F78/LB1.

95. House of Commons Hansard, Third Series, vols 101–92 (1848–68) (hereafter HC Hansard), vol. 159, cc. 1237–53; Wood to Canning, 27 June 1860, Wood Papers, Mss. Eur. F78/LB3.

96. Queen Victoria's Proclamation, 1 November 1858, in C. H. Philips (ed.), *The Evolution of India and Pakistan 1858 to 1947: Selected Documents* (London: Oxford University Press, 1962), pp. 10–11.

97. P. Hardy, *The Muslims of British India* (Cambridge: Cambridge University Press, 2007), pp. 62–6.

98. Anon., *What Shall We Do with the Musulmans?* (Calcutta: Sanders, Cones and Co., 1858).

99. E. Arnold, *Education in India: A Letter from the Ex-Principal of an Indian Government College to his Appointed Successor* (London: Bell and Daldy, 1860), pp. 13–16.

100. [Trevelyan], *The Letters of Indophilus to 'The Times'*, p. 75.

101. S. Gopal, *Patna in the 19th Century (A Socio-Cultural Profile)* (Calcutta: B. Mitra, 1996), p. 18

102. Memorandum by the Commissioner of Patna Suggesting Measures for the Diffusion of Knowledge in the Patna Division, n.d., Bengal General Proceedings, State Archives of West Bengal, Kolkata, no. 158 of 28 August 1856.

103. Tayler to the Secretary to the Government of Bengal, 11 July 1857, *Correspondence Connected with the Removal of Mr. W. Tayler from the Commissionership of Patna* (Calcutta: John Gray, 1858), pp. 39–41.

104. W. S. Atkinson, Director of Public Instruction, to the Secretary to the Government of Bengal, 20 September 1860, Bengal Education Proceedings, India Office, British Library, London (hereafter BEP), no. 13 of October 1860.

105. Secretary to the Government of Bengal, to W. S. Atkinson, Director of Public Instruction, 4 October 1860, BEP, no. 15 of October 1860.

2 Education, Religion and State in Ireland and India

1. Resolution of the Government of India on Muslim Education, 7 August 1871, *Selections from the Records of the Government of India, Home Department No. CCV: Correspondence on the Subject of the Education of the Muhammadan Community in British India and their Employment in the Public Service Generally* (Calcutta: Superintendent of Government Printing, 1886), p. 152.

2. W. W. Hunter, *The Indian Musalmans* (1871) (Lahore: Sang-e-Meel Publications, 1999).

3. Hunter, *The Indian Musalmans,* p. 146.

4. Hunter, *The Indian Musalmans,* p. 174.

5. Note on Muslim Education, 26 June 1871, Lord Mayo Papers, Add. MS 7490, Manuscripts Department, Cambridge University Library (hereafter Mayo Papers (India)), Ms. 7490/9/39.

6. See for example F. Robinson, *Separatism Among Indian Muslims: The Politics of the United Provinces' Muslims, 1860–1923* (Cambridge: Cambridge University Press, 1974), pp. 99–100. Robinson suggests that 'the most important source of British awareness' of Indian Muslims was 'the threat they presented to the security of the Raj' and references Hunter's text as confirmation of this point.

7. F. H. Skrine, *Life of Sir William Wilson Hunter, K.C.S.I., M.A., LL.D., a Vice-President of the Royal Asiatic Society, etc.* (London: Longmans, Green and Co., 1901), p. 199.

8. Correspondence in Mayo Papers (India) reveals that the first copy of *Indian Musalmans* to reach India was sent by its author to J. F. Stephen, law member of Mayo's council, and arrived in September 1871 with the request that it be forwarded to the viceroy. In England the book had been read by Stephen's predecessor, Henry Maine, who left India in 1869 and occupied a position on the council of the secretary of state for India. On the day that the arrival of the text in India was first noted, 20 September 1871, J. P. Norman, officiating chief justice of the Calcutta High Court and the man responsible for hearing the appeals of the seven Wahabi suspects convicted at Patna earlier that year, was killed on the steps on the court. Though extensive investigations uncovered no evidence of a connection between the assassin, a Pathan named Abdullah and the Wahabis, the event was widely considered to be a further manifestation of Wahabi conspiracy and induced something akin to panic in the British community in India. News of the assassination greatly increased public interest in Hunter's book in England, provoking a second edition to be swiftly published. However, in Mayo's council the possible harm to be done by the circulation of the text was discussed. Notes passed between Mayo, J. F. Stephen and John Strachey indicate that the idea of censuring *Indian Musalmans* was entertained but rejected by government. Lord Mayo, who admitted to having read only half of the book, recorded that its suppression might prove practically impossible. Official opinion on Hunter's text was far from universally favourable. The lieutenant governor of the North-Western Provinces (hereafter NWP), William Muir, suggested to Mayo that *Indian Musalmans* was 'not only exaggerated but misguided', adding that it 'appears to me calculated to do much mischief, and create panic and alienation on both sides'. Muir's assessment shared much in common with that of the most prominent Muslim educationalist in the NWP, Sayyid Ahmad Khan. On the assassination of Norman, see Mayo Papers (India), Ms. 7490/39. For reaction to Hunter's book, see Stephen to Mayo, 20 September 1871, Mayo Papers (India), Ms. 7490/140/35; Strachey to Mayo, 21 September 1871, Mayo Papers (India), Ms. 7490/141/207; Mayo to Strachey, 22 September 1871, Mayo Papers (India), Ms. 7490/158/214; Muir to Mayo, 11 November 1871, Mayo Papers (India), Ms.

7490/128/181; and S. A. Khan, *Review on Dr. Hunter's Indian Musalmans: Are They Bound in Conscience to Rebel against the Queen?* (Benares: 1872).

9. 'The Assassination of the Earl of Mayo Viceroy and Governor-General of India', Lord Mayo Papers, Collection List No. 126, National Library of Ireland, Dublin (hereafter Mayo Papers (Ireland)), Ms. 5,167.

10. See Mayo Papers (India), Ms 7490/9/39.

11. T. Ballantyne, 'Race and the Webs of Empire: Aryanism from India to the Pacific', *Journal of Colonialism and Colonial History*, 2:3 (2001), pp. 1–25, on p. 1. Ballantyne suggests a need to reimagine the geographies of the British Empire to take account of the mobile and intertextual nature of imperial knowledge. The metaphor of the 'web' suggests networks for the transmission of ideas, ideologies and identities between metropolitan centre and colonial periphery and also, importantly, between different colonial sites. Indeed, Ballantyne suggests, we might see the empire as an agglomeration of overlapping webs with multiple 'sub-imperial' centres and peripheries. See especially pp. 1–8.

12. On the transfer of nationalist ideas between Ireland and India, see M. Silvestri, *Ireland and India: Nationalism, Empire and Memory* (Basingstoke: Palgrave Macmillan, 2009); J. M. Wright, *Ireland, India and Nationalism in Nineteenth Century Literature* (Cambridge University Press, 2009); K. O'Malley, *Ireland, India and Empire: Indo-Irish Radical Connections, 1919–64* (Manchester: Manchester University Press, 2009); and most of the essays in T. Foley and M. O'Connor (eds), *Ireland and India: Colonies, Culture and Empire* (Dublin: Irish Academic Press, 2006). On aspects of government and administration, see S. B. Cook, *Imperial Affinities: Nineteenth Century Analogies and Exchanges between India and Ireland* (New Delhi: Sage Publications, 1993); N. Mansergh, *The Prelude to Partition: Concepts and Aims in Ireland and India* (Cambridge: Cambridge University Press, 1978); and several of the essays in Foley and O'Connor's volume. For an insightful overview, see C. A. Bayly, 'Ireland, India and Empire: 1780–1914', *Transactions of the Royal Historical Society, Sixth Series*, 10 (2000), pp. 377–97.

13. C. Boylan, 'Victorian Ideologies of Improvement: Sir Charles Trevelyan in India and Ireland', in T. Foley and M. O'Connor (eds), *Ireland and India: Colonies, Culture and Empire* (Dublin: Irish Academic Press, 2006), pp. 167–78. Bayly's 'Ireland, India and Empire' includes a suggestive passage on another Irish peer and Indian viceroy, Lord Dufferin. See pp. 389–92.

14. Lord Mayo was born Richard Southwell Bourke and styled Lord Naas between 1842 and 1867, when he became the sixth earl of Mayo. For clarity I refer to him as Lord Mayo throughout, the title by which he was most commonly known during his viceroyalty.

15. W. W. Hunter, *A Life of the Earl of Mayo, Fourth Viceroy of India*, 2 vols (London: Smith, Elder, & Co., 1875), vol. 1, p. 73. Hunter's two volume biography of Mayo, published three years after his death, remains an important source of information on the Irish and Indian periods of Mayo's career. See also G. Pottinger, *Mayo: Disraeli's Viceroy* (Wilton: Michael Russell, 1990).

16. E. W. Said, *Culture and Imperialism* (London: Vintage Books, 1994), p. 1.

17. Mayo to Strachey, 21 June 1869, Mayo Papers (India), Ms. 7490/149/123.

18. On the establishment and development of the national education system in Ireland, see D. H. Akenson, *The Irish Education Experiment: The National System of Education in the Nineteenth Century* (London: Routledge & Kegan Paul, 1970). The principles upon which the national system was to be established were outlined by Lord Stanley, chief secretary for Ireland, in a letter to the duke of Leinster in October 1831. As Stanley notes, as early as 1812 an Irish education commission had recommended the establish-

ment of a system 'from which should be banished even the suspicion of proselytism, and which, admitting children of all religious persuasions, should not interfere with the peculiar tenets of any'. Lord Stanley to the Duke of Leinster, October 1831, in A. Hyland and K. Milne (eds), *Irish Educational Documents. A Selection of Extracts from Documents Relating to the History of Irish Education from the Earliest Times to 1922*(Dublin: C.I.C.E., 1987), pp. 98–103, on p. 99.

19. A. Shields, *The Irish Conservative Party, 1852–68: Land, Politics and Religion* (Dublin: Irish Academic Press, 2007), p. 108.

20. House of Commons Hansard, Third Series (hereafter HC Hansard), vol. 101, c. 320, 21 August 1848

21. HC Hansard, vol. 101, c. 316, 21 August 1848.

22. HC Hansard, vol. 106, cc. 675–708, 21 June 1849; vol. 112, cc. 153–220, 21 June 1850.

23. HC Hansard, vol. 112, c. 220, 21 June 1850.

24. HC Hansard, vol. 126, cc. 603–4, 26 April 1853.

25. HC Hansard, vol. 126, c. 604, 26 April 1853.

26. Akenson, *The Irish Education Experiment*, pp. 244–74.

27. HC Hansard, vol. 126, c. 604, 26 April 1853: 'It could not be denied', Mayo argued, 'that the rules had been so framed that almost the whole Roman Catholic children of Ireland were included in the schools, and that their effect had been to deprive an influential minority of the advantages of the system'.

28. HC Hansard, vol. 126, c. 604, 26 April 1853.

29. Shields, *The Irish Conservative Party*, p. 144.

30. HC Hansard, vol. 155, c. 305, 22 July 1859; Eglington to Mayo, 19 February 1859, Mayo Papers (Ireland), Ms. 11,031/16; Eglington to Mayo, 22 February 1859, Mayo Papers (Ireland), Ms. 11,031/17.

31. HC Hansard, vol. 189, c. 918, 5 August 1867. See also the draft for the appointment of the royal commission in Mayo's notes: the commission, Mayo noted, was to enquire 'how far the rules of the said National System may be relaxed in reference to religious education so as to enable the Patrons and Friends of Schools of Elementary or Primary Education in Ireland more extensively to avail themselves of the Public Grants for Education in Ireland and to act without conflict with the National System'. Mayo Papers (Ireland), Ms. 43,876/3.

32. The Royal (Powis) Commission produced its final report in May 1870. See Hyland and Milne (eds), *Irish Educational Documents*, pp. 121–7.

33. O. T. Burne, *Memories* (London: Edward Arnold, 1907), p. 86.

34. A. M. Monteath, 'Note on the State of Education in India, 1865–66', in P. Kirpal (ed.), *Selections from Educational Records of the Government of India. Volume I. Educational Reports, 1859–71* (Delhi: Government of India, 1960), pp. 121–298, on p. 149.

35. Burne, *Memories*, p. 86.

36. Note on Muslim Education, 26 June 1871, Mayo Papers (India), Ms. 7490/9/39; E. C. Bayley to the Secretary to the Government of Bengal, 7 August 1871, Bengal Education Proceedings, India Office, British Library, London (hereafter BEP), no. 71 of August 1872.

37. Note on Muslim Education, 26 June 1871, Mayo Papers (India), Ms. 7490/9/39.

38. Note on Muslim Education, 26 June 1871, Mayo Papers (India), Ms. 7490/9/39.

39. T. W. Moody, 'The Irish University Question of the Nineteenth Century', *History*, 43 (1958), pp. 90–109.

40. HC Hansard, vol. 187, cc. 1433–4, 31 May 1867.

41. Strictly Confidential Memorandum on the Catholic University Question, n.d., Mayo

Papers (Ireland), Ms. 43,878/1. Though undated, we can be fairly sure when this memorandum was completed from its forwarding to Disraeli in February 1868. Mayo to Disraeli, 5 February 1868, Benjamin Disraeli Papers (Dep. Hughenden, 1–382), Bodleian Library, University of Oxford (hereafter Disraeli Papers), 90/2, 180–1.

42. Mayo to the Attorney General for Ireland, 3 December 1867, Mayo Papers (Ireland), Ms. 11,217/1; Derby to Mayo, 27 December 1867, Mayo Papers (Ireland), Ms. 43,877/2.
43. HC Hansard, vol. 190, cc. 1381–6, 10 March 1868.
44. Mayo to Disraeli, 11 January 1851, Disraeli Papers, 90/2, 6–9.
45. HC Hansard, vol. 188, c. 55, 18 June 1867.
46. Mayo to the Attorney General for Ireland, 3 December 1867, Mayo Papers (Ireland), Ms. 11,217/1.
47. HC Hansard, vol. 188, cc. 70–1, 18 June 1867.
48. HC Hansard, vol. 187, c. 1440, 31 May 1867; vol. 189, c. 230, 26 July 1867.
49. HC Hansard, vol. 188, c. 67, 18 June 1867.
50. HC Hansard, vol. 190, c. 1382, 10 March 1868.
51. Strictly Confidential Memorandum on the Catholic University Question, n.d., Mayo Papers (Ireland), Ms. 43,878/1.
52. Shields, *The Irish Conservative Party*, pp. 189–92.
53. HC Hansard, vol. 187, c. 101, 7 May 1867.
54. HC Hansard, vol. 187, c. 158, 7 May 1867.
55. HC Hansard, vol. 187, c. 163, 7 May 1867.
56. HC Hansard, vol. 191, cc. 871–2, 3 April 1868; vol. 192, c. 808, 22 May 1868.
57. HC Hansard, vol. 190, c. 1391, 10 March 1868. See also Mayo's notes towards this speech, Mayo Papers (Ireland), Ms. 11,217/2.
58. HC Hansard, vol. 191, cc. 871–2, 3 April 1868.
59. HC Hansard, vol. 192, cc. 807–8, 22 May 1868.
60. Hunter, *A Life of the Earl of Mayo,* vol. 1, pp. 92–3.
61. Mayo to Disraeli, 2 May 1869, Disraeli Papers, 90/3, 95–100; Mayo to Disraeli, 30 May 1871, Disraeli Papers, 90/3, 139–44.
62. W. F. Monypenny and G. E. Buckle, *The Life of Benjamin Disraeli, Earl of Beaconsfield,* 2 vols (London: John Murray, 1929), vol. 2, pp. 345–58.
63. HC Hansard, vol. 190, c. 1764, 16 March 1868.
64. Mayo to Disraeli, 3 January 1869, Disraeli Papers, 90/3, 86–94.
65. Note on Muslim Education, 26 June 1871, Mayo Papers (India), Ms. 7490/9/39.
66. Resolution of the Government of India on Muslim Education, 7 August 1871, *Selections from the Records of the Government of India, Home Department No. CCV*, p. 152.
67. Mayo referred to Wood's dispatch for confirmation of the principle that Arabic and Sanscrit languages and literature might be taught in government institutions 'without any instruction being given in the tenets of either the Hindoo or the Mahomedan religions'. Note on Muslim Education, 26 June 1871, Mayo Papers (India), Ms. 7490/9/39.
68. HC Hansard, vol. 155, cc. 304–5, 22 July 1859.
69. Strictly Confidential Memorandum on the Catholic University Question, n.d., Mayo Papers (Ireland), Ms. 43,878/1.
70. Hunter, *The Indian Musalmans,* p. 179.
71. H. C. Bowen, *Muhammadanism: Its Present Condition and Influence in India* (London: Macmillan and Co., 1873), p. 10.
72. 'Our Mussalman Subjects', *The Spectator*, 19 August 1871, p. 7.
73. Moody, 'The Irish University Question of the Nineteenth Century', p. 97.

74. Hunter, *The Indian Musalmans,* pp. 203–5.
75. On Palgrave, see M. Allan, *Palgrave of Arabia: The Life of William Gifford Palgrave, 1826–88* (London: Macmillan, 1972); and G. Nash, *From Empire to Orient: Travellers to the Middle East, 1830–1926* (London: I.B. Tauris, 2005), pp. 66–73. Palgrave's *Narrative of a Year's Journey Through Central and Eastern Arabia (1862–63)* (London: Macmillan and Co., 1865) was an important resource for officials seeking to understand the origins and doctrinal tenets of the Wahabi movement in India. See J. Talboy's Wheeler, Memorandum on the Wahabees, Mayo Papers (India), Ms. 7490/39/3.
76. W. G. Palgrave, *Essays on Eastern Questions* (London: Macmillan and Co., 1872), pp. 111–41.
77. R. H. Davison, *Reform in the Ottoman Empire, 1856–1876* (Princeton, NJ: Princeton University Press, 1963); and D. Quataert, *The Ottoman Empire, 1700–1922* (Cambridge: Cambridge University Press, 2000), pp. 89–109, 172–91.
78. Davison, *Reform in the Ottoman Empire,* pp. 244–50.
79. Palgrave, *Essays on Eastern Questions,* pp. 116–7.
80. Palgrave, *Essays on Eastern Questions,* p. 140.
81. A. C. Lyall, *Asiatic Studies: Religious and Social* (London: John Murray, 1882), pp. 228–57. On Lyall as representative of his generation of colonial officials and his writings about the Indian Rebellion of 1857–8, see A. Padamsee, *Representations of Indian Muslims in British Colonial Discourse* (Basingstoke: Palgrave Macmillan, 2005), pp. 72–102.
82. Lyall, *Asiatic Studies,* p. 251.
83. Lyall, *Asiatic Studies,* p. 252. Lyall noted the failure of existing policy in this regard: 'It would have been wiser to permit Musalmans ... to graduate in Oriental classics; and we might have continued ample State provision for the religious education of their youth, according to the course of study approved by their customs and their religion'. Lyall, *Asiatic Studies,* p. 249.
84. Lyall, *Asiatic Studies,* pp. 258–86.
85. Lyall, *Asiatic Studies,* p. 273.

3 The Calcutta Madrasa and Muslim Education in Bengal

1. Minute by Warren Hastings, 17 April 1781, Bengal Public Consultations, India Office, British Library, London, 18 April 1781. On the foundation and early years of the Calcutta Madrasa, see S. C. Sanial, 'History of the Calcutta Madrassa', *Bengal Past and Present,* 8 (1914), pp. 83–111, 225–50; and C. Lushington, *The History, Design and Present State of the Religious, Benevolent and Charitable Institutions, founded by the British in Calcutta and its Vicinity* (Calcutta: Hindostanee Press, 1824), pp. 136–41.
2. On the *dars-i-nizami* curriculum in South Asian madrasas, see F. Robinson, *The 'Ulama of Farangi Mahall and Islamic Culture in South Asia* (London: Hurst & Company, 2001), pp. 14–5.
3. Minute of the Governor General, Warren Hastings, 21 January 1785, Sanial, 'History of the Calcutta Madrassa', Appendix C, p. 109.
4. Minute by Cecil Beadon, 26 April 1852, *Selections from the Records of the Government of Bengal, No. 14: Papers relating to the Establishment of the Presidency College of Bengal* (Calcutta: Military Orphan Press, 1854), Appendix V, pp. xxvii–xxxii, on p. xxvii.
5. The Madrasa and Sanscrit College at Benares were what James Mill had in mind when in 1824 he announced that the object of colonial educational efforts 'should not have been to teach Hindoo learning, or Mahomedan learning, but useful learning'. (Court of Directors'

Revenue Department Dispatch to the Governor General in Council, 18 February 1824, in L. Zastoupil and M. Moir (eds), *The Great Indian Education Debate: Documents Relating to the Orientalist-Anglicist Controversy, 1781–1843* (Richmond: Curzon, 1999), p. 116.

6. Matthew Lumsden, Acting Secretary to the Madrasa, to the Members of the Madrasa Committee, 30 May 1823, Bengal Revenue Consultations, India Office, British Library, London (hereafter BRC), no. 15, 3 July 1823.

7. Matthew Lumsden, Secretary to Madrasa Subcommittee, to the General Committee of Public Instruction (hereafter GCPI), 29 March 1824, East India Company Board of Control Records, India Office, British Library, London (hereafter Board Records), vol. 909, no. 25694, pp. 683–6.

8. Matthew Lumsden, Acting Secretary to the Madrasa, to the Members of the Madrasa Committee, 30 May 1823, BRC, no. 15 of 3 July 1823.

9. Matthew Lumsden, Secretary to the Madrasa Subcommittee, to the GCPI, 19 February 1825, Board Records, vol. 909, no. 25695, p. 720.

10. Proceedings of Madrasa Subcommittee, 16 March 1829, General Committee of Public Instruction, State Archives of West Bengal, Kolkata (hereafter GCPICP), Proceedings of the Committee, vol. 5, part 1, p. 368.

11. Report of the Proceedings of the GCP, 27 October 1831, GCPICP, Proceedings of the Committee, vol. 5, part 2, pp. 489–95.

12. For a list of translations undertaken with the patronage of the GCPI between 1823 and 1831, see the report of the proceedings of the GCPI, 27 October 1831, GCPICP, Proceedings of the Committee, vol. 5, part 2, pp. 489–95.

13. List of Students Who Have Left the Madrasa and the Nature of Their Employment, 22 April 1840, GCPICP, Proceedings of the Committee, vol. 5. part 2, pp. 671–80.

14. Minute by Charles Trevelyan Presented at GCPI Meeting on 8 June 1833, GCPICP, Proceedings of the Committee, vol. 2, pp. 57–9.

15. Minute by Charles Trevelyan, 4 February 1834, C. E. Trevelyan et al., *The Application of the Roman Alphabet to All the Oriental Languages; Contained in a Series of Papers Written by Messrs. Trevelyan, J. Prinsep, and Tytler, Rev. A. Duff, and Mr. H.T. Prinsep and Published in Various Calcutta Periodicals in the Year 1834* (Serampore: Serampore Press, 1834), pp. 37–8.

16. Minute by Charles Trevelyan Presented at GCPI Meeting on 8 June 1833, GCPICP, Proceedings of the Committee, vol. 2, pp. 60–1.

17. Note on Education by Trevelyan, n.d., [1834], Trevelyan Papers, CET 102.

18. Proceedings of Madrasa Subcommittee Meeting, 20 April 1834, India Public Consultations, India Office, British Library, London (hereafter IPC), no. 11, 7 March 1835. Minutes by GCPI members were recorded on the resolution in the period July–September 1834 and can be found in IPC, nos. 10 and 13 of 7 March 1835.

19. Minute by H. T. Prinsep, 9 July 1834, IPC, no. 10, 7 March 1835.

20. Proceedings of Meeting of the GCPI, 21 March 1835, GCPICP, Proceedings of the Committee, vol. 2, pp. 87–90.

21. Minute by Lieutenant Colonel William Morison, 18 February 1835, IPC, no. 17, 7 March 1835.

22. Extract from the diary of H. T. Prinsep, n.d., in H. Sharp (ed.), *Selections from Educational Records. Part I: 1781–1839* (Calcutta, Superintendent Government Printing, 1920), pp. 132–4.

23. Petition of the Mussulman Inhabitants of Calcutta and its Environs, n.d., IPC, no. 9, 13 March 1835. According to the index to the consultations, this petition was dated 21

February 1835. See Zastoupil and Moir (eds), *The Great Indian Education Debate*, p. 192.

24. Note by H. T. Prinsep, 15 February 1835, Zastoupil and Moir (eds), *The Great Indian Education Debate*, pp. 174–88; Minute by H. T. Prinsep, 20 May 1835, IPC, no. 8 of 3 June 1835.

25. 'I give my entire concurrence to the sentiments expressed in this Minute', wrote Bentinck, at the bottom of the copy of Macaulay's minute in the government consultations. See IPC, no. 15, 7 March 1835.

26. Draft Resolution on Education, n.d., Bentinck Papers, Jf 1334.

27. Resolution of the Governor General of India in Council, 7 March 1835, IPC, no. 19, 7 March 1835.

28. H. T. Prinsep, Secretary to the Government of India, to the Muslim Petitioners, 9 March 1835, IPC, no. 10, 13 March 1835.

29. H. T. Prinsep, Secretary to the Government of India, to the Muslim Petitioners, 9 March 1835, IPC, no. 10, 13 March 1835.

30. Petition of the Moosliman Inhabitants of Bengal, n.d., IPC, no. 17, 24 August 1836; Minute by the Governor General, 24 August 1836, IPC, no. 20, 24 August 1836; James Prinsep to H. H. Wilson, 5 July 1838, H. H. Wilson Papers, Mss. Eur. E301, India Office, British Library, London, Mss. Eur. E301/3/139–40.

31. Minute by the Governor General on the Promotion of Education among the Natives of India, 24 November 1839, IPC, no. 2, 8 January 1840.

32. Matthew Lumsden, Acting Secretary to the Madrasa, to the Members of the Madrasa Committee, 30 May 1823, BRC, no. 15, 3 July 1823.

33. Matthew Lumsden, Secretary to Madrasa Subcommittee, to the GCPI, 29 March 1824, Board Records, vol. 909, no. 25694, pp. 683–6.

34. A. Duff, *The Rev. Dr. Duff's Letters, Addressed to Lord Auckland, on the Subject of Native Education: With his Lordship's Minute (for the Sake of Reference) Prefixed* (Calcutta: Baptist Mission Press, 1841), pp. 51–75.

35. *Report of the General Committee of Public Instruction of the Presidency of Fort William in Bengal, for the year 1836* (Calcutta: Baptist Mission Press, 1837), pp. 82–8.

36. '[T]he great object of the students in the Sanscrit and Arabic Colleges of the Government has been to rise to office as Law Pundits and Moulvies in the Courts. *The knowledge which gains for men reputation and profit among the Native community, as great religious Teachers, or among the Hindoos as proficients in Astrology, is not to be acquired at those Colleges,* and will best be obtained elsewhere from private Native instructors'. Minute by the Governor General on the Promotion of Education among the Natives of India, 24 November 1839, IPC, no. 2, 8 January 1840, my emphasis. Auckland's role overseeing the removal of religious subjects from the Arabic course of the Madrasa was later recounted by Frederick Halliday, then a member of the GCPI. See the evidence of F. J. Halliday, 25 July 1853, *Sixth Report from the Select Committee on Indian territories,* House of Commons Parliamentary Papers (hereafter HCPP), 1852–3, 897, xxix.1, pp. 56–7.

37. F. J. Mouat, Secretary to the Council of Education, to Cecil Beadon, Secretary to the Government of Bengal, 4 August 1853, *Selections from the Records of the Government of Bengal,* pp 1–30, on p. 2.

38. On Sprenger's career, and in particular his time as principal of the Delhi College, see G. Minault, 'Aloys Sprenger: German Orientalism's "Gift" to Delhi College', *South Asia Research*, 31:1 (2011), pp. 7–23; and M. I. Chaghatai, 'Dr Aloys Sprenger and the Delhi College', in M. Pernau (ed.), *The Delhi College: Traditional Elites, the Colonial State, and Education before 1857* (New Delhi: Oxford University Press, 2006), pp. 105–24.

39. F. J. Mouat, Secretary to the Council of Education, to the Government of Bengal, 4 January 1851, Bengal Education Consultations, India Office, British Library, London (hereafter BEC), no. 3, 29 January 1851.

40. Minault, 'Aloys Sprenger'.

41. A. Sprenger, 'Plan of Study for the Mudrissa', *Selections from the Records of the Government of Bengal,* Appendix 4, pp. xvi–xxiii, on p. xvi.

42. A. Sprenger, *The Life of Mohammad, from Original Sources* (Allahabad: Presbyterian Mission Press, 1851), pp. 1, 44, 91.

43. Sprenger, 'Plan of Study for the Mudrissa', *Selections from the Records of the Government of Bengal*, Appendix 4, p. xix.

44. A. Sprenger, *A Catalogue of the Arabic, Persian and Hindu'sta'ny Manuscripts, of the Libraries of the King of Oudh, Compiled by Order of the Government of India* (1854) (Osnabruck: Biblio Verlag, 1979), p. xiii.

45. On the Delhi College, see G. Minault, 'Qiran al-Sa'adain: The Dialogue between Eastern and Western Learning at Delhi College', in J. Malik (ed.), *Perspectives of Mutual Encounters in South Asian History, 1760–1860* (Leiden: Brill, 2000), pp. 260–77; M. Hasan, *A Moral Reckoning: Muslim Intellectuals in Nineteenth-Century Delhi* (New Delhi: Oxford University Press, 2007), pp. 115–27; and the collection of essays in M. Pernau (ed.), *The Delhi College: Traditional Elites, the Colonial State, and Education before 1857* (New Delhi: Oxford University Press, 2006).

46. F. Boutros to C. Beadon, 24 January 1851, BEC, no. 11, 26 March 1851.

47. A. A. Powell, 'Scholar Manqué or Mere Munshi? Maulawi Karimu'd-Din's Career in the Anglo-Oriental Education Service', in M. Pernau (ed.), *The Delhi College: Traditional Elites, the Colonial State, and Education before 1857* (New Delhi: Oxford University Press, 2006), pp. 203–31, on p. 208.

48. 'Three Remarks on the Education of the Natives of India', *Friend of India*, 4 April 1844 and 11 April 1844.

49. Chaghatai, 'Dr Aloys Sprenger and the Delhi College', pp. 115–9.

50. Sprenger, 'Plan of Study for the Mudrissa', *Selections from the Records of the Government of Bengal*, Appendix 4, pp. xviii–xxi.

51. List of Books Prepared in Urdu at Delhi, *Selections from the Records of the Government of Bengal*, Appendix 5, p. l.

52. Sprenger, 'Plan of Study for the Mudrissa', *Selections from the Records of the Government of Bengal*, Appendix 4, pp. xvi–xx.

53. M. S. Dodson, *Orientalism, Empire and National Culture: India, 1770–1880* (Basingstoke: Palgrave Macmillan, 2007), pp. 87–117.

54. Sprenger, 'Plan of Study for the Mudrissa', *Selections from the Records of the Government of Bengal*, Appendix 4, p. xvi.

55. Sprenger, 'Plan of Study for the Mudrissa', *Selections from the Records of the Government of Bengal*, Appendix 4, pp. xvi–xx.

56. M. Pernau, 'Introduction: Entangled Translations: The History of the Delhi College', in M. Pernau (ed.), *The Delhi College: Traditional Elites, the Colonial State, and Education before 1857* (New Delhi: Oxford University Press, 2006), pp. 1–31, on p. 25.

57. S. Liddle, 'Azurda: Scholar, Poet and Judge', in M. Pernau (ed.), *The Delhi College: Traditional Elites, the Colonial State, and Education before 1857* (New Delhi: Oxford University Press, 2006), pp. 125–44, on p. 130.

58. Sprenger, 'Plan of Study for the Mudrissa', *Selections from the Records of the Government of Bengal*, Appendix 4, p. xviii.

59. Minute by Cecil Beadon, 26 April 1852, *Selections from the Records of the Government of Bengal*, Appendix 5, p. xxx.
60. Minute by J. W. Colville, 3 March 1852, *Selections from the Records of the Government of Bengal*, Appendix 5, pp. xxv–xxvi, on p.xxv.
61. Minute by J. W. Colville, 3 March 1852, *Selections from the Records of the Government of Bengal*, Appendix 5, p. xxv.
62. Minute by F. J. Halliday, 16 March 1852, *Selections from the Records of the Government of Bengal*, Appendix 5, p. xxvi.
63. Cecil Beadon, Secretary to the Government of Bengal, to F. J. Mouat, Secretary to the Council of Education, 21 October 1853, *Selections from the Records of the Government of Bengal*, pp. 31–38, on p. 35.
64. 'Disturbance in the Mudrissa', *Selections from the Records of the Government of Bengal*, Appendices 2 and 3, pp. viii–xv, on pp. ix–x.
65. F. Hayes, Officiating Secretary to the Council of Education, to J. P. Grant, Secretary to the Government of Bengal, 26 March 1851, BEC, no. 7, 2 April 1851.
66. 'Disturbance in the Mudrissa', *Selections from the Records of the Government of Bengal*, Appendices 2 and 3, p. ix.
67. W. N. Lees, Principal, Calcutta Madrasa, to W. G. Young, Director of Public Instruction, 11 May 1858, India Education Proceedings, National Archives of India, New Delhi (hereafter IEP), nos 1–8, July 1860.
68. W. N. Lees, *A Biographical Sketch of the Mystic Philosopher and Poet Jami Being the Preface to his 'Lives of the Mystics'* (Calcutta: W. N. Lees's Press, 1859).
69. W. N. Lees, Principal, Calcutta Madrasa, to W. S. Atkinson, Director of Public Instruction, 1 September 1860, Bengal Education Proceedings, India Office, British Library, London (hereafter BEP), no. 18, March 1864.
70. Principal's Report on the Calcutta Madrasa, 26 June 1855, IEP, no. 2a, April 1870.
71. Under-Secretary to the Government of Bengal, to the Director of Public Instruction, 15 September 1855, IEP, no. 2a, April 1870.
72. F. Halliday, *Minute by F.J. Halliday on Necessary Reforms at the Madrusseh, or Mahommedan College, Calcutta* (Calcutta: 1858).
73. Halliday, *Minute by F.J. Halliday on Necessary Reforms at the Madrusseh.*
74. W. G. Young, Director of Public Instruction, to C. T. Buckland, Junior Secretary to the Government of Bengal, 15 October 1858, IEP, nos. 1–8, July 1860; G. Smith, Doveton College, Calcutta, to the Government of Bengal, 12 March 1858, Bengal Education Reports, India Office, British Library, London (hereafter BER), 1857–8, Appendix D.
75. Secretary's Note on the Proposal of the Lieutenant Governor of Bengal to Abolish the Arabic Department of the Calcutta Madrasa, 6 December [1858], IEP, nos 1–8 of July 1860.
76. Minute by Lord Canning, 20 June 1860, IEP, nos 1–8 of July 1860.
77. Secretary's Note on the Proposal of the Lieutenant Governor of Bengal to Abolish the Arabic Department of the Calcutta Madrasa, 6 December [1858], IEP, nos 1–8 of July 1860.
78. Secretary's Note on the Proposal of the Lieutenant Governor of Bengal to Abolish the Arabic Department of the Calcutta Madrasa, 6 December [1858], IEP, nos 1–8 of July 1860.
79. Evidence of C. E. Trevelyan, 28 June 1853, *Second Report from the Select Committee of the House of Lords*, HCPP, 1852–3, 627–I, xxxii.1, p. 197; Brief Memorandum on the Subject of Government Education in India by Alexander Duff, 25 January 1854, Charles Wood Papers, Mss. Eur. F78, Borthwick Institute, University of York, Mss. Eur. F78/25.
80. W. N. Lees, Principal, Calcutta Madrasa, to W. S. Atkinson, Director of Public Instruction, 1 September 1860, BEP, no. 18, March 1864.

81. The Muslim teachers of the Madrasa, Lees recorded, had been informed that those of them 'who tenaciously adhere to teaching their pupils to commit to memory, like so many parrots, the texts of a certain number of class books – a system that has long since been exploded in Europe – have no business here'. W. N. Lees, Principal, Calcutta Madrasa, to W. S. Atkinson, Director of Public Instruction, 1 September 1860, BEP, no. 18 of March 1864.

82. Examination Paper for the First and Second Class of the Madrasa, cited in the Report of the Madrasa Reform Committee, 1 December 1869, BEP, January 1870, Appendix A.

83. William Nassau Lees to the Director of Public Instruction, 11 December 1862, IEP, no. 2a, April 1870.

84. Maulvi Abdul Majid to Matthew Lumsden, n.d. [February 1824], GCPICP, Proceedings of the Committee, vol. 4, pp. 154–8.

85. 'Disturbance in the Mudrissa', *Selections from the Records of the Government of Bengal*, Appendices 2 and 3, pp. x–xi.

86. 'Disturbance in the Mudrissa', *Selections from the Records of the Government of Bengal*, Appendices 2 and 3, p. xi.

87. W. N. Lees, Principal, Calcutta Madrasa, to W. S. Atkinson, Director of Public Instruction, 1 September 1860, BEP, no. 18, March 1864.

88. W. N. Lees, Principal, Calcutta Madrasa, to the Secretary to the Government of Bengal, 4 February 1870, IEP, no. 2, April 1870.

89. S. R. Mehrotra, *The Emergence of the Indian National Congress* (Delhi: Vikas Publications, 1971), pp. 1–106.

90. M. Fisher, 'The Office of Akhbar Nawis: The Transition from Mughal to British Forms', *Modern Asian Studies*, 27:1 (1993), pp. 45–82.

91. Minault, 'Qiran al-Sa'adain', pp. 268–72.

92. M. Pernau, 'From a 'Private' Public to a 'Public' Private Sphere: Old Delhi and the North Indian Muslims in Comparative Perspective', in G. Mahajan (ed.), *The Public and the Private: Issues of Democratic Citizenship* (New Delhi: Sage Publications, 2003), pp. 103–29, on p. 111.

93. R. Ahmed, *The Bengal Muslims 1871–1906: A Quest for Identity* (New Delhi: Oxford University Press, 1988); A. K. Chakraborty, *Bengali Muslim Literati and the Development of Muslim Community in Bengal* (Shimla: Indian Institute of Advanced Study, 2002); T. M. Murshid, *The Sacred and the Secular: Bengal Muslim Discourses, 1871–1977* (Calcutta: Oxford University Press, 1995).

94. Little previous research has been undertaken into the Anjuman-i-Islam. See M. Y. Abbasi, *Muslim Politics and Leadership in South Asia, 1876–92* (Islamabad: Institute of Islamic History, Culture and Civilization, 1981), pp. 50–1; and Mehrotra, *The Emergence of the Indian National Congress*, pp. 212–16.

95. Ahmed, *The Bengal Muslims*, p. 36; Chakraborty, *Bengali Muslim Literati and the Development of Muslim Community in Bengal*, pp. 14–15.

96. 'The Mahomedan Association', *The Englishman*, 8 May 1855.

97. 'Unjuman-i-Islamee, or Mahomedan Association', *The Englishman*, 1 November 1855.

98. 'The Education of Moonsiffs', *Friend of India*, 11 October 1855.

99. 'Unjuman-i-Islamee, or Mahomedan Association', *The Englishman*, 1 November 1855.

100. 'Unjuman-i-Islamee, or Mahomedan Association', *The Englishman*, 1 November 1855.

101. 'Mahomedan Reform Association', *Friend of India*, 26 July 1855.

102. Address to Her Majesty the Queen by the Mahomedan Association of Calcutta, 14 November 1858, in J. K. Majumdar (ed.), *Indian Speeches and Documents on British Rule*,

1821–1918 (Calcutta: Longmans, Green & Co., 1937), pp. 79–81.

103. 'Unjuman-i-Islamee, or Mahomedan Association', *The Englishman*, 1 November 1855.

104. Report of the Bengal Council of Education for the Year 1843–4, *Second Report from the Select Committee of the House of Lords*, HCPP, 1852–3, 627–I, xxxii.1, Appendix N, pp. 511–13.

105. A. Latif, 'A Short Account of My Public Life', *Nawab Bahadur Abdul Latif, C.I.E.* (Calcutta: Thacker Spink & Co., n.d. [1915]), pp. 165–206, on p. 199.

106. A. Latif, 'A Minute on the Hooghly Mudrussah Written at the Request of the Hon'ble Sir J. P. Grant, K.C.B., Lieutenant Governor of Bengal', in E. Haque (ed.), *Nawab Bahadur Abdul Latif: His Writings & Related Documents* (Dacca: Samudra Prokashani, 1968), pp. 19–42, on p. 20.

107. Latif, 'A Minute on the Hooghly Mudrussah', p. 22.

108. M. Ali, *Short Essays by Moulvee Mohommed Ulli, An English Teacher of the Calcutta Government Madrassa College* (Calcutta: I.C. Bose & Co., 1858).

109. Latif, 'A Minute on the Hooghly Mudrussah', pp. 23–4.

110. A. Latif, *A Paper on Mahomedan Education in Bengal Read by Mouvlie Abdool Luteef Khan Bahadoor at the Second Session of the Bengal Social Science Association, Held at the Town Hall of Calcutta, on the 30th January 1868* (Calcutta: 1868), pp. 15–17.

111. MLS to the Madrasa Reform Committee, 22 September 1869, BEP, January 1870, Appendix A.

112. [Mahomedan Literary Society], *A Quarter Century of the Mahomedan Literary Society of Calcutta. A Resumé of its Work from 1863 to 1869, etc.* (Calcutta: 1889), p. 6.

113. [Mahomedan Literary Society], *A Quarter Century of the Mahomedan Literary Society of Calcutta*, p. 6.

114. A. Latif, 'A Short Account of My Humble Efforts to Promote Education, specially among the Mahomedans', in E. Haque (ed.), *Nawab Bahadur Abdul Latif: His Writings & Related Documents* (Dacca: Samudra Prokashani, 1968), pp. 187–242, on p. 196.

115. [Mahomedan Literary Society], *A Quarter Century of the Mahomedan Literary Society of Calcutta*, p. 7.

116. Latif, *A Paper on Mahomedan Education in Bengal*, pp. 15–7.

117. W. N. Lees, Principal, Calcutta Madrasa, to the Secretary to the Government of Bengal, 4 February 1870, IEP, no. 2, April 1870.

118. W. N. Lees to the Director of Public Instruction, 21 May 1864, IEP, no. 2a, April 1870.

119. On the specific charges levelled against Lees, including his mixing of the accounts of the Calcutta Madrasa with those of his private printing press, see 'The Abuses in Warren Hastings' Madrissa', *Friend of India*, 17 February 1870.

120. Responses to the Madrasa reform committee are collected in *Selections from the Records of the Government of India, Home Department No. CCV*, pp. 1–149, and BEP, January 1870, Appendix A.

121. MLS to the Madrasa Reform Committee, 22 September 1869, BEP, January 1870, Appendix A.

122. Mahomedan Improvement Association, Mirzapur, to the Madrasa Reform Committee, 8 September 1869, *Selections from the Records of the Government of India, Home Department No. CCV*, pp. 134–5; Scientific Society of Bihar, Muzaffarpur, to the Madrasa Reform Committee, 17 September 1869, *Selections from the Records of the Government of India, Home Department No. CCV*, pp. 106–8.

123. Sayyid Amir Hossain to the Madrasa Reform Committee, 9 September 1869, *Selections from the Records of the Government of India, Home Department No. CCV*, pp. 141–2; Mu-

hammad Allahdad Khan to the Madrasa Reform Committee, 19 November 1869, *Selections from the Records of the Government of India, Home Department No. CCV*, pp. 97–101.

124. Sayyid Serajooddeen Ahmad to the Madrasa Reform Committee, 22 September 1869, *Selections from the Records of the Government of India, Home Department No. CCV*, pp. 101–2.

125. Inhabitants of Gaya to the Madrasa Reform Committee, n.d., *Selections from the Records of the Government of India, Home Department No. CCV*, p. 104; Inhabitants of Patna to the Madrasa Reform Committee, n.d., *Selections from the Records of the Government of India, Home Department No. CCV*, pp. 121–2; Inhabitants of Patna to the Madrasa Reform Committee, n.d., *Selections from the Records of the Government of India, Home Department No. CCV*, p. 123.

126. Evidence of Maulvi Muhammad Ilahdad, 14 August 1869, *Selections from the Records of the Government of India, Home Department No. CCV*, p. 60.

127. Evidence of Maulvi Golam Kadir, 17 August 1869, *Selections from the Records of the Government of India, Home Department No. CCV*, p. 63; Evidence of Qazi Abdul Bari, 31 August 1869, *Selections from the Records of the Government of India, Home Department No. CCV*, pp. 75–7.

128. Petition of Muhammad Bajuir and Other Students, 4 October 1869, *Selections from the Records of the Government of India, Home Department No. CCV*, pp. 129–34, on p. 131.

129. Evidence of Maulvi Gholam Yehyiah, 28 August 1869, *Selections from the Records of the Government of India, Home Department No. CCV*, pp. 74–5.

130. Evidence of Maulvi Murhumut Hossain, 25 August 1869, *Selections from the Records of the Government of India, Home Department No. CCV*, p. 72; Evidence of Fuzl-I Ali, 24 August 1869, *Selections from the Records of the Government of India, Home Department No. CCV*, pp. 70–1.

131. Pernau, 'Introduction', p. 25.

132. Evidence of Maulvi Muhammad Mazhar, 25 August 1869, *Selections from the Records of the Government of India, Home Department No. CCV*, p. 71.

133. Latif, *A Paper on Mahomedan Education in Bengal*, p. 6.

134. MLS to the Madrasa Reform Committee, 22 September 1869, BEP, January 1870, Appendix A.

135. Petition of Students of the Arabic Department of the Madrasa, n.d., *Selections from the Records of the Government of India, Home Department No. CCV*, pp. 135–8.

136. Murhumut Hossain to the Madrasa Reform Committee, 1 September 1869, *Selections from the Records of the Government of India, Home Department No. CCV*, p. 101–2.

137. Ameer Ali to the Madrasa Reform Committee, 2 September 1869, *Selections from the Records of the Government of India, Home Department No. CCV*, pp. 102–4.

138. Scientific Society of Bihar, Muzaffarpur, to the Madrasa Reform Committee, 17 September 1869, *Selections from the Records of the Government of India, Home Department No. CCV*, p. 107.

139. W. N. Lees, *Indian Musalmans: Being Three Letters Reprinted from the 'Times', with an Article on the Late Prince Consort and Four Articles on Eucation, Reprinted from the 'Calcutta Englishman'* (London: William and Norgate, 1871). See also W. N. Lees to the Director of Public Instruction, 4 September 1866, IEP, no. 2a, April 1870.

140. MLS to the Madrasa Reform Committee, 22 September 1869, BEP, January 1870, Appendix A.

141. Ameer Ali to the Madrasa Reform Committee, September 1869, *Selections from the Records of the Government of India, Home Department No. CCV*, p. 103.

142. Latif, 'A Short Account of My Humble Efforts to Promote Education', p. 210.

143. R. H. Wilson, Officiating Under-Secretary to the Government of Bengal, to the Direc-

tor of Public Instruction, 29 September 1871, BEP, no. 37, September 1871.

144. Note by C. Bernard, Officiating Secretary to the Government of Bengal, 22 January 1872, *Selections from the Records of the Government of India, Home Department No. CCV*, pp. 186–7.

145. W. S. Atkinson, Director of Public Instruction, to the Secretary to the Government of Bengal, 12 January 1872, BEP, no. 91, August 1872.

146. R. H. Wilson, Under-Secretary to the Government of Bengal, to J. Sutcliffe, 29 September 1871, BEP, no. 38, September 1871.

147. W. S. Atkinson, Director of Public Instruction, to the Secretary to the Government of Bengal, 12 January 1872, BEP, no. 91, August 1872; J. Sutcliffe to R. H. Wilson, Officiating Under Secretary to the Government of Bengal 8 November 1871, BEP, no. 83, August 1872.

148. Note by C. Bernard, Officiating Secretary to the Government of Bengal, 22 January 1872, *Selections from the Records of the Government of India, Home Department No. CCV*, pp. 186–7.

149. Minute by G. Campbell on Education in Government Schools, 4 December 1871, BEP, no. 14, December 1871.

150. C. Bernard, Officiating Secretary to the Government of Bengal, to the Director of Public Instruction, 30 August 1872, BEP, no. 96, August 1872.

151. Report of the Madrasa Reform Committee, 1 December 1869, BEP, January 1870, Appendix A.

152. Minute by George Campbell, Lieutenant Governor, 13 April 1871, BEP, no. 41, April 1871.

153. Nawab Abdul Latif, Secretary to the Committee for the Supervision and Management of the Calcutta and Hooghly Madrasas, to the Director of Public Instruction, 16 June 1871, BEP, no. 6, August 1871.

154. G. C. Kozlowski, *Muslim Endowments and Society in British India* (Cambridge: Cambridge University Press, 1985), p. 131–55; K. Zachariah, *History of the Hooghly College, 1836–1936* (Alipore: Bengal Government Press, 1936); J. Kerr, *A Review of Public Instruction in the Bengal Presidency from 1835 to 1851*, 2 vols (London: W. M. H. Allen & Co., 1853), vol. 2, pp. 96–107.

155. Note by C. Bernard, 12 January 1872, *Selections from the Records of the Government of India, Home Department No. CCV*, p. 176.

156. Latif, 'A Minute on the Hooghly Mudrussah', pp. 37–40.

157. Petition of the Mahomedans of Hooghly, 15 August 1869, *Selections from the Records of the Government of India, Home Department No. CCV*, p. 122.

158. Resolution of the Government of Bengal, 17 August 1872, BEP, no. 67, August 1872.

159. C. Bernard, Officiating Secretary to the Government of Bengal, to the Secretary to the Government of India, 17 August 1872, *Selections from the Records of the Government of India, Home Department No. CCV*, pp. 171–4, on p. 173.

160. Resolution of the Government of Bengal, 29 July 1873, BEP, no. 87, August 1873.

161. C. Bernard, Officiating Secretary to the Government of Bengal, to the Director of Public Instruction, 30 August 1872, BEP, no. 152, August 1872.

162. C. Bernard, Secretary to the Government of Bengal, to the Commissioners of Rajshahye, Dacca and Chittagong, 11 September 1873, BEP, no. 87 (10), September 1873.

163. Muslim responses thanking the Bengal government for this decision included M. Obaidulla, *The Madrasah Scheme* (Calcutta: Urdoo Guide Press, 1873) and Latif, 'A Short Account of My Humble Efforts to Promote Education', p. 216.

164. BER, 1874–5, pp. 98–104.

4 Religious Education and State Withdrawal in the Punjab

1. Punjab Education Reports, India Office, British Library, London (hereafter PER), 1885–6, pp. 7–8.

2. *Report of the Indian Education Commission Appointed by the Resolution of the Government of India Dated 3ʳᵈ February 1882* (Calcutta: Superintendent of Government Printing, 1883), pp. 44–6.

3. S. A. Khan, *Translation of the Report of the Members of the Select Committee for the Better Diffusion and Advancement of Learning among Muhammadans in India* (Benares: Medical Hall Press, 1872), pp. 2–3.

4. Abdul Latif to Sayyid Ahmad, n.d. [1863], in Y. Husain (ed.), *Selected Documents from the Aligarh Archives* (London: Asia Publishing House, 1967), pp. 6–7.

5. D. Lelyveld, *Aligarh's First Generation: Muslim Solidarity in British India* (Princeton, NJ: Princeton University Press, 1978), pp. 102–46; S. Y. Shah, *Higher Education and Politics in Colonial India: A Study of Aligarh Muslim University (1875–1920)* (Delhi: Renaissance, 1996), pp. 139–71; M. S. Jain, *The Aligarh Movement* (New Delhi: Icon Publications, 2006), pp. 1–128.

6. Khan, *Translation of the Report*, pp. 8–30.

7. [Muhammadan Anglo-Oriental College Management Committee], *Scheme for the Proposed Mahomedan Anglo-Oriental College* (n.p., n.d. [1872]).

8. A. A. Powell, *Scottish Orientalists and India: The Muir Brothers, Religion, Education and Empire* (Woodbridge: The Boydell Press, 2010), pp. 232–9.

9. [Muhammadan Anglo-Oriental College Management Committee], *Scheme of Studies for the Mahomedan Anglo-Oriental College, Aligarh* (Benares: Medical Hall Press, 1875).

10. Sayyid Ahmad participated in the activities of the Delhi Vernacular Translation Society while based at Delhi in the later 1840s. In 1846 he translated a Persian treatise on mathematics into Urdu. The preface of the work acknowledged his debt to Aloys Sprenger. See M. I. Chaghatai, 'Dr Aloys Sprenger and the Delhi College', in M. Pernau (ed.), *The Delihi College: Traditional Elites, the Colonial State, and Education before 1857* (New Delhi: Oxford University Press, 2006), pp. 121–2.

11. Speech by Sayyid Ahmad before the MLS, October 1863, in S. Muhammad (ed.), *The Aligarh Movement. Basic Documents: 1864–1898*, 3 vols (Meerut: Meenakshi Prakashan, 1978), vol. 1, p. 3.

12. Lelyveld, *Aligarh's First Generation*, pp. 113–8.

13. T. Allender, *Ruling through Education: The Politics of Schooling in the Colonial Punjab* (New Delhi: New Dawn Press, Inc., 2006), pp. 17–53; H. R. Mehta, *A History of the Growth and Development of Western Education in the Punjab, 1846–1884* (Punjab: Govt Record Office, 1971), pp. 30–1.

14. A. M. Monteath, 'Note on the State of Education in India, 1865–66', in P. Kirpal (ed.), *Selections from Educational Records of the Government of India. Volume I. Educational Reports, 1859–71* (Delhi: Government of India, 1960), pp. 167–9.

15. PER, 1861–2, p. 16.

16. 'Report of the Anjuman-i-Punjab for the year 1865', *Lahore Chronicle*, 13 January 1866, pp. 28–9.

17. F. Mir, *The Social Space of Language: Vernacular Culture in British Colonial Punjab* (Berkeley, CA: University of California Press, 2010), pp. 56–61.

18. 'Report of the Anjuman-i-Punjab for the year 1865', *Lahore Chronicle*, 13 January 1866, pp. 28–9.

19. S. M. Latif, 'A Brief Account of the History and Operations of the Anjuman-i-Punjab from its Foundation in 1865 to the End of the Year 1877', Supplement to the *Civil and Military Gazette*, Lahore, 12 January 1878.

20. 'Report of the Anjuman-i-Punjab for the Year 1865', *Lahore Chronicle*, 13 January 1866, pp. 28–9.

21. T. H. Thornton, Secretary to the Government of the Punjab, to E. C. Bayley, Secretary to the Government of India, 27 May 1868, *Reports and Correspondence on Progress of Education in India, 1866–70*, House of Commons Parliamentary Papaers (hereafter HCPP), 1870, 397, lii.1, pp. 312–5.

22. Notification No. 472 on the Creation of the Lahore Government College, 8 December 1869, in J. P. Naik (ed.), *Selections from Educational Records of the Government of India Vol. II. Development of University Education, 1860–87* (Delhi: Government of India, 1963), pp. 58–63.

23. Allender, *Ruling through Education*, pp. 123–57.

24. J. M. Diamond, 'The Orientalist-Literati Relationship in the Northwest: G. W. Leitner, Muhammad Hussain Azad and the Rhetoric of Neo-Orientalism in Colonial Lahore', *South Asia Research*, 31:1 (2011), pp. 25–43, on p. 28; T. Allender, 'Bad Language in the Raj: The "Frightful Encumbrance" of Gottlieb Leitner, 1865–1888', *Paedagogica Historica*, 43:3 (2007), pp. 383–403, on p. 388.

25. J. M. Diamond, 'Narratives of Reform and Displacement in Colonial Lahore: The *Inti-kaal* of Muhammad Hussain Azad', *Journal of Punjab Studies*, 16:2 (2009), pp. 159–77.

26. Diamond, 'The Orientalist-Literati Relationship in the Northwest', pp. 31–7.

27. G. W. Leitner, *The Theory and Practice of Education with Special Reference to Education in India* (Lahore: Indian Public Opinion Press, n.d. [1870]), pp. 29–30.

28. Leitner, *The Theory and Practice of Education*, p. 30.

29. G. W. Leitner, *A Lecture on the Races of Turkey (Both of Europe and Asia,) and the State of their Education: Being, Principally, a Contribution to Muhammadan Education* (Lahore: Indian Public Opinion Press, 1871), p. 7.

30. For biographical details, see J. H. Stocqueler, *A Review of the Life and Labours of Dr G. W. Leitner* (Brighton: Tower Press, 1875); and C. Whitehead, *Colonial Educators: The British Indian and Colonial Education Service, 1858–1983* (London: I.B. Tauris, 2003), pp. 33–4.

31. On the teaching of Muslim law at the Punjab University College and the appeals of Got-tlieb Leitner and Punjabi Muslim elites for the wider application of *shari'at* in colonial courts, see R. Ivermee, 'Shari'at and Muslim Community in Colonial Punjab, 1865–85', *Modern Asian Studies*, 48:4 (2014), pp. 1068–95. Many of the individuals negotiating co-lonial educational provisions in this period were also involved in an ultimately successful campaign for the appointment of *qazis* (Muslim law officers) by the Punjab government and the more extensive administration of *shari'at* in the colonial judicial system.

32. Leitner, *The Theory and Practice of Education*, p. 31.

33. O. Chadwick, *The Secularization of the European Mind in the Nineteenth Century* (Cambridge: Cambridge University Press, 1975), pp. 229–37.

34. Evidence of G. W. Leitner, n.d., *Report by the Panjab Provincial Committee; With Evi-dence Taken before the Committee, and Memorials Addressed to the Education Commis-sion* (Calcutta: Supt. of Govt. Printing, 1884), pp. 352–87, on p. 358.

35. A. Howell, *Education in British India, prior to 1854, and in 1970–71* (Calcutta: Super-intendent of Government Printing, 1872), pp. 34–5.

36. Howell, *Education in British India*, pp. 95–104.

37. Leitner, *The Theory and Practice of Education*, p. 30.

38. Evidence of G. W. Leitner, n.d., *Report by the Panjab Provincial Committee*, p. 352.
39. Evidence of G. W. Leitner, n.d., *Report by the Panjab Provincial Committee*, p. 352. The term 'laïcité' was enshrined in French law in 1905.
40. PER, 1871–2, p. 7.
41. Evidence of G. W. Leitner, n.d., *Report by the Panjab Provincial Committee*, p. 364.
42. G. W. Leitner, *History of Indigenous Education in the Panjab Since Annexation and in 1882* (Calcutta: Superintendent of Government Printing, 1882), part 1, p. 5.
43. G. W. Leitner, 'Native Self-Government in Matters of Education', *Journal of the East India Association*, 9 (1876), pp. 1–46, on p. 14.
44. Leitner, 'Native Self-Government in Matters of Education', pp. 14–5.
45. Evidence of G. W. Leitner, n.d., *Report by the Panjab Provincial Committee*, pp. 354–8.
46. Powell, *Scottish Orientalists and India*, pp. 226–7.
47. Leitner, *History of Indigenous Education*, part 1, p. 14.
48. Leitner, *History of Indigenous Education*, part 1, p. 25.
49. Evidence of G. W. Leitner, n.d., *Report by the Panjab Provincial Committee*, pp. 354–6.
50. Latif, 'A Brief Account of the History and Operations of the Anjuman-i-Punjab'.
51. C. Pearson, Officiating Registrar of the Punjab University College, to the Officiating Secretary to the Government of the Punjab, 8 July 1872, Punjab Home Proceedings, India Office, British Library, London (hereafter PHP), no. 37, April 1872.
52. Views of the Muhammadan Members of the Senate, n.d. [1872], PHP, no. 37, April 1872.
53. Evidence of the Anjuman-i-Punjab, 15 July 1882, *Report by the Panjab Provincial Committee*, pp. 505–16, on p. 505.
54. Resolution of the Anjuman-i-Punjab on the Subject of Religious Education, 4 December 1880, *Report by the Panjab Provincial Committee*, p. 585.
55. Memorandum by Muhammad Latif on Muhammadan Education in India, n.d. [1882], *Selections from the Records of the Government of India, Home Department No. CCV*, pp. 310–2.
56. Evidence of Rahim Khan, n.d., *Report by the Panjab Provincial Committee*, pp. 414–21, on p. 415.
57. Leitner to Lytton, 12 December 1876, First Earl of Lytton Papers as Viceroy of India, Mss. Eur. E218, India Office, British Library, London, Mss. Eur. E218/30/23.
58. Resolution of the Government of India Appointing the Education Commission, February 1882, *Report of the Indian Education Commission*, Appendix A, pp. 623–8, on p. 625.
59. A. Jalal, *Self and Sovereignty: Individual and Community in South Asian Islam Since 1850* (London: Routledge, 2000) pp. 114–22.
60. *Report by the Panjab Provincial Committee*, pp. 126–602.
61. E. D. Churchill, 'Muslim Societies of the Punjab, 1860–1890', *Panjab Past and Present*, 8:1 (1974), pp. 69–91, on p. 77; N. G. Barrier, 'Muslim Politics in the Punjab, 1870–1890', *Panjab Past and Present*, 5:1 (1971), pp. 84–127, on p. 86.
62. Muhammad Barkat Ali Khan, Secretary to the Anjuman-i-Islam, Lahore, to the Secretary to the Government of the Punjab, 1 August 1882, *Selections from the Records of the Government of India, Home Department No. CCV*, pp. 314–8.
63. Churchill, 'Muslim Societies of the Punjab', pp. 77–8.
64. *Aligarh Institute Gazette*, 15 December 1891.
65. In 1893 the MAO College was attended by 324 students, 218 of whom derived from the NWP and 87 from the Punjab. See *Aligarh Institute Gazette*, 18 July 1903. For a more extensive enquiry into the derivation of Aligarh students, see Lelyveld, *Aligarh's First Generation*, pp. 179–85.
66. Evidence of G. W. Leitner, n.d., *Report by the Panjab Provincial Committee*, p. 384.

67. Evidence of the Anjuman-i-Punjab, 15 July 1882, *Report by the Panjab Provincial Committee*, pp. 505–6.
68. Evidence of the Lahore Arya Samaj, n.d., *Report by the Panjab Provincial Committee*, pp. 466–85, on p. 473.
69. Evidence of the Anjuman-Hamdardi-Islamia, n.d., *Report by the Panjab Provincial Committee*, pp. 132–40, on p. 132.
70. Evidence of the Anjuman-i-Islam, Amritsar, n.d., *Report by the Panjab Provincial Committee*, pp. 146–9, on p. 147.
71. Evidence of Mirza Fath Muhammad Beg, n.d., *Report by the Panjab Provincial Committee*, pp. 209–11, on p. 211.
72. *Report of the Indian Education Commission*, pp. 585–602.
73. J. Johnston, *Abstract and Analysis of the Report of the 'Indian Education Commission', with Notes, and 'The Recommendations' in Full* (London: Hamilton, Adams & Co., 1884), pp. 66–81.
74. Evidence of J. G. Cordery, n.d., *Report by the Panjab Provincial Committee*, pp. 184–91, on p. 185.
75. Evidence of W. Coldstream, n.d., *Report by the Panjab Provincial Committee*, p. 174–194, on p. 80; Evidence of Rev. Worthington Jukes, n.d., *Report by the Panjab Provincial Committee*, pp. 296–303, on p. 297.
76. *Report by the Bengal Provincial Committee; with Evidence Taken before the Committee, and Memorials Addressed to the Education Commission* (Calcutta: Supt. of Govt. Printing, 1884), pp. 209–12; see especially questions 4, 6, 7, 8, 16, 17, 18, 23, 24, 36, 37, 38, 49, 64, 68, 69 and 70.
77. W. W. Hunter to the Secretary to the Government of the Punjab, n.d., Punjab Education Proceedings, India Office, British Library, London (hereafter PEP), no. 4, July 1882; *Report of the Indian Education Commission*, pp. 621–2.
78. Evidence of W. R. M. Holroyd, n.d., *Report by the Panjab Provincial Committee*, pp. 592–602.
79. *Report of the Indian Education Commission*, pp. 585–602.
80. Speech of Lord Ripon to the members of the MAO College Fund Committee, 18 November 1884, in Muhammad (ed.), *The Aligarh Movement*, vol. 3, pp. 716–26, on p. 723.
81. L. Wolf, *Life of the First Marquess of Ripon, K.G., P.C., G.C.S.I, D.C.I., etc*, xx vols (London: John Murray, 1921), vol. 1, pp. 230–6; A. Denholm, *Lord Ripon 1827–1909: A Political Biography* (London: Croom Helm, 1982), pp. 87–8.
82. Speech at Bishop Cotton School, Simla, 25 September 1880, in K. P. S. Gupta (ed.), *Speeches of the Marquis of Ripon, Viceroy and Governor General of India*, xx vols (Calcutta: Star Press, 1883), vol. 1, pp. 23–6, on p. 24.
83. Hunter to Primrose, 25 December 1882, Ripon Papers, Ms. Add. 43,617, Western Manuscripts, British Library, London (hereafter Ripon Papers), Ms. Add. 43,617/121.
84. Hunter to Primrose, 28 September 1882, Ripon Papers, Ms. Add. 43, 617/113.
85. Hunter to Primrose, 28 September 1882, Ripon Papers, Ms. Add. 43, 617/113.
86. *Report of the Indian Education Commission*, pp. 483–507.
87. W. W. Hunter to Sayyid Ahmad, 4 July 1882, Muhammad (ed.), *The Aligarh Movement*, vol. 2, p. 512.
88. Hunter to Ripon, 5 April 1883, Ripon Papers, Ms. Add. 43,617/125.
89. A. Croft, *Review of Education in India in 1886, with Special Reference to the Report of the Education Commission* (Calcutta: Superintendent of Government Printing, 1888), pp. 343–4.

90. PER, 1885–6, pp. 7–8.
91. Minute of the Lieutenant Governor on the Punjab Education Report of 1881–2, n.d., PEP, no. 1, November 1882.
92. See the collection of correspondence in PEP, no. 22, March 1884.
93. K. W. Jones, *Socio-Religious Reform Movements in British India. The New Cambridge History of India III.1* (Cambridge: Cambridge University Press, 1989), p. 98; Churchill, 'Muslim Societies of the Punjab', p. 77.
94. On the Anjuman-i-Himayat-i-Islam, see particularly [Anon.], *Anjuman-i-Himayat-i-Islam Lahore: A Short History and Account of its Constructive Activities* (Lahore: Anjuman-i-Himayat-i-Islam, n.d.); and S. R. Wasti, *Muslim Struggle for Freedom in British India* (Delhi: Renaissance Publishing House, 1993), pp. 218–29. Both Ayesha Jalal and Kenneth Jones have erred in suggesting that the Anjuman-i-Himayat-i-Islam was founded in 1866. Jones writes that the Anjuman was established by Muhammad Shafi and Mian Shah Din – supporters of Sayyid Ahmad Khan – in this year. Muhammad Shafi and Mian Shah Din were born in 1869 and 1868 respectively, studied law in England and were active in the foundation of the London Anjuman-i-Islam in 1889. Both returned to the Punjab in the early 1890s to become leading public figures in the cause of Muslim educational progress. See Jalal, *Self and Sovereignty*, p. 53; Jones, *Socio-Religious Reform Movements in British India*, p. 95; and on Muhammad Shafi and Mian Shah Din, S. M. Ikram, *Indian Muslims and Partition of India* (New Delhi: Atlantic Publishers, 1992), pp. 216–19.
95. Wasti, *Muslim Struggle for Freedom in British India*, pp. 220–3.
96. *Anjuman-i-Himayat-i-Islam Lahore*, pp. 9–10; M. S. Din, 'Mohamedan Societies in the Punjab', *Indian Magazine*, 208 (1888), pp. 186–92, on p. 191.
97. *Anjuman-i-Himayat-i-Islam Lahore*, pp. 9–10.
98. *Report of the Indian Education Commission*, pp. 194–7.

5 The Campaign for a Muslim University

1. G. Minault and D. Lelyveld, 'The Campaign for a Muslim University, 1898–1920', *Modern Asian Studies*, 8:2 (1974), pp. 145–89, on p. 145.
2. Minault and Lelyveld, 'The Campaign for a Muslim University', p. 145.
3. S. Y. Shah, *Higher Education and Politics in Colonial India: A Study of Aligarh Muslim University (1875–1920)* (Delhi: Renaissance, 1996), p. 174.
4. Minault and Lelyveld, 'The Campaign for a Muslim University', p. 145; Shah, *Higher Education and Politics in Colonial India*, p. 174.
5. On the MEC, see A. R. Khan, *The All India Muslim Education Conference: Its Contribution to the Cultural Development of Indian Muslims 1886–1947* (Karachi: Oxford University Press, 2001); M. S. Jain, *The Aligarh Movement* (New Delhi: Icon Publications, 2006), pp. 148–86; D. Lelyveld, *Aligarh's First Generation: Muslim Solidarity in British India* (Princeton, NJ: Princeton University Press, 1978), pp. 300–17; and E. D. Churchill, 'The Muhammadan Educational Conference and the Aligarh Movement 1886–1900', *Panjab Past and Present*, 8:2 (1974), pp. 366–81. The MEC was founded as the Muhammadan Educational Congress before its name was changed to the Muhammadan Educational Conference in 1890. Five years later it became the Muhammadan Anglo-Oriental Educational Conference, and later still the All India Muslim Educational Conference. For clarity I refer to it as the Muslim Educational Conference (MEC) throughout.
6. *Aligarh Institute Gazette*, 4 May 1886.

7. Sayyid Ahmad's opposition to the Congress was recorded in his exchanges with the pre-eminent Muslim Congress supporter, Badruddin Tyabji. See for example Sayyid Ahmad to Tyabji, 24 January 1888, Badruddin Tyabji Papers, National Archives of India, New Delhi (hereafter Tyabji Papers), no. 858.

8. *Aligarh Institute Gazette*, 8 May 1888.

9. *Aligarh Institute Gazette*, 18 February 1890.

10. *Aligarh Institute Gazette*, 4 February 1888 and 15 January 1889. That Muslims in the Punjab had taken far more enthusiastically to the MEC than in the NWP was noted by Theodore Beck and others. See *Aligarh Institute Gazette*, 2 July 1889.

11. *Aligarh Institute Gazette*, 10 January 1893.

12. Mohsin-ul-Mulk had settled at Aligarh in 1893 after retiring from public service in the state of Hyderabad, and from 1896 he travelled across India publicizing the MEC's objectives. For an overview of his public life, see S. M. Ikram, *Indian Muslims and Partition of India* (New Delhi: Atlantic Publishers, 1992), pp. 75–87.

13. Report on the First Meeting of the MEC, Aligarh, December 1886, in S. Muhammad (ed.), *The Aligarh Movement. Basic Documents: 1864–1898*, xx vols (Meerut: Meenak-shi Prakashan, 1978), vol. 3, p. 772–3, on p. 772.

14. *Aligarh Institute Gazette*, 15 January 1889.

15. Report on the First Meeting of the MEC, Aligarh, December 1886, in Muhammad (ed.), *The Aligarh Movement*, vol. 3, p. 773; Report on the Second Meeting of the MEC, Lucknow, December 1887, in Muhammad (ed.), *The Aligarh Movement*, vol. 3, pp. 774–7, on p. 775.

16. Report on the Second Meeting of the MEC, Lucknow, December 1887, in Muham-mad (ed.), *The Aligarh Movement*, vol. 3, p. 775.

17. *Aligarh Institute Gazette*, 15 January 1889.

18. A. P. MacDonnell, Secretary to the Government of India, to all Local Governments and Administrations, 31 December 1887, India Education Proceedings, National Archives of India, New Delhi (hereafter IEP), no. 37, January 1888.

19. L. D. Wurgaft, *The Imperial Imagination: Magic and Myth in Kipling's India* (Middle-town, CT: Wesleyan University Press, 1983), pp. 159–68.

20. A. P. MacDonnell, Secretary to the Government of India, to all Local Governments and Administrations, 31 December 1887, IEP, no. 37, January 1888.

21. See the collection of responses to the Government of India's December 1887 letter in *Selections from the Records of the Government of India, Home Department, No. CCLXV*, pp. 1–231.

22. H. E. M. James, 'Reflections on the Way Home', *National Review*, 22 (1893–4), pp. 335–51.

23. *Aligarh Institute Gazette*, 15 December 1893.

24. Alfred Croft, Director of Public Instruction, Bengal, to the Secretary to the Govern-ment of Bengal, 28 October 1888, *Selections from the Records of the Government of India, Home Department, No. CCLXV*, pp. 140–56, on pp. 151–5.

25. D. Duncan, Principal of the Presidency College, Madras, to the Director of Public Instruction, n.d. [1888], *Selections from the Records of the Government of India, Home Department, No. CCLXV*, pp. 33–41, on p. 36.

26. Opinion of the Lord Bishop of Bombay, 15 March 1888, *Selections from the Records of the Government of India, Home Department, No. CCLXV*, pp. 79–80.

27. Minute by A. P. Howell, Officiating Resident at Hyderabad, 25 June 1888, *Selections from the Records of the Government of India, Home Department, No. CCLXV*, p. 226.

28. Minute by A. P. Howell, Officiating Resident at Hyderabad, 25 June 1888, *Selections from*

the *Records of the Government of India, Home Department, No. CCLXV*, pp. 226–7.

29. Babu Peary Mohun Mookerjee, Secretary to the British Indian Association, to the Secretary to the Government of Bengal, 22 March 1888, *Selections from the Records of the Government of India, Home Department, No. CCLXV*, pp. 125–9, on p. 126; Resolution of the Government of India on Discipline and Moral Training in Schools and Colleges in India, 17 August 1889, *Selections from the Records of the Government of India, Home Department, No. CCLXV*, pp. 1–9, on p. 8.

30. Rev. J. Mayr, Rector of St. Xavier's College, Bombay, 13 March 1888, *Selections from the Records of the Government of India, Home Department, No. CCLXV*, pp. 95–7, on p. 96.

31. Rev. W. G. Peel, Acting Secretary, Church Missionary Society, Madras, to the Director of Public Instruction, n.d. [1888], *Selections from the Records of the Government of India, Home Department, No. CCLXV*, pp. 69–70.

32. E. Marsden, Inspector of Schools, Madras, to the Director of Public Instruction, n.d. [1888] *Selections from the Records of the Government of India, Home Department, No. CCLXV*, pp. 55–8, on p. 56; H. L. Johnson, Commissioner of the Assam Valley Districts, to the Secretary to the Chief Commissioner, Assam, 28 April 1888, *Selections from the Records of the Government of India, Home Department, No. CCLXV*, pp. 211–2; T. G. Clarke, Commissioner of Coorg, to the Secretary to the Chief Commissioner of Coorg, 11 April 1888, *Selections from the Records of the Government of India, Home Department, No. CCLXV*, pp. 221–2.

33. A. P. MacDonnell, Secretary to the Government of India, to All Local Governments and Administrations, 31 December 1887, IEP, no. 37, January 1888.

34. *Aligarh Institute Gazette*, 10 January 1888.

35. Proceedings of the General Educational Conference, Punjab Education Proceedings, India Office, British Library, London (hereafter PEP), July 1888, Appendix 5.

36. Orders of the Lieutenant Governor on the Proceedings of the General Educational Conference, PEP, no. 5, July 1888.

37. *Aligarh Institute Gazette*, 15 January 1889.

38. On Viqar-ul-Mulk's public life, see Ikram, *Indian Muslims and the Partition of India*, pp. 101–14.

39. *Aligarh Institute Gazette*, 10 January 1893.

40. Nawab Abdul Latif to the Secretary to the Government of Bengal, 24 September 1888, *Selections from the Records of the Government of India, Home Department, No. CCLXV*, pp. 133–6, on p. 135.

41. Nawab Mushtaq Husain to the Secretary to the Government of the NWP, 22 September 1894, NWP Education Proceedings, India Office, British Library, London (hereafter NWPEP), no. 6, July 1895.

42. Nawab Mushtaq Husain to the Secretary to the Government of the NWP, 13 June 1895, NWPEP, no. 12, July 1895.

43. Extract from a Letter by Nawab Mushtaq Husain, 14 October 1894, NWPEP, no. 15, July 1895. For a more extensive analysis of the strategy employed by Viqar-ul-Mulk as he negotiated with the government, see R. Ivermee, 'Islamic Education and Colonial Secularism: The Amroha Experiment of 1895–96', *South Asian History and Culture*, 5:1 (2014), pp. 21–36, on pp. 29–32.

44. E. White, Director of Public Instruction, to the Secretary to the Government of the NWP, 17 September 1899, NWPEP, no. 5, June 1890.

45. Secretary to the Government of the NWP to the Chairmen of All District Boards, 23 May 1890, NWPEP, no. 9, June 1890.

46. W. C. Bennett, Secretary to the Government of the NWP, to the Secretary to the Government of India, 18 July 1888, *Selections from the Records of the Government of India, Home Department, No. CCLXV*, pp. 156–8.

47. T. C. Lewis, Director of Public Instruction, to the Secretary to the Government of the NWP, 16 May 1895, NWPEP, no. 11, July 1895.

48. Secretary to the Government of the NWP to the Director of Public Instruction, 13 August 1896, NWPEP, no. 31, August 1896.

49. *Aligarh Institute Gazette*, 13 August 1895.

50. F. Robinson, *Separatism among Indian Muslims: The Politics of the United Provinces' Muslims, 1860–1923* (Cambridge: Cambridge University Press, 1974), pp. 133–41; Hardy, *The Muslims of British India*, 142–6.

51. Newspapers including the *Punjab Observer* (17 April 1897) suspected MacDonnell of deliberately excluding Muslims from government employment – a suspicion entirely justified. See Antony Patrick MacDonnell Papers, MS Eng. hist. c. 352–64, Bodleian Library, University of Oxford (hereafter MacDonnell Papers), Newspaper cuttings, Ms. Eng. hist. c. 364, 35; and for confirmation of MacDonnell's intentions, MacDonnell to Elgin, 22 August 1897, MacDonnell Papers, Ms. Eng. hist. c. 353.

52. MacDonnell to Curzon, 31 August 1900, George Nathaniel Curzon Papers, Mss. Eur. F111–2, India Office, British Library, London (hereafter Curzon Papers), Mss. Eur. F111/202/89.

53. MacDonnell to Curzon, 3 December 1900, Curzon Papers, Mss. Eur. F111/202/200.

54. MacDonnell to Elgin, 16 July 1897, MacDonnell Papers, Ms. Eng. hist. c. 353; MacDonnell to Elgin, 22 August 1897, MacDonnell Papers, Ms. Eng. hist. c. 353.

55. Speech Delivered at the Convocation of the Allahabad University, 8 March 1899, A. P. MacDonnell, *Selections from Speeches of Sir A.P. MacDonnell, G.C.S.I., Lieutenant-Governor, N.W.P., and Chief Commissioner of Oudh, from 1895 to 1901* (Naini Tal: N.W. Provinces and Oudh Government Camp Branch Press, 1901), pp. 95–115, on pp. 98–9.

56. Minute by MacDonnell to his Successor, n.d. [1901], MacDonnell Papers, Ms. Eng. hist. c. 363.

57. Speech Delivered on Occasion of the Laying of the Foundation Stone of the Hindu Boarding House for Students of the Muir College, Allahabad, 29 July 1901, *Selections from Speeches of Sir A. P. MacDonnell, G.C.S.I., Lieutenant-Governor, N.W.P., and Chief Commissioner of Oudh, from 1895 to 1901* (Naini Tal: N.W. Provinces and Oudh Government Camp Branch Press, 1901), pp. 205–13, on p. 205.

58. Speech at Gathering of Residents of Allahabad, 22 December 1895, MacDonnell Papers, Newspaper cuttings, Ms. Eng. hist. c. 363.

59. Secretary to the Government of the NWP to the Secretary to the Local Committee, La Martiniere College, Lucknow, 6 July 1896, NWPEP, no. 14, July 1896.

60. Speech Delivered at the Convocation of the Allahabad University, 8 March 1899, *Selections from Speeches*, p. 103.

61. Reply to an Address Presented by the Trustees of the MAO College, Aligarh, 24 January 1896, *Selections from Speeches*, pp. 16–17, on p. 17.

62. Speech Delivered at the Convocation of the Allahabad University, 8 March 1899, *Selections from Speeches*, p. 106.

63. For the original copy of this address, see MacDonnell Papers, Ms. Eng. hist. c. 358, folio 7.

64. Reply to an Address Presented by the Trustees of the MAO College, Aligarh, 24 January 1896, *Selections from Speeches*, p. 17.

65. Secretary to the Government of the NWP to the Director of Public Instruction, 6 July

1895, NWPEP, no. 16, July 1895.

66. Nawab Mushtaq Husain to the Secretary to Government of the NWP, 18 May 1896, NWPEP, no. 22, August 1896.

67. Secretary to the Government of the NWP to the Director of Public Instruction, 9 June 1896, NWPEP, no. 24, August 1896.

68. Head Master, Anglo-Vernacular High School, Amroha, to the Inspector of Schools, Fourth Circle, 4 April 1896, NWPEP, no. 18, August 1896.

69. Draft Circular Prepared by W. N. Boutflower, July 1896, NWPEP, no. 30, August 1896.

70. Secretary to the Government of the NWP to the Director of Public Instruction, 6 July 1895, NWPEP, no. 16, July 1895.

71. Head Master, Anglo-Vernacular High School, Amroha, to the Inspector of Schools, Fourth Circle, 4 April 1896, NWPEP, no. 18, August 1896; Head Master, Anglo-Vernacular High School, Amroha, to the Director of Public Instruction, 29 May 1896, NWPEP, no. 26, August 1896.

72. T. C. Lewis, Director of Public Instruction, to the Secretary to the NWP Government, 16 May 1895, NWPEP, no. 11, July 1895.

73. W. N. Boutflower, Officiating Director of Public Instruction, to the Secretary to the Government of the NWP, 26 June 1896, NWPEP, no. 27, August 1896.

74. NWP Education Reports, India Office, British Library, London (hereafter NWPER), 1897–8, p. 33; NWPER, 1899–1900, p. 65.

75. *Aligarh Institute Gazette*, 16 January 1897.

76. 'Proposed Memorial to the Late Sir Syed Ahmad', *Moslem Chronicle*, 9 April 1898.

77. 'Rules of the Sir Syed Ahmad Memorial Fund', *Moslem Chronicle*, 11 February 1899.

78. On the corporate life of the MAO College in the 1880s and 1890s, see Lelyveld, *Aligarh's First Generation*, pp. 253–99.

79. Lord Curzon's Address at Aligarh, 23 April 1901, in T. Raleigh (ed.), *Lord Curzon in India: Being a Selection from his Speeches as Viceroy and Governor-General of India, 1898–1905* (London: Macmillan and Co., 1906), pp. 474–9, on p. 478.

80. Lelyveld, *Aligarh's First Generation*, pp. 113–8.

81. *Aligarh Institute Gazette*, 15 August 1893.

82. 'Speech by Theodore Beckat College Prize-Giving', *Mahomedan Anglo-Oriental College Magazine*, September 1892.

83. *Aligarh Institute Gazette*, 16 February 1886.

84. *Aligarh Institute Gazette*, 16 July 1889.

85. 'Principal's Report for 1894–1895', *Mahomedan Anglo-Oriental College Magazine*, July 1895.

86. *Aligarh Institute Gazette*, 16 July 1889.

87. *Aligarh Institute Gazette*, 2 January 1886.

88. 'Principal's Report for 1894–1895', *Mahomedan Anglo-Oriental College Magazine*, July 1895.

89. 'Report of the Principal for 1899–1900', *Mahomedan Anglo-Oriental College Magazine*, September 1900.

90. Lelyveld, *Aligarh's First Generation*, p. 276.

91. T. Morison, *Imperial Rule in India: Being an Examination of the Principles Proper to the Government of Dependencies* (Westminster: Archibald Constable & Co., 1899), p. 116.

92. Morison, *Imperial Rule in India*, p. 118.

93. *Aligarh Institute Gazette*, 19 February 1901. Boarding houses named after successive lieutenant governors of the United Provinces, Antony MacDonnell and James La

Touche, were opened at the college in 1904–5.

94. Morison, *Imperial Rule in India*, p. 125.

95. T. Morison, 'Scheme on the Proposed Mohamedan University', n.d. [1898], Sayyid Husain Bilgrami Papers, Nehru Memorial Library, New Delhi (hereafter Bilgrami Papers), Subject File 5.

96. T. Morison, 'A Muhamadan University', *National Review*, 32 (1898–9), pp. 243–9.

97. 'Muhammadan Educational Conference', *Moslem Chronicle*, 14 January 1899 and 4 February 1899.

98. 'Muhammadan Educational Conference', *Moslem Chronicle*, 14 January 1899 and 4 February 1899.

99. 'Muhammadan Educational Conference', *Moslem Chronicle*, 14 January 1899 and 4 February 1899; and Beck, 'The Proposed Mahomedan University'.

100. In addition to the resolution 'That this Conference approves the establishment of a Muhammadan University' the conference would pass a general resolution on the importance of religious education for Muslim pupils. See 'Muhammadan Educational Conference', *Moslem Chronicle*, 14 January 1899 and 4 February 1899.

101. Tyabji to Mohsin-ul-Mulk, 21 December 1898, Tyabji Papers, no. 109.

102. For biographical details, see S. H. Imadi, *Nawab Imad-ul-Mulk (Social and Cultural Activities of Nawab Imad-ul-Mulk Syed Husain Bilgrami in Hyderabad* (Hyderabad: Government of Andhra Pradesh, 1978).

103. *Administration Report of His Highness the Nizam's Dominion for 1294 Fasli (1884–85)* (Bombay: 'Times of India' Steam Press, 1886), p. 192.

104. *Report of the Administration of His Highness the Nizam's Dominion for 1303 Fasli (8th October 1893 to 7th October 1894)* (Bombay: 'Times of India' Steam Press, 1895), pp. 193–8.

105. 'A Brief History of the Dairatul Maarif', Bilgrami Papers, Subject File 3.

106. S. H. Bilgrami, 'Moral and Religious Education', *Addresses, Poems and Other Writings of Nawwab Imadul-Mulk Bahadur (Sayyid Husayn Bilgrami, C. S. I.)* (Hyderabad: Government Central Press, 1925), pp. 21–4, on p. 21.

107. *Administration Report of His Highness the Nizam's Dominion for 1294 Fasli*, p. 193.

108. Leitner had by this point returned to England to found the Oriental Institute at Woking, and sought the patronage of the Nizam to build a mosque attached to the Institute. See Leitner to Bilgrami, 2 November 1888, Bilgrami Papers, Leitner Correspondence File.

109. *Aligarh Institute Gazette*, 7 January 1890.

110. Beck to Bilgrami, 30 August 1888, Bilgrami Papers, Beck Correspondence File; Bilgrami to Sayyid Ahmad, 20 August 1888, Bilgrami Papers, Speeches and Writings by Bilgrami, File 3.

111. Beck to Bilgrami, 13 September 1888, Bilgrami Papers, Beck Correspondence File.

112. Presidential Address at the Eleventh MEC, 30 December 1896, *Addresses, Poems and Other Writings*, pp. 54–66, on pp. 59–61.

113. *Aligarh Institute Gazette*, 16 January 1897.

114. S. H. Bilgrami, 'The Mahomedan University', n.d. [1898], Bilgrami Papers, Subject File 5.

115. See Bilgrami's Presidential Address at the Fourteenth Meeting of the MEC, *Addresses, Poems and Other Writings*, pp. 90–110, on p. 97.

116. Bilgrami, 'The Mahomedan University', Bilgrami Papers, Subject File 5.

117. 'The Mohammedan Educational Conference', *Mahomedan Anglo-Oriental College Magazine*, February 1901.

118. Reply to an Address Presented at Aligarh, 18 February 1900, Bilgrami Papers, Speeches and Writings by Bilgrami, File 8.

119. Morison to Bilgrami, 10 November 1900, Bilgrami Papers, Morison Correspondence File. This appeal was repeated three years on: see Morison to Bilgrami, 9 October 1903, Bilgrami Papers, Morison Correspondence File.
120. 'The Sir Syed Memorial Meeting', *Moslem Chronicle*, 18 March 1899.
121. Amir Ali to Tyabji, 28 November 1887, Tyabji Papers, no. 39.
122. 'The Muhammadan Educational Conference', *Moslem Chronicle*, 11 November 1899.
123. Note by Amir Ali on the Mahomedan University proposal, n.d. [1898], Bilgrami Papers, Subject File 5.
124. A. Ali, *The Life and Teachings of Mohammed, or the Spirit of Islam* (London: W. H. Allen & Co., 1891); A. Ali, *The Spirit of Islam, or the Life and Teachings of Mohammed* (Calcutta: S. K. Lahiri & Co., 1902).
125. Presidential Address at the Thirteenth MEC, Calcutta, December 1899, in S. Muhammad (ed.), *The All-India Muslim Educational Conference (Select Presidential Addresses) 1886–1947* (New Delhi: A.P.H. Publishing Corporation, 2003), pp. 15–31.
126. 'The Muhammadan Educational Conference: The Thirteenth Session', *Moslem Chronicle*, 28 December 1899.
127. 'Meeting at Town Hall: Sir Syed Memorial Fund Association', *Moslem Chronicle*, 6 January 1900.
128. L. Fraser, *India under Curzon & After* (London: William Heinemann, 1911); D. Dilks, *Curzon in India* (London: Rupert Hart-Davis, 1969–70); and M. Edwardes, *High Noon of Empire: India under Curzon* (London: Eyre & Spottiswoode, 1965).
129. Proceedings of the Educational Conference held at Simla, September 1901, IEP, notes to nos 47–61, November 1901.
130. Address at the Simla Educational Conference, December 1901, in Raleigh (ed.), *Lord Curzon in India*, pp. 313–39.
131. *Indian Education Policy: Being a Resolution Issued by the Governor-General in Council, on the 11th March 1904* (Calcutta: Office of the Superintendent, Government Printing, 1904).
132. Address at the Simla Educational Conference, December 1901, in Raleigh (ed.), *Lord Curzon in India*, pp. 319–28.
133. Secretary to the Government of India, Home Department, to the Secretary of State for India, 3 September 1903, IEP, no. 84, December 1903.
134. Address at the Convocation of the Calcutta University, 11 February 1905, in Raleigh (ed.), *Lord Curzon in India*, pp. 489–99, on p. 495.
135. Minute by the Viceroy on University Reform, 28 February 1901, IEP, notes to nos. 122–9, December 1901.
136. On the debate in England leading to this decision, see N. Harte, *The University of London 1836–1986: An Illustrated History* (London: Athlone), pp. 119–61.
137. Note by T. Raleigh, 2 February 1900, IEP, notes to nos. 122–9, December 1901.
138. Proceedings of the Educational Conference held at Simla, September 1901, IEP, notes to nos. 47–61, November 1901.
139. Minute by the Viceroy on University Reform, 28 February 1901, IEP, notes to nos. 122–9, December 1901.
140. Address at the Simla Educational Conference, December 1901, in Raleigh (ed.), *Lord Curzon in India*, p. 337.
141. W. R. Lawrence to Annie Beasant, 19 January 1899, Curzon Papers, Mss. Eur. F111/199/12.
142. Address at the Simla Educational Conference, December 1901, in Raleigh (ed.), *Lord Curzon in India*, p. 337.

143. Address at Aligarh, 23 April 1901, in Raleigh (ed.), *Lord Curzon in India*, p. 477.
144. Curzon also stated at Aligarh that Queen Victoria had expressed sympathy for the Muslim University plan. This was almost certainly the result of Rafiuddin Ahmad, who had travelled to England from Poona in the 1890s to study law in London. While in the capital he and Munshi Abdul Karim became acquaintances of Victoria. Rafiuddin Ahmad was a founder member of the Muslim Patriotic League of London, and would be among the first to advance the Muslim University plan in England. See R. Ahmad, 'The Proposed Muslim University in India', *Nineteenth Century*, 44 (1898), pp. 915–21; and on Rafiuddin Ahmad's relationship with Victoria, M. N. Qureshi, *Pan-Islam in British Indian Politics: A Study of the Khilafat Movement, 1918–1924* (Leiden: Brill, 1999), p. 43.
145. Draft Commission Questions, 18 March 1902, Bilgrami Papers, Subject File 22.
146. *Report of the Indian Universities Commission* (Simla: Government Central Printing Office, 1902), p. 1; 'The Problem of Indian Education', *The Pioneer*, 21 August 1902.
147. *Aligarh Institute Gazette*, 9 January 1902; see also 'Muhammadan Educational Conference', *Moslem Chronicle*, 11 January 1902.
148. This plan had been devised by the Madras Board of Muhammadan Education and carried the support of H. T. Boddam, a judge at the Madras High Court and in 1901 the first European to preside over an annual meeting of the MEC. See his Presidential Address at the Fifteenth MEC in Madras, December 1901, in Muhammad (ed.), *The All-India Muslim Educational Conference*, pp. 81–102, on p. 93; and *Aligarh Institute Gazette*, 9 January 1902.
149. *Aligarh Institute Gazette*, 20 March 1902. For the lieutenant governor's response, see J. La Touche, *Selections from Speeches of Sir J.J.D. La Touche, K.C.S.I., Lieutenant-Governor of the United Provinces from 1901 to 1906* (Naini Tal: United Provinces Government Camp Press, 1906), pp. 1–6.
150. *Aligarh Institute Gazette*, 17 April 1902.
151. *Aligarh Institute Gazette*, Supplement to 29 May 1902.
152. *Report of the Indian Universities Commission*, p. 6.
153. H. D. Griffin, Secretary to the Government of the United Provinces, to the Secretary to the Government of India, Home Department, 2 January 1903, IEP, no. 72, December 1902.
154. *Report of the Indian Universities Commission*, pp. 15–19.
155. *Report of the Indian Universities Commission*, p. 20.
156. *Report of the Indian Universities Commission*, pp. 8–10; Note by H. W. Orange and H. H. Risley, 18 June 1903, IEP, notes to nos. 67–86, December 1903.
157. *Report of the Indian Universities Commission*, pp. 60–3.
158. See the extensive administrative notes attached to IEP, no. 67, December 1902.
159. Note by Lord Curzon, 20 July 1902, IEP, no. 67 of December 1902.
160. *Report of the Indian Universities Commission*, p. 8.
161. Raleigh to Lawrence, 21 April 1900, Bilgrami Papers, Raleigh Correspondence File.
162. Raleigh to Lawrence, 21 April 1900, Bilgrami Papers, Raleigh Correspondence File.
163. Note by Lord Curzon, 20 July 1902, IEP, no. 67, December 1902.
164. S. Tejani, *Indian Secularism: A Social and Intellectual History, 1890–1950* (Ranikhet: Permanent Black, 2007), pp. 113–43.
165. 'Mahomedan Educational Conference: Bombay', *Moslem Chronicle*, 16 January 1904.
166. A. Hydari, 'A Mahomedan University in India', *East and West*, 3:34 (1904), pp. 765–73.
167. Minault and Lelyveld, 'The Campaign for a Muslim University', p. 157.
168. Hydari, 'A Mahomedan University in India', pp. 772–3.
169. 'Provincial Educational Conference', *Moslem Chronicle*, Supplement to 16 April 1904.
170. 'The Mahommedan Educational Conference', *Aligarh Monthly*, February 1903; M.

Hayat, 'The Proposed Mohammadan University in India', *East and West*, 1:13 (1902), pp. 1379–84.

171. 'The Indian Universities Commission', *Moslem Chronicle*, 15 November 1902.

172. *Aligarh Institute Gazette*, 14 February 1903; Presidential Address at the Sixteenth MEC, Delhi, December 1902, in Muhammad (ed.), *The All-India Muslim Educational Conference*, pp. 115–28.

173. Hayat, 'The Proposed Mohammadan University in India', p. 1384.

174. *Aligarh Institute Gazette*, 14 February 1903.

175. 'The Indian Universities Commission', *Moslem Chronicle*, 15 November 1902.

176. *Aligarh Institute Gazette*, 21 March 1903 and 25 July 1903.

177. Hayat, 'The Proposed Mohammadan University in India'.

178. *Aligarh Institute Gazette*, 8 February 1904.

179. Morison, *Imperial Rule in India*, pp. 125–7.

180. T. Morison, *The History of the M.A.O. College, Aligarh: From its Foundation to the Year 1903; Together with the Annual Report for the Year 1902–1903 and Appendices* (Allahabad: Pioneer Press, 1903), pp. 29–33.

181. Nawab Abdul Latif to the Secretary to the Government of Bengal, 24 September 1888, *Selections from the Records of the Government of India, Home Department, No. CCLXV*, pp. 133–6, on p. 135.

182. *Report of the Administration of His Highness the Nizam's Dominion for 1303 Fasli*, p. 200.

183. *Report on the Administration of His Highness the Nizam's Dominions for the Four Years 1304 to 1307 Fasli. (8th October 1894 to 7th October 1898)* 2 vols (Madras: Lawrence Asylum Press, 1899), vol. 1, p. 308–10.

184. 'Aligarh Old Boys' Association London', *Moslem Chronicle*, 18 July 1903.

185. M. Ali, *My Life, A Fragment: An Autobiographical Sketch of Maulana Mohamed Ali*, ed. A. Iqbal (Lahore: Sh. Muhammad Ashraf, 1946); A. Iqbal, *The Life and Times of Mohamed Ali: An Analysis of the Hopes, Fears and Aspirations of Muslim India from 1778 to 1931* (Lahore: Institute of Islamic Culture, 1974); M. Hasan, *Mohamed Ali: Ideology and Politics* (New Delhi: Manohar, 1981).

186. 'Moslem Aspirations', *The Comrade*, 19 August 1911.

187. 'The Indian National Congress', *The Comrade*, 18 February 1911. For a discussion of Mohamed Ali's later political activity, deriving from his conception of the place of religious community in the Indian nation, see Tejani, *Indian Secularism*, pp. 144–95.

188. Ali, *My Life*, p. 42.

189. M. Ali, *The Proposed Mohamedan University: Being an Address Delivered at the Bombay Presidency Mohamedan Educational Conference, at Ahmadabad, on 16th October, 1904* (Bombay: Caxton Printing Works, 1904), pp. 28–30.

190. Ali, *The Proposed Mohamedan University*, p. 34.

191. 'The Indian National Congress', *The Comrade*, 18 February 1911.

Conclusion: Secularism Contested

1.   *Act No. XVI of 1915: An Act to Establish and Incorporate a Teaching and Residential University at Benares* (Delhi: Superintendent of Government Printing, 1915). On the foundation of Benares Hindu University, see S. L. Dar and S. Somaskandan (eds), *History of the Banaras Hindu University* (Varanasi: Banaras Hindu University Press, 1966), pp. 1–315; L. Renold, *A Hindu Education: Early Years of the Banaras Hindu University* (New Delhi: Oxford University Press, 2005), pp. 1–63; and J. Lütt, *The Movement for the Foundation of the Benares*

Hindu University (Heidelberg: Südasien-Institut der Universität Heidelberg, 1976).

2. On Malaviya's life and career, see S. L. Gupta, *Pandit Madan Mohan Malaviya: A Socio-Political study* (Allahabad: Chugh Publications, 1978); S. R. Bakshi, *Madan Mohan Malaviya: The Man and His Ideology* (New Delhi: Anmol Publications, 1990); and B. J. Akkad, *Malaviyaji (A Brief Life Sketch of Pandit Madan Mohan Malaviya)* (Bombay: Vora, 1948).

3. [M. M. Malaviya], 'The Hindu University of Benares: Why it is Wanted and What it Aims at', in S. L. Dar and S. Somaskandan (eds), *History of the Banaras Hindu University* (Varanasi: Banaras Hindu University Press, 1966), pp. 114–49, on pp. 133–8.

4. [M. M. Malaviya], 'Prospectus of a Proposed Hindu University', in S. L. Dar and S. Somaskandan (eds), *History of the Banaras Hindu University* (Varanasi: Banaras Hindu University Press, 1966), pp. 49–74, on pp. 70–1.

5. Renold, *A Hindu Education*, pp. 43–63.

6. Renold, *A Hindu Education*, p. 63.

7. Nandini Chatterjee reaches a similar conclusion, arguing that 'the Government agreed to modify its policy of a formally secular university system, in the hope of earning political returns through patronage of indigenous, explicitly religious concerns, drawing Indians away from disaffection and nationalism'. N. Chatterjee, *The Making of Indian Secularism: Empire, Law and Christianity, 1830–1960* (Basingstoke: Palgrave Macmillan, 2011), p. 42.

8. L. Fraser, *India under Curzon and After* (London: William Heinemann, 1911), pp. 199–200.

9. P. Hardy, *The Muslims of British India* (Cambridge: Cambridge University Press, 2007), pp. 116–46; F. Robinson, *Separatism among Indian Muslims: The Politics of the United Provinces' Muslims, 1860–1923* (Cambridge: Cambridge University Press, 1974), pp. 133–74.

10. *Aligarh Institute Gazette*, 1 August 1903.

11. Morison to Bilgrami, 5 May 1903, Sayyid Husain Bilgrami Papers, Nehru Memorial Library, New Delhi (hereafter Bilgrami Papers), Morison Correspondence File.

12. S. R. Wasti, *Lord Minto and the Indian Nationalist Movement* (Oxford: Clarendon Press, 1964), pp. 59–88; D. Chakravarty, *Muslim Separatism and the Partition of India* (New Delhi: Atlantic, 2003), pp. 16–41; Robinson, *Separatism among Indian Muslims*, pp. 133–74; Hardy, *The Muslims of British India*, pp. 147–67.

13. F. Shaikh, *Community and Consensus in Islam: Muslim Representation in Colonial India* (Cambridge: Cambridge University Press, 1989), pp. 76–118; Robinson, *Separatism among Indian Muslims*, p. 145.

14. Muslim address to the Viceroy, 1 October 1906, Spencer Harcourt Butler Papers, Mss. Eur. F116, India Office, British Library, London (hereafter Harcourt Butler Papers), Mss. Eur. F116/65.

15. Draft of the Simla Memorial, n.d., Bilgrami Papers, Subject File 10; Proceedings of the Inaugural Session of the All-India Muslim League, 30 December 1906, S. S. Pirzada (ed.), *Foundations of Pakistan: All-India Muslim League Documents: 1906–1947*, 2 vols (Karachi: National Publishing House, 1969), vol. 1, p. 1–15.

16. Muslim Address to the Viceroy, 1 October 1906, Harcourt Butler Papers, Mss. Eur. F116/65.

17. P. Chatterjee, 'On Civil and Political Society in Post-Colonial Democracies', in S. Kaviraj and S. Khilnani (eds), *Civil Society: History and Possibilities* (Cambridge: Cambridge University Press, 2001), pp. 165–78, on p. 172.

18. S. H. Bilgrami, 'The Mahomedan University', n.d. [1898], Bilgrami Papers, Subject File 5; *Aligarh Institute Gazette*, 15 January 1889.

19. 'The Mahommedan Educational Conference', *Aligarh Monthly*, February 1903.

INDEX